Global Auteurs

Intersections in Communications and Culture

Global Approaches and Transdisciplinary Perspectives

Cameron McCarthy and Angharad N. Valdivia
General Editors

Vol. 22

PETER LANG
New York • Washington, D.C./Baltimore • Bern
Frankfurt am Main • Berlin • Brussels • Vienna • Oxford

Brian Michael Goss

Global Auteurs

Politics in the Films of Almodóvar,
von Trier, and Winterbottom

PETER LANG
New York • Washington, D.C./Baltimore • Bern
Frankfurt am Main • Berlin • Brussels • Vienna • Oxford

Library of Congress Cataloging-in-Publication Data

Goss, Brian Michael.
Global auteurs: politics in the films of Almodóvar, von Trier,
and Winterbottom / Brian Michael Goss.
p. cm. — (Intersections in communications and culture; v. 22)
Includes bibliographical references and index.
1. Politics in motion pictures. 2. Auteur theory (Motion pictures)
3. Motion pictures—Political aspects—Europe. 4. Almodóvar, Pedro—
Criticism and interpretation. 5. Trier, Lars von, 1956– —
Criticism and interpretation. 6. Winterbottom, Michael—
Criticism and interpretation. I. Title.
PN1995.9.P6G67   791.4302'330922—dc22   2008043885
ISBN 978-1-4331-0145-8 (hardcover)
ISBN 978-1-4331-0134-2 (paperback)
ISSN 1528-610X

Bibliographic information published by **Die Deutsche Bibliothek**.
Die Deutsche Bibliothek lists this publication in the "Deutsche
Nationalbibliografie"; detailed bibliographic data is available
on the Internet at http://dnb.ddb.de/.

Cover design by Joshua Hanson

The paper in this book meets the guidelines for permanence and durability
of the Committee on Production Guidelines for Book Longevity
of the Council of Library Resources.

© 2009 Peter Lang Publishing, Inc., New York
29 Broadway, 18th floor, New York, NY 10006
www.peterlang.com

Printed in the United States of America

This book is dedicated to my mother, Gladys Ann Goss,
for her sacrifices on behalf of all her children.

CONTENTS

PREFACE

Why am I so interested in politics? If I were to answer you very simply, I would say this: *why* shouldn't I be interested? That is to say, what blindness, what deafness, what density of ideology would have to weigh me down to prevent me from being interested in what is probably the most crucial subject to our existence, that is to say the society in which we live, the economic relations within which it functions, and the system of power which defines the regular forms and regular permissions and prohibitions of our conduct. The essence of our life consists, after all, of the political functioning of the society in which we find ourselves. So I can't answer the question of why I should be interested; I could only answer it by asking why shouldn't I be interested?

        —Michel Foucault (original emphasis; 1974: 167–168)

In Michael Winterbottom's recent *A Cock and Bull Story* (2005), one characteristically witty scene features a university professor's brief monologue that explains the film's source material (namely, the eighteenth-century novel, *The Life and Opinions of Tristram Shandy, Gentleman*). The professor is clad in a garish tie that signifies indifference to the mundane routines of dress; and, in the register of narrative, is summoned to the camera's gaze non-diegetically while, in the plot, the film-within-a-film version of *Tristram Shandy* is being riddled with creative setbacks. In a scholarly office enclave, surrounded by books, the kindly and fastidious professor advances an articulate explanation. He posits, in reasonable and measured terms, that both Tristram and Walter Shandy engage with the Sisyphean errand of trying to plan and impose an order on the chaos that is life.

    Why dwell on this short scene, aside from the mere fact that Winterbottom's corpus of films is one of the topics of this volume? First, it depicts a neat professorial trick to capture and explain what, paradoxically, is posited to be anchored in the ineffably complex. Second, and more importantly, I will assay an arguably grander project in this volume than Winterbottom's professor who ventures explanation of but one "ineffable" text (albeit with greater concision than will be evident here). I seek to address context and text in performing politically alert readings of the more than 40 films that comprise the three directors' bodies of work. More specifically, this book presents a commitment to discussing the economic base via examination of the international film industry; an industry that, from a European vantage point, is characterized by a U.S. behemoth that commandeers a vast amount of space (most notably on screen) and vacuums up a large measure of oxygen (investment, fame, and hype). At the same time, I attempt to reconcile discussion of the material exigencies of the economic base with the ostensibly "individualistic" auteur theory. With one foot each in the domain of industrial analysis and in auteur theory, I ground this investigation of three politically resonant and contemporary filmmakers: Pedro Almodóvar, Lars von Trier and Michael Winterbottom.

Auteur theory "has *won*," claims Robert Stam in peremptory fashion, although some exchanges of fire continue over a paradigm that dwells on the figure in the director's chair (original emphasis; Stam 2000a: 6). At the same time, and in a different register, one may posit that Hollywood has *not won* as the final instance has yet to be reached and new challenges to the major studios' grip are in play from Europe and farther afield.

Following the discussion of the international film industry and the auteur theory, the balance of the book devotes extensive attention to each of the directors. Here, the concept of politics insinuated into text gets fuller expression, animated by the convictions of an organic pan-politicism that Foucault passionately expresses in the epigram. Specific lines of argument with regard to each director will be rehearsed later. For the moment, it will be sufficient to observe that several lines of inquiry figure in the campaign to unpack the films: Theories of ideology, gender, psychoanalysis, and formalism/realism perform heavy lifting in the pages that follow.

Nonetheless, along with marshaling theoretical approaches to tease apart and pull together the films in a director's corpus, there is the usually unstated question that hovers around the margins: *Why?* Why shepherd concepts from the canon of scholarship toward the flickering light and moving images on screen? Is there a risk of overkill? Indeed, films have on occasion been smothered in theoretically dense over-analysis. There is, however, a complementary and still greater danger of under-analyzing films or other widely circulating cultural artifacts: News programs, sporting events, music videos, and so on. On this view, dull anti-intellectualism and cramped literalism insist that, "It's just a film! Move along now, nothing more to see..." Via mobilization and application of theory that fleshes out the film texts, I try to make each director's corpus speak up more clearly with respect to the bedrock, baseline considerations of contemporary issues and politics.

While each of the trio of directors has achieved an international profile via distribution and acclaim, each at times and to various extents straddles the art house niche in the bohemian district and the hulking Cineplex by the exit ramp; that is, each director is both minting cultural capital for self-consciously savvy spectators and reaching broader audiences. North Americans and Europeans alike speak their cultural capital when they exhibit fluency with the fictional worlds that have been conjured by Almodóvar, von Trier, and Winterbottom. I am, however, untroubled by the filmmakers' liminality between "high culture" and popularity as to some extent it heightens a tension that has long been characteristic of film across its history as a medium. Film presents a split identity for being at once widely circulated commercial spectacle, as apotheosized in mainstream Hollywood and Bollywood productions (hence the moral panics surrounding "arousing" content, crystallizing in the decades-long reign of the Hays Office "Production Codes" [Thompson and Bordwell 2003: 216–217]). At the same time, film's uniquely hybridized qualities make any given film an amalgam of elevated art forms. These forms include scriptwriting, photography, acting, editing of moving images, make-up, lighting, and music (among others). Almodóvar, von Trier, and Winterbottom make the popular/elite tension more vibrant in their particular ways.

Each director is also a signature national figure in Spain, Denmark, and the United Kingdom, respectively. However, each is also implicated in the intensification of global interface across the past several decades. In this vein, von Trier has set several films in the United States that are launched as critique of the presumptive global hegemon and has also deployed highly international casts from the start of his career. Winterbottom has, similarly, filmed and set several films in various parts of South East Asia with accompanying story lines that examine internationalized classism clashing with national borders. Almodóvar, the eldest of the three directors, is arguably the most rooted in his nationality. Although his international distribution is also the strongest of the trio, Marvin D'Lugo posits a deeply inscribed "geo-cultural positioning" via pan-Hispanicism at the heart of Almodóvar's cinema (2006).

Like Winterbottom's professor, I am alert to the buzzing, vexing confusion in the external world. But even if the effort occurs in a cascade of paradoxes and Sisyphean moments, I attempt to delineate some order within these films and their interfaces with the world external to them.

ACKNOWLEDGMENTS

With gratitude, I offer the following "shout-outs" of acknowledgment for interventions that have massaged and teased this volume to its final (optimal!) form. Cameron McCarthy and Angharad Valdivia are the "Intersections in Communication and Culture" book series editors who shepherded the project from the germ of suggestion, into a proposal, and finally into a contractual reality. Thereafter, they have exhibited wisdom in being hands-on with assistance and laissez-faire as it enabled my vision of the volume. Mary Savigar, acquisitions editor for Media and Communication Studies at Peter Lang Publishing, has presented continuous patience, good cheer, and perceptive suggestions. Paul Vita, chair of the English and Communication Department at Saint Louis University-Madrid Campus, commandeered course releases and exhortation that have been enabling toward a timely finish. Friends and colleagues furnished comments and questions when called upon to do so on drafts and in "brown bag" fora. For this, I thank Cary Barney, Stephen Cassmier, Daniel Chornet-Roses, Anne Dewey, Glenn Huyck, Matthew Kineen, Anne McCabe, Father James O'Leary, Sofia Poe, and Maura Tarnoff. Sophie Appel, Production Supervisor at Peter Lang, and my colleague Daniel Chornet-Roses have been patient and indispensable during the typesetting process. Thanks to this ensemble of people, writing the book has been more than a monastic and monadic experience and has been enriching in the social dimension of supportive exchange.

CHAPTER 1

Introduction

This is a volume about three filmmakers. It also is not about them, insofar as in discussing even accomplished artists, the stakes do not hinge only on the monadic "genius," but implicate the world that he or she inhabits. In other wor*ds, text* and *context* permeate each other.

Why these three filmmakers? Each is from a distinctly different zone of Europe. In particular: the heat-laden Latin south with its checkered histories of empire and, more recently, transition from dictatorship (Pedro Almodóvar, Spain); the chilly and haunted Reformationist northern Germanic perimeter (Lars von Trier, Denmark); and a historically powerful island, ambivalent about its relation to the nearby continent, that has arguably exerted the most resounding global impact of any nation during the past 500 years (Michael Winterbottom, United Kingdom). Moreover, in the register of contrast, it is an interesting happenstance that each director was born in a different decade (1940s, 1950s, 1960s), although, at the same time, it is only 12 years that separate the oldest (Almodóvar, born 1949) and the youngest (Winterbottom, 1961). One trained at his national film school (von Trier), the second largely learned the craft "hands on" in the industry after university (Winterbottom), and the third is an auto-didact who taught himself to make films in the evenings that followed his respectable day job (Almodóvar).

Linkages between the trio of directors follow from the fact that each is a contemporary fixture in the European industry in a moment when Europe is living through a historically startling degree of integration. Moreover, each director is recognized as being in various moments of compiling a corpus of films widely characterized as interesting and significant.[1] In this vein, Almodóvar, von Trier, and Winterbottom can each wave toward a full award case as well as other forms of recognition: international circulation, article- and book-length treatment, and dedicated fan response. Each of the three directors has also established a production company with partners; the three resultant companies are called El Deseo, Zentropa, and Revolution Films. In doing so, the trio has maintained grounding in their national industries while also gaining a measure of independence that is enabling toward their auteurist inclinations. The discussion of these three directors may also illuminate how filmmakers establish a niche, nationally and globally, while it also unpacks their messages as social commentators.

Despite the acclaim that each has generated, I have made an effort to not compose celebratory panegyrics in what would amount to publicity, academically ventriloquized, for the three directors. While an academic does not typically enact popcorn-stained fandom in print, auteur studies often collapse into their own version of it by gingerly tendering criticisms of their subjects in circumspect ways. In turn, such circumspection lends itself to quickly suturing closed any tears in the final "confirmation" and "approval" of the director's work that may otherwise be destabilized by serious criticism. David Bordwell (1989) has located similar tendencies toward pulling punches in some precincts of the symptomatically oriented film literature. To wit, Bordwell observes that commercial films are usually evaluated more strenuously than "alternative" or auteur cinema that is presumed to be oppositional in the first instance.

Each filmmaker is discussed in a chapter that "stands on its own" with respect to the other chapters. Furthermore, the volume's organization goes against the general trend of following up introductory comments with discussion of an auteur's films arrayed into a single file sequential parade from the first film to the last (as in, e.g., prior, insightful writing on Almodóvar by Acevedo-Muñoz [2007], D'Lugo [2006], and Smith [2000]). In lieu of this temporal/sequential organization, I have organized each chapter thematically around fleshing out themes that I take as deeply inscribed throughout each auteur's corpus of films. This approach squares with the auteur theory that is presented in detail in chapter 3 since thematic motifs are one of the pillars of the theory.

That is how the text is organized. What about content? Politics is one of the title words of this volume—but what does politics mean? Notwithstanding Right-inflected efforts to selectively impose a narrowly crabbed concept of politics (that would, e.g., nonsensically "keep politics out of the classroom"), theorization in recent decades has prompted a more inclusive concept of it that may be called "cultural politics." The cultural studies tradition that originally emerged out of the United Kingdom presents a potent expression of the intersection of politics and everyday life as elaborated in, for example, Dick Hebdige (1988)'s *Subculture: The Meaning of Style* or Stuart Hall et al. (1978)'s *Policing the Crisis: The State, and Law and Order*; and into the present as instanced by a recently launched British journal devoted to the politics of the "everyday" (*International Journal of Media and Cultural Politics*). These inclusive conceptions engage with a much wider swath of activity in the conviction that politics are not as distant as an arcane bill, encased within legalistic jargon and deliberated over in parliament. Rather, politics are regularly negotiated and lived through by subjects in everyday material terms. In turn, expansive concepts of politics are largely parsed from the state and implicate the experience of family life, gender and identity, culture ("high" and "low")—topics on which I will dwell in this volume.

Nonetheless, along with the invaluable insights that it has enabled, the shift from attending to formal (state-centric) politics to cultural politics is not to be celebrated for the mere fact that it has gained considerable traction. In the effort to grasp reality as it is, one must recognize that the state was and is an enormously powerful actor. Across different societies and social models, the state retains a leading part in an array of key social functions (e.g., management of the economy, schooling, health, administration of law and justice, foreign policy). Thus, at times, I emphasize cultural politics in the analyses of the films that follow. In other passages, I pursue discussion of the formalized politics that more directly orients to the state and governance as it intersects with the filmmakers' texts. I do not, in other words, abandon the concept of politics as implicated in formal state activity. At the same time, I put a strong measure of stress on the insights that are enabled by the expansiveness of positing cultural politics and what it reveals about power, ideology, and stress fractures within them.

Power is an unavoidable feature of external reality, and it may operate within a variety of registers. In one such account, power aligns into "economic," "political," "coercive," and "symbolic" forms (Flew 2007: 4–8). While these forms are not mutually exclusive, the taxonomy provides a useful cataloging of the axes along which power may run. Moreover, power need not obey (stop at) fastidiously marked frontiers, thereby bringing actors of varying magnitudes of power into various measures of conflict.

Neo-conservative pundit Charles Krauthammer extends the abstracted description of power into full-throated assertions about its contemporary contours. To his Usonian readership, he claims, "We dominate every field of human endeavor from fashion to film to finance. We rule the world culturally, economically, diplomatically, and militarily as no one has since the Roman Empire" (quoted in Hafez 2007: 83).[2] Krauthammer's smug outburst is of a piece with the neo-conservative Project for a New American Century (PNAC)'s agitation, from the late Clinton era onward, for "full spectrum dominance" to be exercised by the United States within the global arena.[3] Notwithstanding neo-conservative oratory and position papers, across the first decade of the millennium, the United States' long-standing weaknesses have been far more manifest. Broadly speaking, these weaknesses include a profoundly classist economic model that guarantees intractable social conflict, insularity and mass paranoia that stimulate aggression, and indulgence of even the most wild-eyed fundamentalisms. Finally, since 2001, a corrupt administration that is brazen about its hostility toward prevailing material realities (Suskind 2004) has effected startling ("full spectrum") internal and external damage in crude manifestations of these formerly tempered weaknesses.

To take one metric of the United States' long and inevitable relative decline that now shades into absolute decline, consider currency. From January 2, 2002, to June 24, 2008, the euro nearly *doubled* in value against the dollar (i.e., a rise of 73 percent, from 0.90 euros to the dollar to 1.56 euros [www.x-rates.com/cgi-bin/hlookup.cgi])—with no interruption in the entrenched six-year-long pattern at hand. These numbers are striking but hardly compare with the barometric pressure of opinion that one may convey anecdotally and that speaks to regard for the United States that has been devalued in global terms. The effect may be most potent among younger people forming what, in many cases, will be life-long habits of mind; and who, unlike their parents, may not recall an epoch before the corrupt and insipid George W. Bush emblematized the nation. Alongside the anecdotal, the Pew Global Attitudes Project (2006) has made regular efforts to quantify international views on the United States and has found steep declines in favorability, notably in Europe.

Despite the United States' shambolic "Lost Decade" to open the new millennium, its international success on the cinema screen maintains to the present—and likely into the foreseeable future. However, in a related vein, recent scholarship from Terry Flew (2007) of Australia and Kai Hafez (2007) of Germany take pains (up to contortionist postures) in order to damp down what they take as exaggerated assumptions about the current extent of media globalization. Their position may, in part, be a riposte against pretensions of PNAC-style Usonian preeminence within facile assumptions of a globalized media environment. Maneuvers such as those of Flew and Hafez may seem necessary when U.S. investigators' concepts of media globalization frequently collapse into detailing the global distribution of U.S. product—with attendant expectations that it is all other cultures' task and telos to accommodate to U.S. tastes.[4] Nonetheless, even given their theses, neither Flew nor Hafez labors to deny the United States' international prominence on the cinema screen. Instead, they construe film as an exceptional medium within the global mediascape.

In any event, given my national background and given this historical moment, I am attentive to the three auteurs' postures to the United States as it arises in their bodies of films—most notably von Trier and Winterbottom, since Almodóvar is more profoundly grounded in the national. In turn, the U.S.-European distinction is a recurring issue in European film scholarship with regard to the continent's screen culture and industries (e.g., Wayne 2002). I intervene in the issues in, first, assembling a de-mystifying and detailed discussion of the behavior of the international film industry (chapter 2); and, second, for the very emphasis on these European filmmakers (chapter 4–6).

In his magisterial overview of the strategies that academics adopt in order to read films, David Bordwell observes that it is often true that:

> . . . film criticism is legitimated by the virtue of the theory that underwrites it, not by reference to claims about the intrinsic value of cinema or even the strength of particular interpretations. 'Theory' justifies the object of study, while concentration on the object can be attacked as naive empiricism. (1989: 97)

While it is anti-intellectual to dismiss theory, Bordwell's observations are well taken. Many a film analysis (or college-level course) veers toward theory campaigns that talk over the film and/or use it to ventriloquize theoretical breakthroughs. A contrasting approach assays to make the films "speak" for themselves more clearly, using theory as salient and as subordinate to the demands of unpacking what a film (or constellation of films) may mean. In doing so with rigor, theory will prove indispensable as a means of fashioning the conceptual framing that organizes and rigorously tightens up the analysis—and makes it more than a series of elaborate plot summaries punctuated with the periodic "interesting observation." As always, theory should be securely in hand to be wielded as instrument—while the interpreter should be wary of the curious seductions of being wielded by the theory. Toward this end, in the chapters that follow, I draw upon theories of authorship, ideology, psychoanalysis and realism/formalism as need arises in order to tease and massage interpretations into form.

The structure of the volume is as follows: Section I opens with detailed discussion of the international film industry (chapter 2) and then introduces a version of the auteur theory from some of the preexisting parts around the scholar's workbench (chapter 3). These opening moves ground the discussion that follows in section II's treatment of Almodóvar (chapters 4–6), section III's of von Trier (chapters 7 and 8), and section IV's of Winterbottom (chapters 9–11).

More specifically, chapter 2's account of the film industry in international terms is offered in the conviction that analysis limited to film text flickering onscreen is short of enacting a deep grasp of the medium. What, one may ask, is behind the screen? That is, how did this film projected on that screen on the wall of this exhibition space get positioned as such via the production-distribution-exhibition chain? A relatively brief but comprehensive portrait of film production fills the need within this project to account for the material dimension of culture. I survey the United States' longstanding advantages in international film; for example, the boosts that the U.S. industry gets from a wide distribution apparatus, immense investment and advertising budgets, as well as from the *lingua franca* of English. At the same time, ownership of the flagship Hollywood studios has passed into international hands, even if the Los Angelino commercial model still prevails in guiding the industry's behavior. Moreover, the increasing confidence of the European Union (EU) has concomitants in stepped-up European co-production, EU support, and the film festival circuit that endows European cinema with prestige and distribution.

Why study filmmakers—and not devote that same rigor to film genres, or time periods, or national cinemas? What does such an approach enable and at what costs? In furnishing a firm theoretical base for the balance of the investigation, chapter 3 examines the auteur theory. After scoring the classic Andrew Sarris–Pauline Kael confrontation, I telescope in on a method that elucidates style and thematic motifs in the corpus of a filmmaker. Along with this method of reading the auteur that is attentive to the continuities in signature and theme, the big concept around which this chapter revolves is to explain the particular while carefully avoiding unduly romantic individualism. I make the case for positioning the director in his or her timeframe, place, and means of production (that typically implicates a vast team of professionals who collaborate on the film). The director is not alpha and omega, on this view, but an entry point into investigating the culture that extols (and at times disciplines) a given director's contributions for brushing nerves in particular ways.

With guiding context and theory in place, section II surveys and interprets Spain's Almodóvar. Among this trio, Almodóvar's acclaim is the most evident as, for instance, *All About My Mother/Todo sobre mi madre* (1999) has been described as the most award-decorated film in the 110-plus year annals of the medium (D'Lugo 2006: 105). Chapter 4 discusses Almodóvar's stylistic signature. The chapter is also indebted to Louis Althusser (1994)'s concept of the Ideological State Apparatuses as these are the institutions (church, media, family, and gender) on which Almodóvar's films dwell and where substantive social change is incubated. Chapter 5 intensifies the attention to the ISAs in Almodóvar's films before telescoping in on gender. I do not challenge the premise that Almodóvar is a woman-friendly maker of modern cinematic myth but seek to carefully calibrate and qualify this widely circulated assumption. The section concludes with chapter 6's close readings of three recent, highly regarded films (*All About My Mother* [1999], *Talk to Her/Hable con ella* [2002], and *Volver* [*2006*]).

Section III spotlights the corpus of the noted Danish controversialist von Trier. Discussion opens in chapter 7 with attention to von Trier's pronounced stylistic shift from a grand formalism to a more stripped-down Dogme95–New Wave-ish style. Despite this signal change in the signature, I posit that von Trier presents an almost unswerving concern with the thematic motif of characters in trances—and, more significantly, with outsiders and failed idealists. Chapter 8 investigates how the outsider and failed idealist motifs have become crossed with von Trier's characteristically ambitious "U-S-A: Land of Opportunity" trilogy that perceptively depicts a nation that the filmmaker has never visited. While von Trier is a technical filmmaking wizard, I also argue that, as his career has played out, some of the cynicism implicit within his film's presentation of outsiders and idealists has damped down the political insights that the films may offer. Chapter 8's extended closing analysis of *Manderlay* (2005) takes up this particular criticism as it intersects with von Trier's efforts to dissect racism.

Section IV discusses Winterbottom. The British director is the youngest of the three filmmakers and also the latecomer. He delivered his cinematic debut in the mid-1990s when Almodóvar and von Trier were already established (indeed, were revitalizing their careers). As a filmmaker, Winterbottom is marked by his fecundity (more than a film per year, on average), willingness to venture in new directions in generic terms—and by his commitment to human rights and issues of international politics as these impact on "everyday" subjects' lives. Chapter 9 develops an account of Winterbottom's stylistic signature and family/gender relations across his corpus of films. Chapter 10 analyzes the tense and challenging relations that Winterbottom cultivates between fact and fiction (in part, cued by his frequent use of journalists as protagonists). Finally, chapter 11 fixes onto Winterbottom's presentation of the United States and, more broadly, human rights in the international arena. While Winterbottom's *The Claim* (2000), set in nineteenth-century California, is favorable to the United States' image of itself, the documentary *The Road to Guantanamo* (co-directed with Mat Whitecross, 2006) is a straightforward reply to one shard of neo-conservative doctrine. Finally, I discuss Winterbottom's incorporation of human rights as a guiding narrative theme.

Finally, before our main feature, a personal note: composing this volume has been, among other things, an inventory of my lifelong, zig-zagged, and eclectic educational history. I hope that the results contribute to the reader's education in some appreciable measure.

SECTION I
INDUSTRIES AND AUTEURS

CHAPTER 2

The International Film Industry

In this chapter, I take up Miller et al.'s conviction that, "the best cultural studies have worked through the imbrication of power and signification at all points on the cultural continuum" (2001: 2). Subsequent chapters will assay to unpack what the auteurs' films say, for example, in terms of their ideological valence as well as their strains against prevailing ideology. However, discussion of texts without contexts presents a necessarily incomplete account of the world of films, as it does not ground them in their methods of production. At the same time, the assumption that traces of political, economic, and social power are insinuated into film texts is almost a commonplace—even as many investigations do not take the step, in practice, of interrogating power as it intersects with the text. Tracing the circulation of power back to the means of production in international terms is still less frequently realized; for example, prominent political economist of media Robert W. McChesney (1999) devotes scant attention to texts themselves. Exceptions exist that prove the rule, such as Janet Wasko's (2000) book-length study of Disney that examines both text and industry context with rigor.

In surveying the international film industry, one quickly encounters the high profile of the United States and its major studio oligopoly (i.e., "Hollywood"). To wit: The 39 biggest box-office hits in the world in 1998 were U.S. productions (Miller et al. 2001: 49). While the U.S. produced 18 films in 2000 that generated 100 million U.S. dollars (USDs) in international box office outside the home territory, the rest of the world claimed a combined total of *zero* such films (Miller et al. 2001: 5). Turning specifically to the other major pole of global wealth, Europe, one finds that Hollywood has realized striking success. In 1996, Hollywood studios claimed 70 percent of the ticket revenue in the European Union (EU) (Miller et al. 2001: 5). At one point in time, *Titanic* garnered an alarming *24 percent* of total box office revenue in Poland (Jäckel 2003: 140). As of March 2008, The Numbers Web site lists the "All Time Highest Grossing Movies Worldwide"; the 152 top-grossing films are U.S. productions and co-productions (The Numbers 2008). An Australian production, *Crocodile Dundee* (Peter Faiman 1986), enters as the first non-U.S. entry at Number 153 on the list.[1]

U.S. productions saturate European television screens as well, often via films that have exhausted their cinematic runs. Terry Flew (2007) and Kai Hafez (2007) are, however, adamant that, on the small screen, local formats, and talent are advantaged, particularly in the prime viewing hours. Nevertheless, the U.S. capture of the big screen has long been evident (Hobsbawm 1996: 195)—and long resented. In addition to armadas of, for example, overblown and commercially calculated big-budget spectaculars and often charmless comedies, the United States' recent trend toward gore-pornography ("gorno") has given further pause for concern toward seeing film with some potential for audience uplift.

The situation is by no means symmetrical on the other side of the Atlantic. In 2000, Hollywood locked down the domestic box office with a nearly airtight 93 percent of the revenue in its domestic market. By contrast, European films captured a meager 3.9 percent share on U.S. soil; figures that are consistent with long-term trends in which Hollywood functions as a one-way portal from America to the rest of the globe's screens. Hence, regardless of where we are, "We are all experts at understanding Hollywood movies" (Miller et al. 2001: 1). By contrast, in Dimitris Eleftheriotis' offhand appraisal, U.S. films generally do not "demonstrate awareness of their existence in relation to other cultures and other cinemas" (2001: 83). While the U.S. screen industries were increasingly rolling over Europe, barricades against wider domination by the U.S. industry were mainly found in India and China; the two screen-laden population giants have successfully been able to leverage these characteristics to limit U.S. imports (Miller et al. 2001). At the same time, given its constant efforts at global reach and intensifying reliance on foreign box office, Hollywood films also strategically "dis-embed" from North America (Wayne 2002).

The Da Vinci Code, for example, may be characterized as a studio film that has donned the proverbial wig and sunglasses in order to impersonate a European film: Tom Hanks as a Harvard professor notwithstanding, it features European stars (Audrey Tatou, Ian McKellen, Jean Reno) as well as European locales and versions of its histories/mythologies.

Why, specifically, do these trends and patterns matter? In the first line of her book on the topic, Anne Jäckel captures the stakes: "The film industry is unlike any other" because "its products are cultural, public as well as private goods, with a symbolic (historical, national, linguistic, social) significance that cannot be reduced to a mere commodity" (2003: 1). Former French president François Mitterand made the case for culture in these words:

> Creations of the spirit are not just commodities; the elements of culture are not pure business. Defending the pluralism of works of art and the freedom of the public to choose is a duty. What is at stake is the cultural identity of all our nations. It is the right of all peoples to their own culture. It is the freedom to create and choose our own images. A society which abandons to others the way of showing itself, that is the way of presenting itself to itself, is a society enslaved. (quoted in Eleftheriotis 2001: 70)

The stakes are, thus, very high.

The theme has rehearsed many times, but the contrast is generally construed as follows: In the United States' Hollywood-based studio oligopoly, film is a business in the first instance. In Europe, the likely birthplace of film (Barnouw 1993), it is still firstly an art form and thus construed as partly removed from unconditional market relations. Despite the contrast, there has long been cross-fertilization between U.S. and European film. A notable instance: The wedding of German expressionism (sinister nocturnal environments and low-key lighting schemes) to the low-life world of the United States' hard-boiled literature ushered *film noir* to the screen (Shrader 1986). More recently, 1950s Hollywood "B" movies were part of the impetus for French New Wave. In turn, by the late 1960s, this wave had reversed its transatlantic course back to the United States as the "New American cinema" of Arthur Penn, Robert Altman, Francis Coppola, Bob Rafelson et al. (Cook 1990: 874–879). Even given these noteworthy moments of cross-fertilization, Hollywood filmmaking is qualitatively different for the extent to which it is governed by commercial writ in a manner not observed in Europe.[2]

Of course, popular films are not to be scorned merely for having been seen by a public willing to brave a ticket window or video rental line; conversely, many an obscure film is highly deserving of its status for being indulgent, even unwatchable. In this vein, Mike Wayne acknowledges that, "more culturally and politically ambitious cinema always risks making an alliance with elitism" (2002: 21). Wayne reframes the issue, however, by observing that the "elitism versus populism" dichotomy looks in the wrong direction. He posits that analysis should instead focus on an industrial Hollywood oligopoly with global reach that is broadly enabled by the economic doctrines of liberalized market access. He furnishes an analogy. For Wayne, a progressive-in-spirit film perspective that is nonetheless beholden to postmodernism and identity politics, orients to "patterns" of cultural offerings "temporarily arranged by the kaleidoscope." However, he writes, "With each twist a new pattern would order itself while the machine which determines the patterns remains intact" (2002: 128). Following Wayne's charge, in this analysis I want to not only peer at the screen but also to look in detail at the machine that shoots the imagery toward it: namely, the film industry in international terms, with a focus on the machinery of the Hollywood studio oligopoly and the European counters to it.

This chapter unfolds by discussing the methods and deeply inscribed market advantages of the Hollywood studio. Thereafter, I address the evolving European responses to the studio model at the national and supra-national level, including international film festivals. While cognizant of the substantial advantages that Hollywood commands, one purpose is to steer away from positing an endgame in which its studios are fore-ordained to prevail over rivals—like industrial versions of John Rambo or Ethan Hunt.

Hollywood Studios: They Might Be Giants

Why does Hollywood succeed in international markets? A short and direct answer to this question is that Hollywood films do well at the box office, domestically and internationally, because that is what they have been designed to do. It is their alpha and omega, written into their DNA. True, despite the painstaking efforts to generate moneymakers, many films flop. Nevertheless, when the stream of studio films pass through the market environments at home and internationally, in the main, these films perform as programmed and generate revenue.

A large part of the reason that this occurs is because the criterion by which studio film projects are selected to go forward from among other candidate projects strongly favors commercial potential. Films that do not present such potential are unlikely to pass through filters of selection. Specifically, Rick Instrell (1992) details "The Package" that typically constitutes the successful pitch for a film project under the auspices of a Hollywood studio. As shocking as it may seem to those who have gazed upon offerings such as *Click* (Frank Coraci 2006), the U.S. industry is more "selective" than that of Europe with regard to projects in development that it permits to go forward. In Europe about one fourth of projects are estimated to go in to production following the development phase. By contrast, in the United States, the ratio is a stingier one in ten of candidate projects that move through all the commercially calibrated filters (Jäckel 2003: 29–30).

The Package plays upon the "high concept" beginning with a storyline that can be reduced to a transparent phrase. The storyline is expected to present an amalgam of the familiar and the novel. What this means is that the story should not be so original (potentially "far out") that the studio's concept of a spectator will not be able to get his or her head around it. Excesses of originality may also leave marketers at a loss to conjure the right packaging for the film. In the first instance, "neo-phobia" does a great deal to damp down the creative impulse. For example, it is exceedingly unlikely that a "New Wave" will be inaugurated under studio auspices, as the industry is presently constituted. However, being too predictable is also not desirable for triggering the palpable déjà vu of having seen the same film last summer (with a slightly different soundtrack or some other face from the stable of *au courant* leads). Hence, given the safe and conservative criterion for going forward with the production of an expensive one-shot commodity (average cost: upward of 75 million USDs), stress on convention and variations on tried themes tend strongly to trump invention.

Other than coloring within the lines of the familiar (as long as the conventions are not *too* obviously tried and true), Instrell identifies other, more concrete features of The Package. Appealing to the teen audience is part of the formula. As teens are the most frequent filmgoers, appeals to their sensibilities present both a note-worthy constraint on film content as well as a commercially safe strategy. Teens as target audience also impact on release dates. Vacation periods from school (summer, winter holidays) are pre-ferred as they cater to teens' seasonal rhythms.

Bankable stars are another feature of The Package that stresses commerce given the boost that stars furnish for promo-tion. If stars from the "'A'-List" are not at hand, promotional ap-peals based on the director may suffice (or even the producer, although it is not a central artistic role). Tie-in potential also looms large under the rubric of The Package. The potential for spin-off books and comics, video games, soundtracks, tee-shirts, and other accoutrements weigh in a candidate project's favor with respect to going forward into production. Effects-laden big budget spectacu-lars about the apocalyptic terror of brain-eating zombies lend themselves to the presumptive blood-saturated narrative desires of teens and the concomitant sales of action figures and hit single ti-tle songs more than subtle, irony-laden independent films about middle age, such as *Sideways* (Alexander Payne 2004) or *Safe* (Todd Haynes 1995).

An established commercial track record associated with a film is part and parcel of its potential for synergy. The candidate pro-ject that has achieved prior success and pre-standing name recog-nition as a book, television program, video game or amusement park ride, or as a previous installment of the film franchise, is ad-vantaged for presenting already established commercial synergy. In this vein, fourteen of the top fifteen highest grossing films of all time in global box office are entries in a franchise (to wit, *Lord of the Rings*, *Pirates of the Caribbean*, *Harry Potter*, *Star Wars*, *Ju-rassic Park*, *Shrek*, and *Spider-Man*)(The Numbers 2008). Other features of the package include a "catchy" title and a positive end-ing; accoutrements that can be tweaked as necessary should they initially be found lacking. Film titles, in particular, may need re-finements when going into circulation abroad due to the intrinsic difficulties of translation between languages or in an effort to ap-peal to local tastes.[3]

Given the rigors of The Package to prompt sales, artistic merit can be thoroughly epiphenomenal to the box office success of a Hol-lywood studio product. However, beyond any given film's compati-bility with The Package, an even wider battery of materially grounded industrial logics presents built-in advantages to the Hollywood studios over other competitors in the international arena. Below, I discuss these deeply embedded systematic factors in detail.

Business "Plan It" Hollywood: Investment and Budgets

The U.S. film industry features massive investment as compared with other nations. Large investment brings big budgets in its train. More specifically, the U.S. film industry accounts for a staggering 74 percent of global film investment (Wayne 2002: 6). Big budgets in turn translate into more star power marshaled to the screen, with astronomical salaries devoted to stars. By contrast, Europeans are often ambivalent or phobic about being stars at least within their national terrains (Finney 1996: 58–59). Big budgets also prompt highly polished production values. In a more speculative vein, these qualities may, over time, relentlessly shape the paradigm of what audiences come to expect from a film—and do so on the terms that are favorable to the Hollywood industry. On this view, the big budget paradigm generates a barrier to market entry in itself by reigning as the default template that fosters widely held expectations for what constitutes a film: recognizable stars and expensive screen spectacle via, for example, special effects and exotic locations (Wayne 2002). While this does not eliminate low-budget production, it pushes it further to the margins.

Bigness is manifest in other forms. Hollywood studios have long commanded an oligopoly with regard to the domestic market, alongside the studios' striking success in generating box office revenue abroad. At present, however, several of the studios are subsidiaries of larger non-U.S. multinational companies (MNCs). For example, Universal Studios is a unit of France's Vivendi (after stints under Japanese and Canadian parent companies) while Columbia is owned by Sony (Japanese) (Thompson and Bordwell 2003: 706). A large share of investment in the studios' films comes from international sources as well. Between these considerations, and the studio's intensifying pursuit of revenue abroad, one might claim that Hollywood is in the process of being dissolved via the solvent of globalization. However, "control of the studio output remains in California and New York . . . where its actual product development and management are domiciled" (Miller et al. 2001: 46).

Moreover, the demands of The Package continue their reign since "there is not a single executive in Hollywood who, under pressure from the parent firm and financiers would make a movie that lacks elements congenial with the ability to market, advertise, promote" (Miller et al. 2001: 169). In turn, the majors have long relied on a great deal of subcontracting that puts the studio in charge of the "design," distribution and marketing while in effect "farming out" many other functions including post-production and animation (Instrell 1992; Miller et al. 2001: 55).

Despite big budgets on one hand, Miller et al. discuss the extent to which the studios are eager to pinch a buck, particularly for "below the line" labor that does not make the credit sequence. For instance, construction workers on the set of *The Mexican* (Gore Verbinski 2001) were paid 12 USDs per diem, while above the line laborers Brad Pitt and Julia Roberts made ends meet on a combined salary of 40 million USDs (Miller et al. 2001: 76). Particularly when the dollar was "hard" in the Clinton 1990s, the major studios ramped up production in Czech Republic, Canada, and Australia and realized savings via a favorable exchange rate for the dollar while also tapping skilled, nonunionized labor. To take one case, shooting *The Matrix* (Andy and Larry Wachowski 1999) in Australia presented savings of up to 30 percent over Los Angeles' costs (Miller et al. 2001: 68).

Marketing "Über Alles"

The average studio film budget was 75.6 million USDs by 1997 (Miller et al. 2001: 83). In turn, promotion accounts for about 30 percent of the budget, making film the United States' third most advertised industry by 1999 (Miller et al. 2001: 48, 150). Expenditure for advertising far outdistances European promotion even as its budgets for hype have spiked upward in recent years (Jäckel 2003: 99). By contrast, the average UK film production presents an advertising budget of 250,000–300,000 British pounds (Wayne 2002: 6) or about 360,000–435,000 USDs at 2002 exchange rates (www.x-rates.com/cgi-bin/hlookup.cgi). Promotion clearly does not reduce to spectators entranced by ads toward which they have no resistance; nonetheless, Hollywood films achieve a high profile abroad via billboards, broadcast, and print ads. By 2008, an entire Madrid metro stop in the city center was turned over to wall-to-wall promotion of the Doug Liman–directed stinker, *Jumper*; promotion so over-the-top as to suggest hysteria that the film would not be noticed on merit (positive reviews and/or word-of-mouth). Along with hyperbolic promotion, various forms of viral campaigning are part of the toolkit. As Jäckel (2003) observes, promotion via the relatively low-cost Internet may level the field somewhat although this strategy is not a panacea within a crowded Internet milieu.

Promotion is so central to a Hollywood project that synergetic concepts for a blockbuster film may be worked out in advance of having a script written as was the case for *Armageddon* (Michael Bay 1998)(Miller et al. 2001: 155). On the other hand, consider the low-budget success of *The Full Monty* (Peter Cattaneo 1997). Fox Searchlight—subsidiary of Hollywood major Twentieth Century Fox—trumpeted the low-budget British comedy-with-touches-of-grit via a promotional budget that exceeded production costs by *tenfold* (Jäckel 2003: 100). The film thus enacted the "have it all" paradox of the low-budget/lavishly advertised feature. Furthermore, almost everything within a studio film's diegesis is a result of a marketing arrangement. By the turn of the millennium, 35 companies were available for the purpose of combing through scripts to locate moments with product placement potential (Miller et al. 2001: 155).

Beyond marketing any given film, a nation's film industry also tunes the commercial climate to the nation's favor. Miller et al. observe that, "As early as 1912, Hollywood exporters were aware that where their films traveled, demand was created for other US goods" as each foot of film exported was said to cascade into an additional dollar spent on U.S. manufacturing (2001: 26). These observations speak to the economic and "sociological propaganda" that an internationally prominent film industry commands (Ellul 1965). For such reasons, the South Korean Motion Picture Promotion Corporation currently promotes the national cinema's international profile and circulation by furnishing monies for translations, prints, and film festival participation (Shin 2005).

Bigness Is a Growth Factor for . . . Further Bigness

The studios present a striking measure of vertical integration (notably with regard to production and distribution) as well as horizontal integration (that enables spin-offs into synergy). Studios are also parts of larger MNCs that in turn ease the synergies that make the film the hub of a rapidly spinning commercial wheel. In a case study of 200-proof commercial synergy, Janet Wasko covers the staggering array of promotions that accompanied Disney's roll-out of its 1997 film, *Hercules* (Ron Clements and John Musker). Hype for the film included tie-ins (food, hotels, cars); 6,000–7,000 licensed products manufactured by 100 different firms; *Hercules on Ice*; a two-mile parade through Manhattan with City Hall coopera-tion; and extensive coverage on the ABC network, E!, Disney Channel, and Arts and Entertainment Channel (Disney-owned venues all)(Wasko 2002: 72–82).

Also notice that, at first blush, the growth of ancillary markets (DVD, cable television) would seem to be good news for small-scale production by furnishing more channels to fill. However, there is a strong countervailing force: Films are released into their first and most prominent distribution channel, the cinema, with a tight window of time and attenuated exhibitor patience for attracting an audience. Films that open badly at the box office move into DVD circulation more rapidly while missing their first and best oppor-tunity for impact. This, in turn, presents a further disadvantage for small-budget productions in their cinema exhibition phase as they are already at the margins with a lower profile for their less readily detected promotional campaigns. Moreover, films that are "different" and/or challenging often require more time to build word-of-mouth that a box-office driven quick hook from the cinema works against. By contrast, "quirky" or challenging films that are studio-supported may be strategically boosted with a gradual "platform release." In cases such as *American Beauty* (Sam Mendes 1999), limited exhibition commences in the cultural center cities in order to generate favorable appraisal from cosmopolitan critics as well as the gold-dust of favorable word-of-mouth that moves later-ally. By contrast, a massive saturation booking for the opening can present a strategy to short circuit what the studio anticipates will be bad word-of-mouth abetted by negative critical response. Hence, the critically savaged *Matrix Revolutions* (Andy and Larry Wa-chowski) premiered in November 2003 with a coordinated *world-wide* release date that stayed one step ahead of the critical/word-of-mouth lynch mob.

Where bigness is concerned, the very size of the United States (about 300 million residents) also presents a built-in advantage for its film industry. By contrast, Germany is the most populous

European nation with approximately 80 million residents. When "medium sized" European nations, such as Portugal or The Netherlands, are one-thirtieth (or less) the size of the U.S. market, "the very existence of a film industry is largely dependent on government regulation and subsidies" (Jäckel 2003: 47). With a large internal market, generally high disposable income and relatively low linguistic diversity, the U.S. studios are in a strong position to recover costs in the domestic market and export for "pure profit." By contrast, with a population less than Illinois and a cultural/linguistic fracture along Latin-Germanic lines, Belgium enjoys no such advantages. Finally, as profit-oriented businesses that have been successful in the past, the Hollywood studios avail themselves of low-interest loans, thereby reinforcing the pre-existing advantages. Wayne observes that U.S. studios may borrow capital at interest rates as low as 2.75 percent as compared with 8–9 percent in the United Kingdom (2002: 6).

During the 1990s, the Dutch media corporation PolyGram launched a serious effort to construct a major studio with international reach via its subsidiary company, Working Titles. In turn, Working Titles realized success with some youth-oriented European films: *Four Weddings and a Funeral* (Mike Newell 1994), *Shallow Grave* (Danny Boyle 1994), and *Trainspotting* (Danny Boyle 1996). The company also supported edgy independent U.S. films *The Usual Suspects* (Bryan Singer 1995) and *Fargo* (Joel Coen 1996). However, the company's successes were not enough to counter its ambitious flops. By 1998, Seagrams purchased PolyGram to absorb the company's music division (Thompson and Bordwell 2003: 711). Kristin Thompson and David Bordwell posit that European "micro-studios" have, by contrast with PolyGram's grander ambitions through Working Titles, proven more successful for their critical success and financial viability. They cite Lars von Trier's innovative Zentropa studio as a notable instance.

Distribution

Distribution, distribution, distribution—that's the issue...the whole business of people saying to European producers that you just need to make films audiences want to see is complete crap. There are American movies that should not be in 100 theaters, ghastly movies with terrible reviews that no one cares about, but because a major has the muscle they get them on the screen.

—Uberto Pasolini (quoted in Miller et al. 2001: 148)

Without a distribution channel, a film will not reach an audience and it effectively becomes the tree that fell unnoticed in the forest. In this vein, part of the relative weakness of the UK industry is reflected in its spotty distribution. In any given year in the United Kingdom, a mere 20 to 50 percent of films that are in the can even realize a cinematic release (Wayne 2002: 8); fewer still realize what can be characterized as wide release with numerous prints in circulation. Thus, distribution is a crucial moment in the film industry—and, in turn, Hollywood's global reach.

The Hollywood studio's production oligopoly is tightly linked up to its distribution oligopoly. Distribution entails the determination and negotiation of the release pattern (e.g., saturation booking, with as many screens as possible for the film's debut) and type of exhibition space that will be favored. Crucially, the distributor furnishes the costly film prints to be exhibited. Promotional campaigns are also arranged by a film's distributor. Furthermore, the distributor may script a film's further movements into other distribution channels by obtaining licenses for broadcast television, cable, and video/DVD (Jäckel 2003). In effect, the first print of the film is the most expensive, and each additional one is amortized across all of these revenue channels (further tilting the scales in favor of bigness). Moreover, an independent filmmaker may have neither the capital for numerous prints, nor the acumen or connections to arrange wide exhibition: hence, the dependence upon distributors.

In Jäckel's appraisal, the international arms of Hollywood studios "dominate the distribution sector in Europe" (2003: 91). These companies include Buena Vista International (Disney), Columbia Tri-Star, and United Pictures International (a consortium of Paramount and Universal). Given that many films do not make money at the box office, distribution comes with a measure of risk. For this reason, bigness in the distribution network is favored within the ostensible "market environment." That is, a distributor with wider reach may cover its "losing bets" via the relatively few films that realize bountiful returns. By contrast, small-scale distributors have been sunk by even one large-scale flop that takes the whole company down with it (Jäckel 2003: 107). As a result, the market necessarily becomes less competitive when left to its own mechanisms that favor lumbering behemoths able to absorb regular losses.

Because the studio distribution arms are in effect stocking the exhibitors' shelves with most of its product, distributors may use their leverage to negotiate favorable deals. Films get "bundled" together so that if exhibitors want to screen any given (artistically, commercially) desirable film, they must also agree to exhibit a turkey or two as part of the bundle of product for their screens. In Miller et al.'s phrase, "you only get the Spielberg film if you take the Jean Claude Van Damme movie" (2001: 151). Once again, bigness begets and reinforces bigness.

"In Spain," Miller et al. observe (2001: 148), "there is not a single national distributor that is not a subsidiary of a Hollywood major." Neighboring France, by contrast, features Europe's strongest national film industry that is also characterized by a pattern of concentration in its distribution apparatus. French firms GBVI, Pathé and UFD combined to capture 39 percent of their domestic distribution market in 1999. They did so, in part, by locally distributing Hollywood product (e.g., *The Mummy*, Stephen Sommers 1999). Moreover, studio arms UIP and Warner Brothers were just behind the French entries in the market share chart for distribution as they combined for 23 percent of the market (Jäckel 2003: 106–107). Jäckel concludes that the continuing reign of bigness in the distribution sector bodes ill for European cinema since smaller distributors tend to behave as better guardians of European culture.

The immersion of film within the exigencies of a commercial milieu presents itself even in the final moment of the production-distribution-exhibition circuit. Hence, exhibition venues where the films are screened present another area in which the studio majors have sought to make further inroads into Europe. Thompson and Bordwell observe that, within the United States, the seductions of the multiplex stimulated more filmgoing behavior in the public via the accretion of further pleasures of consumption onto it (2003: 709). Given the emphasis on bigness, the studios were seized by the idea that "many screens under one roof, a single box office, centralized concession sales, and other economies of scale" would play out in Europe as they had in the U.S. domestic market (2003: 709). Jäckel cites an employment notice for a manager at the U.S.-owned AMC megaplex in Dunkirk, France. Today's "battle" in Dunkirk is waged to vacuum cash from patrons' wallets, as indicated by the ad that reads in part: "'You should provide evidence of holding a successful management post in an economic sector where the number of customers is the main factor of success'" (quoted in Jäckel 2003: 132). By contrast, Jäckel observes that locally grounded independent exhibitors are apt to "emphasize the cultural, social and educational role of the cinema" even as they hope to make ends meet (2003: 132).

The National Entertainment State.

Along with the enormous private resources of the major studios and the MNCs in which they are embedded, the Hollywood industry is also backed by a state that is zealous about promoting its film industry and maximizing its export potential. On one hand, even local governments in the United States "go on offense" to furnish an array of subsidies for filmmaking. In one such case, the Minnesota Film Board attempts to entice filmmakers through a rebate on wages related to production, free first class travel and accommodation for producers abetted by an array of tax breaks (Miller et al. 2001: 10).[4]

On the other hand, the United States also effectively plays "defense." Miller et al. comment that, "US governments and businesses continue to assault other countries' attempts to assert rights to national self-determination on screen via barriers to imports" into the United States (Miller et al. 2001: 9). The World Trade Organization (WTO) has proven to be a useful instrument for such (Miller et al. 2001: 34–41). The United States' efforts at "policing" the national screen "perimeter" from alien celluloid have included setting the world standard in the use of WTO trade complaint mechanisms to police copyrights and erect barriers that keep international media beyond the moat.

Beyond profit, film export avails the United States of a significant measure of sociological propaganda that positions it as the world's vanguard society in part through its sheer visibility and unmissible presence. Following Jacques Ellul (1965)'s conceptualization, films channel "sociological propaganda" that is aligned with and promotes a national "way of life." Moreover, as Miller et al. observe, films "address our very frameworks of taste and politics" (2001: 1). Similarly, in the United Kingdom, analysts posit that, "British media output is like a national advertising campaign" (Wayne 2002: 39) while Jäckel observes that, more generally, "Governments have latched onto the reality that films are big business and excellent promotional tools for your country'" (2003: 65). Given such considerations, the interminable Uruguay Round of the General Agreement on Tariffs and Trade (GATT) in 1993 nearly collapsed over disagreements about liberalization of markets for the screen industries. Even while contentious issues like agriculture had been settled, the clash between the U.S.- and France-led Europe over culture speaks to the U.S. government's vigilance on behalf of Hollywood; and to the stiff opposition that the U.S. posture provokes when culture is unidimensionalized as a commodity that is more-or-less like any other product (e.g., socks, grapefruits) and *not* regarded as a uniquely resonant expression of a culture's specificities.

Talent Poaching

For generations, Hollywood has been advantaged by the allure of its "benjamins" and "bling"—that is, of the material rewards that surround money and exposure. During most of the twentieth century, the United States' wealth, its relative political stability, and its imperviousness to armed conflict on its own soil also presented built-in advantages. By contrast, the exodus of talent from Central Europe to Hollywood during the rise of Euro-fascism in the 1930s implicated figures such as Billy Wilder, Douglas Sirk, Michael Curtiz, Fritz Lang, and Otto Preminger.

In the 1960s, Hollywood faced crisis due to a business model that produced yawn-inducing, big-budget "spectacles" that catered to the older segment of a public that increasingly stayed home and watched television (Cook 1990). However, in this case, the studios were again the beneficiaries of good fortune from Europe; "arty" imports from the "Old World" partly revived the industry via their energetic New Waves. These imports included particular films as well as talent lured, permanently or transiently, to the Hollywood studio; even Jean-Luc Godard ventured a Hollywood film, *Contempt/Le Mépris* (1963)! The trend continues into the third millennium as national celebrities are often judged to have "made it" as international celebrity figures upon gaining the imprimatur of the Southern California–grounded studios (Turner et al. 2000). As co-produced and co-financed films continue to gain traction in a world that is becoming increasingly multipolar in its centers of economic and cultural influence, the gravitation toward New York and Los Angeles will likely become far less obligatory as pilgrimages en route to certifiable global fame; for the moment, however, there is continuity with the past on this score.

Goode Olde English

While construing the English language as a distinct advantage may seem curious, it is palpable—in part for being an enduring residue of an English-speaking nation's global hegemony across the past three centuries (United Kingdom before WWII; thereafter, its former colony, the United States). The English language has in itself become a lead export for its nation of origin in the form of services (teaching, translation) and materials (books). In 2005, UK Chancellor Gordon Brown estimated that the English language accounted for about 1 percent of the United Kingdom's Gross Domestic Product (GDP) at over 10 billion pounds (Branigan 2005); or about 19 billion USDs at 2005 exchange rates (www.x-rates.com/cgi-bin/hlookup.cgi). Not surprisingly, economic and cultural power interpenetrate with each other via a wide array of manifestations. For instance, 26 Nobel Laureates in literature have been native English speakers (twice the nearest competitor, French) while four of the five most translated authors of all time composed their original works in English (Bingham 2007). Where film is concerned, as of March 2008, the top 36 grossing productions in global box office history are in the English language (The Numbers 2008); and the thirty-seventh is Mel Gibson's production, *The Passion of the Christ* (2004), a U.S. film shot in Aramaic, Latin, and Hebrew. In such ways, the enthronement of English and the Anglophile heritage is globally extended and reproduced.

In the international arena, the film industry picks up on the English language's cachet and utility. A telling case: The French comedy *Mon père, ce héros* (1991), starring Gérard Depardieu, generated 300,000 admissions on its release in Germany. A year and a half later, an English-language, scene-by-scene Hollywood remake called *My Father the Hero*—also starring Depardieu—was greeted with a near threefold upward spike to 850,000 cinema admissions in Germany (Jäckel 2003: 100–101)! Jäckel notes a similar pattern in Spain—even though *both* versions of the film (French and Hollywood) were dubbed into Spanish (!). Thus, more than language is at stake in accounting for the box office figures, even if the currency of the English language is one part of Hollywood's reach.

As ABBA-ization of the screen continues, "[e]very significant film-producing country is now making films in the English language" including ten such films in notably Francophile France in 2000 (Jäckel 2003: 63). Similarly, Spain's 2006 Goya Award winner for "Best Film" (*Mejor pelicula*) was an English-language Spanish production, starring Tim Robbins and Sarah Polley and directed by Catalan Isabel Coixet (*The Secret Life of Words /La vida secreta de las palabras* 2005). To take another notable case, about half of native Dane Lars von Trier's film corpus is in English.

Once again, the language boulevard largely runs one way, since U.S. audiences are resistant to reading subtitles—or, at least, are seldom given opportunities to demonstrate otherwise. Recently, U.S. films feature occasional bursts of dialogue in New World Spanish (e.g., Steven Soderbergh's *Traffic* [2000], Robert Rodriguez's *Once Upon a Time in Mexico* [2003]). These are the exceptions that prove the rule in U.S. films and add a touch of the (near-at-hand) "exotic" without making undue linguistic demands on U.S. audiences. Also notice that the biggest box office attractant among international films in U.S. history, with a gross of 128 million USDs, was actually a Taiwan–Hong Kong–United States–China co-production: *Crouching Tiger, Hidden Dragon/Wo hu cang long* (2000)(The Numbers 2001). Director Ang Lee is Taiwanese-born and a U.S.-educated, Westchester County (New York) resident who has worked extensively in both nations' industries. Moreover, co-scriptwriter and producer James Schamus is Usonian. Thus, while a mainly Asian production, *Crouching Tiger, Hidden Dragon* presents influences that made it more accessible to a U.S. audience.

Fighting Back

What is it like to pull a film production together in Europe? Notwithstanding a recognized auteur on board the project, and even given slight budgets, European productions can become very complicated. Lars von Trier's bust-out film, *Breaking the Waves* (1996) required the collaboration of *twenty-two* co-financiers (Finney 1996: 228). While such a vast array of collaboration makes for an extensive opening sequence of title cards for acknowledgment, *Breaking the Waves* was completed with a final budget of 7.5 million USDs (Finney 1996: 224); a very modest sum by U.S. industry

standards. Following initial support from the Danish Film Institute and the European Script Fund, the co-financing net was
hoisted toward Denmark's Nordic neighbors before fanning out
further. Moreover, unconventional techniques were employed to
secure investors. During the Gottenburg Film Festival, producers
Peter Aalbæk Jensen and Vibeke Windelov gathered potential financiers "in a very big room that was very hot, with no daylight
anywhere. We locked the door and told them: Nobody is leaving
until we have the final money on the table"—thus securing public
verbal agreement in part via peer pressure (1996: 225). Securing
French financing along the way was a mixed blessing since, "In
France, cheap solutions do not exist" and Gallic funds actually
raised the film's cost by 150,000 USDs (1996: 227).

What do such narratives illustrate? International cooperation
is necessary for many European projects. Nonetheless, part of
Europe's difficulty in keeping up with the Hollywood studios is
paradoxically linked to the strength of the continent's devotion to
localism (i.e., nationalism—and subnational localism, as in the
case of Spain and Cataluña). As Wayne states, "*national* borders
within Europe have historically been the prime mode in which social, economic, political and cultural life have been organized"
(2002: vii; original emphasis). For such reasons, "'Europe' is a
slippery term'" (Eleftheriotis 2001: 1). Europe's torturous path toward unity has been further complicated by linguistic division and
lengthy ledgers of historical conflict. By contrast, the United
States presents substantial linguistic commonality within the confines of hot-housed nationalism that defies a 3,000-mile expanse
between east and west coasts. Thus, in Eleftheriotis' appraisal, EU
reports speak in an "overwhelmingly anxious tone" when the topic
turns to the effort to pull the long fractious continent together
(2001: 2). As a result, the following Euro-heritage references are
frantically marshaled for cameos in the course of *one paragraph* of
an EU document: "Graeco-Judiac origins," "Roman Empire," "Renaissance," "compass," "printing machine," "age of Reason," "democracy,   a   progressive   theory   of   history,   human   rights,"
"Christendom," "materialist and secular" (quoted in Eleftheriotis
2001: 3). In a more direct expression of contemporary doubt about
the European project, Rosalind Galt quotes Belgian director Chan-
tal Ackerman: "I don't think there is such a thing as European
identity"—in contrast with the strategic unity that contrives co-

production finance schemes for filmmaking (2006: 104). Galt posits a deeper problem that a popular basis for the lived experience of feeling European is not (yet) at hand.

At the same time, the widely assumed division among Europeans may be changing before everyone's eyes, on the ground, with the advent of a rising generation that has grown up with the EU. Young Europeans are coming of age in an environment with ever more exchange across what had only recently (i.e., for their parents) been very starkly defined templates of nationality. Moreover, with the influx of immigrant populations, being European may become less of an ethnic/racial construct and more dependent on the feelings and values that drive identity as in the longer-standing polyglot populations of the United States and Canada. For the moment, however, one may provisionally accept that the continent-wide tendency toward cultural distinction disadvantages European challenges to U.S. screen incursions.[5]

Despite these vexing circumstances, efforts in support of national and European filmmaking are in evidence. What constitutes these efforts? Co-production presents perhaps the leading method of boosting European film. At the same time, Jäckel comments that co-production "is a much abused term" since in fact "few films produced in Europe today are financed solely by one production company. Most are co-productions" (2003: 58). However, many co-productions are actually "co-financing" arrangements in which only money is dedicated to the project—and not substantive creative input. Moreover, co-financing often reduces to a film's prearranged sale to television for broadcast following its cinematic run.

The term co-production also implicates international co-productions, a form of collaboration that is becoming more common in an increasingly integrated Europe. While nations like Belgium have long depended on international co-productions to get films to the screen, the larger EU states have stepped up international co-productions. In Spain, for example, international co-production spiked from 14 percent of its films in 1988 to 28 percent in 1998. On this score, Spain also has the advantage of relatively easy collaboration with numerous New World nations with which it shares language as an enduring residue of the Columbian era. Germany and France also witnessed increases in international co-productions to varying degrees (Jäckel 2003: 60) while the United Kingdom's co-production possibilities have proliferated due to the ascendancy of its native tongue as an international currency (con-sidered earlier). The United States has also been a willing interna-tional co-production partner with EU projects.

Co-productions may be conducted on an entirely privatized ba-sis. However, public programs have also been facilitators of Euro-pean film production in general and co-production in particular. Governments (local and national) may support film production via a wide array of methods. These include: Grants, loans, tax shel-ters, concessions and rebates, cash bonuses based on box office per-formance, subsidies, and recognition via awards (Jäckel 2003: 46–55). State-sponsored facilities are also useful with respect to stu-dios, provision of extras (e.g., military and police), transport and other aspects of production such as securing locations. Taxes that are levied on tickets are also ploughed back into national produc-tion with schemes that differ in their details across national bor-ders.

A Survey of Continent-Wide Initiatives

What has the EU been doing for film? The European Community (precursor to the EU) launched the MEDIA program to boost its film industries in the 1980s. Miller et al. betray disdain for these interventions as "largely ineffective" (2001: 93), for being over-whelmed by the scale of private European investment that places its bets on financing Hollywood product. Miller et al.'s palpable eye-rolling also stems from the EU's enablement of what they take to be culture as driven by stone-faced culturecrats. Despite their left-leaning trappings, by the end of their study, Miller et al. am-bivalently enthrone the market and their version of its mytholo-gized "sovereign consumer" (Goss 2003). In making these moves, Miller et al. at once acknowledge and dismiss their empirical ob-servation that today's wealthy core of nations achieved their status via massive, strategic State intervention in markets. The G7 has, in other words, unashamedly guided and subsidized the vaunted "invisible hand" with spectacular success in many targeted indus-tries—including film.

Where specifics are concerned, Europe's pilot MEDIA program was initiated in 1988 with a modest budget (Jäckel 2003: 68). The program pursued new initiatives in the 1990s that included im-proved exhibition for the European films of the future as well as enhanced conservation and restoration of films of the past. In

1994, the successor MEDIA II program was endowed with a larger budget and a revised mission to maintain Europe's linguistic diversity while supporting film production in regions with lower output. During the program's five-year run, MEDIA II made contributions to 281 production houses encompassing 1,690 audiovisual productions (Jäckel 2003: 73). Distribution of films beyond their nation of origin also spiked upward from 246 in 1996 to 456 in 1999 (Jäckel 2003: 74). MEDIA Plus was inaugurated as the successor program to facilitate European production with more money and some new foci such as assisting the transition to new (i.e., digital) technologies in the film industry.

The boost from MEDIA has mainly been directed toward smaller nations with more vulnerable industries; hence, by design, Ireland reaps more benefits than France. MEDIA and national film schools have also stepped up coverage of the business side of production. Jäckel comments that, "'Watching as many films as possible at the *cinematheque*'. . . is no longer regarded as a reasonable approach to acquire film-making skills" (2003: 34)—essential as it may be to the artistic side. Curricula include courses on how to develop the script and fashion a business plan. Nonetheless, given the studio behemoths' pre-standing advantages, discussed earlier, the EU programs did not turn the battleship around for Europe's industries. Critics have also questioned whether MEDIA is a "half measure" intervention that cannot support the needs of European cinema—and thus a form of sop that fights yesterday's battles (Jäckel 2003: 89).

Eurimages is the Council of Europe's most assertive program to promote international co-production between European partners and is designed to reduce risk for producers. According to its executive secretary in 1992, the program's objective is "not to get its money back but to support an activity which is both industrial and cultural, and which asserts Europe's identity" (Ryclef Rienstra, quoted in Jäckel 2003: 76). Interest-free loans are advanced to filmmakers once they have already lined up most of the financing with an average contribution of 10 percent of targeted films' budgets. The loans are referred to as "advances in receipts" since sums are to be repaid once profits are realized; given these generous, non-market procedures, some loans are never repaid. Co-productions in low film output areas are prioritized while, on the other hand, some high profile directors have gained assistance (e.g., Belgium's Ackerman, Denmark's von Trier) (Miller et al. 2001: 91).

While undoubtedly helpful, Eurimages' contributions to co-produced films' budgets generally cover only the additional cost of initiating a co-production (roughly, 10 percent of the budget) that include transport and translation services (Wayne 2002). Co-productions also bring risk of, on one hand, the much-feared blandness of what Galt derisively refers to as the "Euro-pudding" of culturally compromised, diluted product on one hand (or, as Galt embellishes it in classic Euro-skeptic fashion, "the filmic correlative of Brussels bureaucracy" [2006: 2]); and, on the other hand, there is risk of clashes punctuated with what Wayne calls nationalistic "investor bullying" (2002: 18). Wayne cites the co-production, *The Disappearance of Finbar*, to which Swedish investors would contribute only if there was some dialogue in Swedish. However, the United Kingdom's Channel Four would not invest unless there were no subtitles, thereby privileging spoken English. The dilemma was finessed by using Swedish dialogue for passages in which the meaning was transparently obvious or for humorous effect when the English-speaking characters were gobsmacked with non-understanding.

Eurimages as well as MEDIA have been active on the exhibition front in addition to interventions on behalf of production. Europa Cinemas were introduced in 1992 as a means of constructing European- and diversity-dedicated theaters in Europe. By 2008, the network consists of 685 cinemas in 392 cities with a total of 1,702 screens (Europa Cinemas 2008). The difference that the Europa Cinemas herald can be read right off the titles of the films' posters in the "Now Playing!" display case. In 1999, participating cinemas in the network were programming European films 64 percent of the time with box office takings of 100 million euros (Jäckel 2003: 89).

What difference does an exhibition venue make? Consider two theaters in Madrid. The first is the Verdi cinema and the second is Yelmo Ideal. The former is a Europa exhibition house and the later is operated by Loews, a U.S. firm. Both are in fairly central locations and both are relatively newly constructed exhibition spaces. Moreover, in contrast with the overwhelming majority of Spanish exhibition, both exhibition houses show films in *la version original*—"original version"—with subtitles for non-Spanish language productions. When patrons opt for original version cinema, it is a clear marker of distinction given that the overwhelming tendency of Spain's cinemas, even in Madrid, is to exhibit dubbed prints. While the two cinemas share the subtitling distinction, the contrast between Verdi (Europa) and Yelmo Ideal (Loews) is augured on the marquee. The Europa cinema favors international films with a European accent while the U.S.-owned cinema is essentially a local house organ for Hollywood. Table 2.1 details what is being exhibited at the two exhibition houses during the week that I am writing this in Autumn 2007. At Yelmo Ideal, 16 of 21 films screened during the weekend are U.S. productions or co-productions. By contrast, all five of Verdi's offerings are European and South American. Although the program is modest in scope at present, and the Loews cinema houses have far more screens on average (Jäckel 2003: 125), the Europa Cinemas present a material (brick and mortar) intervention against studio mono-culture.

The sum of these efforts is that European cinema has taken steps to at least hold its lines in the combat for screen space. Nonetheless, on a continent where commercial success had not been the alpha and omega (or even a matter to overly fret about) some analysts posit that European cinema has embarked on a path with perils; one that may endgame with becoming "Hollywood Lite" via an ironing out of particularity for a slightly greater measure of box office success (Jäckel 2003). On the other hand, European films display willingness to examine their own societies and even venture what Mike Wayne has called "anti-national national cinema" (2002: 26) to an extent not observed in the United States. These penetrating examinations of Europe, without U.S.-style cloying special effects or pieties, bode well for substantive expression in European film; recent exemplars include the United Kingdom's *This Is England* (Shane Meadows 2006), Germany's *The Lives of Others/Das Leben der Anderen* (Florian Henckel von Donnersmarck 2006), and Romania's *4 Months, 3 Weeks, 2 Days/4 luni, 3 saptamani si 2 zile*) (Cristian Mungiu 2007).

Festival Friendly

Along with national and EU-driven programs, the international film festival circuit is significant in nurturing the European film industries (as well as the United States' independent sector). Presently, there are more film festivals in Europe than days of the year

(Elsaesser 2005: 86) with Cannes, Venice, Berlin, and San Sebastián leading the way in prestige and visibility.

Table 2.1 Films Exhibited (Week of September 28–October 4, 2007)
Yelmo Cines Ideal-Madrid (Loews)
Film Title, Country/ies of Origin (Number of Showings per day/weekend)

Sin reservas / No Reservations, United States–Australia (4)
Mataharis, Spain (6)
La gran estafa /The Hoax, United States (6)
Planet terror, United States (1)
Babel, France–United States–Mexico (1)
El coronel Macià, Spain (1)
Un corazón invencible /A Mighty Heart, United States–United Kingdom (4)
Dos dias en Paris / Two Days in Paris, France-Germany (1)
Los Simpson / The Simpsons Movie, United States (1)
Disturbia, United States (2)
El ultimatum de Bourne / The Bourne Ultimatum, United States (2)
Zodiac, United States (1)
Ratatouille, United States (1)
La jungle 4.0 / Live Free or Die Harder, United Kingdom–United States (1)
Conversaciones con mi jardinero, France (2)
El buen pastor / The Good Shepherd, United States (1)
Harry Potter y el orden del fénix / Harry Potter and the Order of the Phoenix, United Kingdom–United States (1)
Caótica Ana, Spain (2)
Death Proof, United States (3)
Hairspray, United States (4)
La extraña que hay en ti /The Brave One, United States–Australia (5)

Verdi-Madrid (EUROPA CINEMA)
Film Title, Country/ies of Origin (Number of Showings per day/weekend)

Chanson d'amour, France (2)
Fraulein, Germany–Switzerland–Bosnia-Herzegovina (2)
Transylvania, France (4)
Qué tan lejos, Ecuador (4)
Conversaciones con mi jardinero, France (4)
En la ciudad de Sylvia, Spain (4)

Europe knew film festivals before WWII, although their stature crystallized, in the 1950s and 1960s. Festivals are implicated in the political climate out of which they have emerged; for instance, the Berlin Film Festival originated in the former Eastern zone and presented a Cold War gesture toward demonstrating the superiority of socialist culture (Elsaesser 2005). Given festivals' prestige as cultural events alongside the economic rise of Asia, the trajectory of festival hosting has extended to, for example, Hong Kong and Pusan, South Korea. Along with the possibilities a festival presents for a filmmaker, the cost of attending a festival was estimated in 1995 at 80,000–100,000 USDs (Jeckel 2003: 114). For this reason, governments such as that of South Korea have intervened to furnish filmmakers with a subsidy in order to attend festivals and thus effectively promote filmmakers' careers as well as the national fare (Shin 2005).

While film festivals present a generally inhospitable environment for the high-concept production, festivals should not be construed as "revolutionary" fora. The festivals are marked by commercial aspects that at least resemble what they are arrayed against, even as they enable an alternative path to visibility and distribution. Nevertheless, differences with the studio formula are substantial since festivals enable a spotlight on films that are not defined in the first instance by strands of high concept DNA. Moreover, many film festivals accent identities outside the "mainstream" (Gay-Bisexual-Lesbian, ethnic minority) and/or devote attention to national industries that are internationally marginal. In this vein, Cristian Mungiu 's Romanian film, *4 Months, 3 Weeks, 2 Days* was awarded the 2007 *Palme d'Or*, in the same year as the nation's EU ascendancy; events that reverberate within and beyond Romania for signaling its emergence within Europe and on the world's stage after the long nightmare of Ceausescu. In testimony to the hunger for global exposure and recognition, the mere appearance of the South Korean film *Old Boy* (Park Chan-Wook 2004) at Cannes gets prominent play on the "Extra" DVD distributed with the feature film by the United Kingdom's Tartan Video. Finally, alongside a nation's presence in the prestige and recognition economy, individual auteurs have also been clear beneficiaries of the rise of film-fests (from e.g., Luis Buñuel, Jean-Luc Godard, Werner Herzog to, more recently, Robert Rodriguez and Stephen Soderbergh).

Films are often made-to-order for debut dates and expectations associated with a festival. Financing may also be linked to the festival's temporal demands and expectations since the festival's close-up furnishes needed "visibility and...attention for films that neither command the promotional budgets nor rely on a sufficiently large internal market (such as India) to find its audience and recoup its investment" (Elsaesser 2005: 88–89). As all films are seeking audiences, they may be showcased in festivals in order to realize subsequent distribution deals. Deals are, in turn, often studio affiliated. Far from bringing Hollywood down, the studio-distributed independent and international films may in turn become effectively subcontracted talent farms and testing grounds for new concepts. In other words, festivals are highly enabling fora for new filmmaking—and, at the same time, are not an existential threat to Hollywood. The studios can in some measure swallow and digest the festival films, their concepts and talent.

While the festivals promote films, the films reciprocally promote the festival as they move into wider circulation. Film festival logos appear on the films' opening title cards, promotional poster, trailer and print ad for the film "as prominently displayed as Hollywood productions carry their studio logo" (Elsaesser 2005: 87). The festival's imprimatur may be taken as a signifier of quality and thus present an essential part of the films' promotion. In turn, festival management is fussy about the display of the logo. For example, Cannes has 8 pages of instructions on how it is to be done with respect to, for example, font, color scheme, and the number of leaves in the palm branch (Elsaesser 2005).

To an extent, all film festivals may be taken as confrontations with Hollywood's grip on the global industry (including the U.S. independent festivals). However, as noted above, Europe's films must "swim in the same waters" as the studio-backed productions—or at least to establish a comfortable niche within them.

In Europe, Jäckel writes, "directors continue to be hailed as the greatest strength of European cinema"—or, she counters, as "keeping the European cinema stuck in a rut of artistic indulgence" (2003: 28). That is, Europe has been conceptualized as promoting a "cinema of directors"—stubborn artisans in *boinas* pursuing idiosyncratic projects with unswerving integrity. This model stands in opposition to America and its "cinema of producers." In turn, producers are understood as the savvy business operators behind the scenes swinging deals, calculating demographic appeals, cutting checks, and reaping box office "benjamins" in a cacophony of ringing cash registers. The contrast is, of course, at once real and an over-simplification since both commercial and non-commercial behavior are in evidence on each side of the Atlantic. Moreover, some filmmakers embody both sides of the dichotomy as signature artists of their time and successful box office attractions; for example, Hitchcock in the past, Almodóvar in the present. Thus, the auteur theory, considered in the next chapter, also and necessarily intersects with the examination of film as an international industry. At this moment, we turn and orient to the figure of the auteur in international film.

CHAPTER 3
The Auteur Theory

One can well imagine a culture where discourse can exist without authorship. One would no longer entertain the questions that have been rehashed for so long: Who is really speaking? Is it really he and not someone else? With what authenticity, or with what originality? And what has he expressed? But other questions like these would arise: What are the modes of existence of this discourse? Where did it come from? How does it circulate? Who can appropriate it? What sites are prepared for possible future subjects? Who can take over the diverse functions of agency? And behind all these questions one would hardly notice the stirring of an indifference: "What difference does it make who is speaking?"
—*Michel Foucault (2001: 290)*

If their theory dictates that the author is dead, a great many symptomatic critics continue to hold séances.
—*David Bordwell (1989: 102)*

The basement of the Museum of the Paths (*Museo de los Caminos*) in Astorga, Castilla y León, Spain features striking works from almost 2 millennia past; engraved tablets, for example, that transmit the Gaelic mythologies that an early wave of migrants brought to what is now northern Spain. In turn, the myths are expressed in a Latinate language, the heritage of an earlier Roman invasion, that eventually mutated into the modern Castilian Spanish language. Hence, the museum's presentation of the tablets includes the original Latinate text as well as the translation into today's vernacular.

Despite the painstaking presentation, what the tablets *do not* present is a hint of authorship: whose hand chiseled the tablet? Or, more telling, who composed these mythologies? Given the time that has elapsed since they were inscribed in stone, the tacit assumption is that the individual author(s), or the hand(s) that chiseled, do not matter and that the texts convey broadly cultural, not individualistic, expression from the distant past. On this view, from the perspective of the early third millennium, the importance of the tablets resides in the cultural residues conveyed by mythologies with Gaelic origins and a Roman *lengua*; these, in turn, index Spain's heritage as a nation built on a series of invasions (Roman, Visigoth, Moroccan) across centuries with the attendant palimpsest of influences.

Presiding ceremonially over "the death of the author," Roland Barthes insists that "the author is a modern figure, a product of society insofar as, emerging from the Middle Ages with English empiricism, it discovered the prestige of the individual, of , as more nobly put, 'the human person'" (2001: 209). Barthes posits that the rise of the category of author proceeded in parallel with the enthronement of the critic—and at the expense of audiences whom he construes as finally enervating the text via their investments of meaning within it. Although neither Foucault (in the epigram) nor Barthes is discussing the museum in Astorga, their insights reverberate with the interpretation offered above, give it sense and force. Similarly one may wonder, looking beyond the author toward the horizon of discourse, (why even ask): Who is the author of common law? Of the Catholic liturgy? Of a newspaper? Of a fad?

However, before dismissing the author as passé and a musty anachronism, consider advances in film knowledge that have emerged from the study of directors under the rubric of auteur theory; a theory that in turn dwells on the contribution of the director to the finished film. One director, Alfred Hitchcock, will serve for purposes of illustration. Hitchcock is, moreover, an appropriate exemplar to use since the auteur theory was originally developed in response to his corpus of films and those of some of his noteworthy contemporaries. Furthermore, one can literally see seconds of a Hitchcock film and recognize the traces of authorship. In the decades since auteur theory was launched, Hitchcock has been implicated in analyzing the supra-individual domains of the political economy and national cinema (Thompson and Bordwell 2003: 242), elaboration of psychoanalytic paradigms (Rothman 1982), as well as in studies of ideology, the classical structure of narrative and their subversion (Wood 2002). Moreover, studies of Hitchcock's collaborators have also been analyzed in formal terms for their contributions to the characteristic look and sound of the films that make them "Hitchcockian" (Brown 1985). Stepping back further from the 50-year patrimony of the corpus of Hitchcock-directed films, one sees the profound impact that he has had on the cultural terrain. Even film audiences who eschew "old" movies have been witness to Hitchcock homage and references (Wolcott 1999). The tendency is sufficiently strong that scholars are even seized to *overstate* Hitchcock's influence (e.g., Ernesto Acevedo-Muñoz on his impact on Almodóvar [2007: 95–117). The widely circulating discourse on Hitchcock necessarily conditions even the casual spectator's reactions to the films, more than 30 years after the final clapboard sounded in his last film. Furthermore, for a more committed student of cinema, Hitchcock's corpus is like a schoolhouse with lesson plans that revolve around signature concepts such as the "MacGuffin" (Truffaut 1984: 98–100), suspense (Bordwell and Thompson 2001: 358–361), and identification (Wood 2002). Auteurism is a wide-open portal into this array of knowledges opened via the author.

What, then, is auteurism? In its most simplified form, auteur theory posits that the director is often the single most important figure in the production of a film. Moreover, directors of distinction often exhibit patterns in the films that bear their names. Notice, however, that the concept immediately encounters difficulties since the director is not equivalent to the "lone artist"—that is, the poet, novelist, painter, or sculptor ("loners" who, nonetheless, often enlist assistants, researchers, and editors).[1]

In stepping through the fundamentals of auteur theory, first, what is meant by the phrase "of distinction"? Auteurism assumes that some directors are noteworthy, at least across some portion of their careers. Other directors may be sorted as able craftspeople; that is, a "safe pair of hands" to whom the production of an expensive cultural commodity may be entrusted. Other directors are hacks. As Pauline Kael acidly observes (1985), an earlier auteur literature pivoted on largely unenlightening, oracular assertions of taste to collate directors into these and other more finely graded categories. Nonetheless, it will suffice to say that auteur theory is at least implicitly evaluative as revealed, for example, in the choice of objects of study. When one looks toward existing literature, it is clear that there is a consensus that Lars von Trier is deemed more important and interesting to grapple with than, e.g., Jonathan Demme given the quantity of articles and volumes devoted to each.

Second, what is one to make of the "patterns" referred to above? These patterns can be roughly parsed into stylistic signature and thematic motifs. Signature refers to the particular use of the art forms—photography, editing, diegetic and non-diegetic sound, scriptwriting, mise-en-scene—that compose a film as it is inscribed on film stock. Specific instances of distinctive use of these constituent art forms include, for example, a penchant for wide angle lens photography that creates striking depth to the shots in Orson Welles' corpus of films; these shots are often enveloped within long takes such as the four-minute opening sequence of *Touch of Evil* (1958) that proceeds without cuts. Beyond signature, thematic motifs refer to themes that are revisited and worked over by a filmmaker across films. Thematic motifs are exemplified by Satyajit Ray's attention to the clash between liberalism and tradition that repeatedly animates his corpus of Bengali films (Wood 1971) or the formation of surrogate family relations that permeates Paul Thomas Anderson's smaller corpus of films (Goss 2002). Geoffrey Nowell-Smith claims that, even as artists may shift with respect to some of their concerns and forms of expression across their careers, such thematic patterns form "a structural hard core of basic and often recondite motifs" (2001: 137).

As straightforward as the theory appears at first blush, it has been a theoretical battleground across six decades. Simplistic, idealizing author- reductionism has vexed some renditions of the auteur theory and has occasioned understandable resistance. In her exhaustive account of auteur studies, Janet Staiger finds other currents that have gone against auteurism; namely, what she declares to be "the final victory of poststructuralist thinking" (2003: 27) heralded by theorists such as Barthes and Foucault (superstar authors in their own right). In turn, post-structuralism implicates an associated "death of the author problem" that is abetted by the rise of mass media-saturated intertextuality such that suprapersonal discourse is assumed to reign (2003: 27). Nevertheless, as an auteur theorist, Staiger claims, "Yet authorship does matter" (2003: 27) and to say otherwise "dodges the material reality of human actions"—although her careful taxonomy of auteurism does not much elaborate the question of *how* or *why* it matters, as I will assay to do below (2003: 49).[2]

Despite an unfavorable critical climate for it in some respects, by 2000, Robert Stam concludes that "Auteurism no longer provokes polemics partially because it has *won*" (original emphasis; Stam 2000a: 6). One reason that auteurism has weathered the critical fusillades directed toward it is that auteurism presented a notable step forward theoretically when it was first introduced. From the start, auteurism was a methodological improvement since a large share of prior film criticism implicated the "impressionism" of the critics' "glandular" responses as given films did/did not stimulate personal taste. Similarly, auteurism trumped "sociologism" that reduced characters and storylines to presumptively positive or negative social messages (Stam 2000a: 6); a vector that persists into the present via readily mobilized moral panic and that animates some "morality"-steered vetting of films.

Moreover, auteurism is no longer what it was as formulated by Andrew Sarris in his provocative and flawed, "Notes on the Auteur Theory in 1962." After the auteur paradigm was articulated, Stam explains the new and complexified terrain: "Most contemporary auteur studies have jettisoned the romantic and individualist baggage to emphasize the ways a director's work can be both personal *and* mediated by extrapersonal elements such as genre, technology, studios, and the linguistic procedures of the medium" (original emphasis; 2000a: 6): a vector that I will flesh out below.

Origins

Stam interprets the rise of auteurism as part of the film community's "search for artistic legitimation" as a newer art form that does not present the longer rich heritage of, for example, painting or literature (2000a: 1). At its beginnings in 1951, the French journal *Cahiers du cinema* quickly assumed the mantle of being the principal organ of auteurism. In turn, auteurism was marked at the outset by a romantic streak expressed via "its adulation of the creative genius of authors" (Stam 2000a: 2). Peter Wollen (1985) characterizes the original rise of auteur theory, centered on *Cahiers*, as having further lines of causality. Following the Vichy era, the resumption of U.S. films on screen in France "came with a force—and an emotional impact" that was not experienced in the films' native country (Wollen 1985: 553). Part and parcel to this impact was the early French auteurists' anti-elitist impulses that harbored less suspicion toward commercially viable film. The iconoclasm was aligned with scorn for France's stuffy, officially valorized "cinema of quality" (e.g., Truffaut 1976). Auteurists contended that "masterpieces were made not only by a small upper crust of directors . . . but by a whole range of authors, whose work had previously been dismissed and consigned to oblivion" (Wollen 1985: 553). Furthermore, the expansive French *cinemathèque* presented valuable cultural infrastructure as it furnished an exceptional range of offerings from film history to cultivate the formation of the committed auteur-oriented *cinéphile*. It did so long before the advent of television/cable/VHS/DVD distribution channels with the resultant promiscuous (albeit, private and domestic) possibilities for surveying the long sweep of film history that new technology occasioned.

While "artist" status had effectively been realized in prior annals of film history (e.g., Sergei Eisenstein, D.W. Griffiths), auteur theory was provocative for its examination and celebration of commercial studio directors: Howard Hawks, John Ford, Vincente Minnelli, Hitchcock—or, more scandalous, titans of the "B"-movie lot such as Nicholas Ray and Samuel B. Fuller! Rather than being ground down by the gears of the studio system, auteurists posited that these directors insinuated artistic statements into their films from within the commercial studio. As Edward Buscombe (2001) observes, the early auteur theorists posited that anyone could make a good film with the right script; however, it was the auteur who had the brio to enhance indifferent source material with a personal thumbprint. As a result, auteur theory pushed through the roadblock between "high" and "low" art. Via auteurism, a significant swath of film directors and even genres were thus rescued from, "literary high art prejudice against them" (Stam 2000a: 6). In the present, Battleship Auteurism has turned so that auteur theory is still engaged in being an instrument of the "intellectual outlaw" (Hughes and Phillips 2000: 26–31) in opposition to an unsatisfactory status quo. However, the terms of its commitments have turned so that auteur theory is regularly cast in the role of champion of non-commercial (often European or Europhile) cinema that stands in defiant distinction against market *über alles* Hollywood studios. Rather than being opposed to starchy tastefulness, as the *Cahiers* group was, auteurism is now mobilized against crass commercialism and its attendant vulgarities. Despite the newly fashioned terms of auteurism's opposition to the status quo, European commentators are often ambivalent about the resultant alignment between auteurism and art house cinema (e.g., Eleft-heriotis 2001).

Along with recognizing auteurs, the theory acknowledged that under the conditions of perfect artistic/industrial storm, an ordinary "safe pair of hands" director could steer a superior film; for instance, Michael Curtiz claims director's credit for *Casablanca* (1942). Conversely, highly regarded auteurs also shepherd indifferent or poor efforts to the screen. However, auteurs consistently made for the "fortuitous intersection of talent and historical moment," in a formulation that weighs both a director's skill and the extrapersonal social climate in which films are made (Stam 2000a: 2).

Despite *Cahiers'* image as an auteurist house organ, in Buscombe's appraisal (1981), the publication regularly oriented to a wide array of filmmaking issues including the industry, genre, and technology. For example, *Cahiers'* 1970 monograph-length study of John Ford's (1939) *Young Mr. Lincoln* features auteurist passages (A Collective Text by the Editors of *Cahiers du cinema* 1985). However, these passages arise within a study that mainly locks onto the film as ideologizing and mythologizing for a U.S. audience, with psychoanalytic methodology in a substantial supporting role. *Cahiers* thus participated in and amplified some of the later developments in auteur studies. As with other film phenomena, auteurism went transnational in short order.

Within a generation, auteurism was transmitted beyond France and the French language through organs such as *Film Culture* in the United States, *Movie* in the United Kingdom, and *Filme Cultura* in Brazil (Stam 2000a: 3).

Battle Royale

In tracing the arc of the auteur theory, and its theoretical particulars, a detailed review of a famous confrontation over it will help clarify the terms and the stakes; namely, Andrew Sarris' "Notes on the Auteur Theory in 1962" and Pauline Kael's response, "Circles and Squares." Both Sarris and Kael suffer theoretical pratfalls in the exchange. However, careful consideration of their donnybrook is instructive as to what auteurism was and is.

Consistent with the anti-elite ethos of its recent French origins, Sarris insists that auteurism is a gesture against the cultural gatekeepers in the taste-making machinery. He cites the rigidity of contemporaneous arch-conservative *New York Times* critic Bosley Crowther in this vein. In doing so, Sarris anticipates further critique of the cultural climate that enabled the rise of youth-oriented cinema by the decade's end. After years of big-budget Hollywood spectacles and formulaic musical flops that did not hail an increasingly "hip" and college-educated population, the studio industry was on the verge of financial collapse by the mid-1960s (Cook 1990). Saviors arrived from unexpected quarters in the form of unconventional younger filmmakers with quasi-European sensibilities—Robert Altman, Peter Bogdonovich, Stanley Kubrick, Mike Nichols, Arthur Penn—who helped save the industry from itself. Their films presented innovation in a stagnant industry with respect to nonlinear narratives and generic pastiche. As the climate shifted, gobsmacked cultural gatekeeper Crowther demonstrably did not "get" the films that he was reviewing (e.g., his histrionic series of attacks on *Bonnie and Clyde* [Crowther 1967a, 1967b]). Auteur theory may also be construed as part of this broad cultural shift.[3]

Substantively, Sarris presents a model of "concentric circles" that circumscribe the auteur. The two circles on which I focus are "signature" (or "personality") and "interior meaning." The former of the two concentric circles implicates "the distinguishable personality of the director as criterion of value" (1985: 537). This means that, beyond mere competence in getting the finished film into the canister, a director of note will exhibit recognizable style in how the film "looks and moves" that should, in turn, be driven by the way the director "thinks and feels" (1985: 538). The looks and moves are achieved by consistently skillful orchestration of film's formal elements with a recognizable touch. David Bordwell (1989) posits that, in devoting attention to style, Sarris displays a concern that many auteur theorists overlook in the almost exclusive stress on films' thematic content. Moreover, signature enables a framework and a formal vocabulary with which to differentiate one director from another—and it rings true to the film-viewing experience. Consider, for example, Stephen Soderbergh's characteristically kaleidoscopic flashback-flashforward montages in *The Limey* (1999), *Out of Sight* (1998), and *Solaris* (2002) (Goss 2004). Furthermore, as succeeding generational waves of filmmakers and cinema audiences have grown up with metastasizing media channels and intensifying visual sophistication, signature assumes added importance in parsing what is on screen.

Signature also underscores the collaborative nature of film authorship since it may be accounted for, in part, by directors' tendency to work with some of the same artists. An array of celebrated examples announces themselves: Akira Kurosawa and Toshirô Mifune in the domain of acting or Hitchcock and Bernard Herrmann's score-writing partnerships. The auteur's collaborations in turn become part of the pleasure in seeing the films and in recognizing tendencies within them. Moreover, these elements of form are not simply eye-candy and stylistic hand-waving when form is tightly articulated to the content that it is marshaled to convey in the noteworthy film that plays a full artistic hand.

The latter circle, interior meaning, is embedded within the first. Here, the hard core of auteurism crystallizes for Sarris since he anoints "interior meaning" as "the ultimate glory of the cinema as an art" (1985: 538). However, despite its importance in his theory of concentric circles, Sarris is nebulous about what interior meaning is. In taking a stab at explanation, Sarris says that interior meaning

> . . . is not quite the vision of the world a director projects nor quite his attitude toward life. It is ambiguous, in any literary sense, because it is embedded in the stuff of the cinema and cannot be rendered in noncinematic terms . . . Dare I come out and say what I think it to be is an *élan* of the soul. (original emphasis; 1985: 538)

Sarris' citation of Jean Renoir fleshes out the concept with clarity: "As Renoir has observed, a director spends his life on variations of the same film" (1985: 539). That is, when surveying the films in the director's corpus, themes and variations on them may crystallize for the careful observer. For example, across many films in Hitchcock's corpus, a wrongly accused (but not fully innocent) man outmaneuvers the State and the mob in what becomes an amalgam of romance and journey of self-discovery (e.g., *39 Steps* [1935], *Young and Innocent* [1937], *Saboteur* [1942], *To Catch a Thief* [1955], *North by Northwest* [1959]). In turn, extracting out patterns and themes enables further analysis of them via symptomatic readings as I will discuss later.

A Rip-roaring Rejoinder

Quickly warming to polemic in response to Sarris, Kael observes that one may "take it for granted" that directors exhibit common threads across their films, using Hitchcock as an example (1985: 542). However, in minting the claim about taken for granted consistencies, Kael does not refute auteur theory but rather affirms its basic assumptions—albeit, while dismissing the existence of motifs and patterns as being obvious.

Kael trains her fire elsewhere in critiquing what she takes as auteurists' submission to the law of the instrument—the proverbial "clue that solves all crimes." Distinguished film critics, she posits, use "their full range of intelligence and intuition, rather than relying on formulas" such as an appeal to the prestige already bequeathed (or denied) to the auteur's corpus (1985: 543); a claim that is indeed well taken in the service of a rigorous auteurism that implicates multiple foci and methodologies. Kael's warning about merely identifying patterns within a director's films is similarly well taken since the scholar should assay to unpack the patterns with respect to more widely circulating cultural formations (Bordwell 1989).

Kael's discussion of the final circle—the "holy of holies" of the auteur in Sarris' original formulation—pirouettes between identifying Sarris' theoretical weaknesses and unashamed elitism. She characterizes the *élan* that Sarris celebrates as at once ineffable and as presenting apologetica for "the frustrations of a man (sic)"— the director—"working against the given material" typically due to commercial studio constraint (1985: 548). Kael also portrays Sarris as unable to account for a director who works on his or her scripts (e.g., John Huston, Ingmar Bergman). That is, Kael smokes out the almost arbitrary location of tension that Sarris emphasizes (i.e., between a director and a script that is handed to him or her). By contrast, a fecund reformulation of auteur theory may dwell upon creative tensions between the director and his or her prevailing social climate (of which the script and the industry are constituent parts).

A great deal of Kael's article is composed of *ad hominem* against auteur theorists and is thus a step removed from engaging with the theory itself. Along with deriding auteurists' ostensible "cult of personality," she also attacks auteurists for identifying what she calls "pathetic little link(s)" between one film by a given director and another (e.g., with respect to similar scenes or shots [1985: 548]). Here, she assays to negate one of Sarris' thoughtful points that engages with a spectator's phenomenal experience of pleasure in exhibiting mastery over the corpus and registering connections between films; connections that are, in turn, useful for further analysis. Kael otherwise outbids the auteurists even as she attacks them. She posits that "often the works auteur critics call masterpieces are ones that seem to reveal the contempt of the director for the audience"—citing no examples or method for determining this, even as (here and elsewhere) she unwittingly positions the director as sole agent of the filmmaking process such that his or her presumed "contempt" suffuses all (1985: 546). As a result, Kael also mints evaluative judgments as auteurism demands; albeit, in a further hit and run mode (e.g., Otto Preminger's films are "consistently superficial and facile" without reasoning or method to back this claim [1985: 551]).

More pointedly, Kael suggests that auteur theorists are devoted to thrashing through the bargain bin to find ostensibly unpolished gems. She characterizes auteurists as "connoisseurs of trash" who idealize "the man (sic) who signs a long-term contract, directs any script handed to him, and expresses himself by shoving bits of style up the crevasses of the plots" (1985: 548). Colorful phrasing notwithstanding, Kael harshly criticizes the judgment and tastes of contemporaneous auteurist theorists even as she tacitly accepts the central premise of the director's importance. On this view, her polemic collapses into a plea for auteur theory that is guided by elitist tastes and sensibilities. Inviting the charge of crass classism, Kael links the auteur theorist's appreciation of "mindless, repetitious commercial products" with "the restless, rootless men who wander on Forty-Second Street and in the Tenderloin of all our big cities just because they could respond to them without thought" (1985: 552). Hence, decades after the exchange, Stam finds that for all the heat of Kael's response to Sarris, it "masked their shared premise"—to wit, the idea that film theory/criticism should be "evaluative," albeit without specifying how the director may be rigorously put into close-up.

Aftermath and Critique

Kael's openly "angry" (1985: 549) appraisal of Sarris and his version of auteurism was not the final word with respect to the indignation that it aroused. Critic Dwight Macdonald quit writing his regular column at *Film Quarterly* when Sarris was brought on board—penning his resignation with, in Richard Corliss' over-the-top phrase, "a venom that suggested an angry redneck burning a cross on the lawn" (1985: 592). In addition, Sarris was slapped disapprovingly with the white glove in being excluded from anthologies that did include Kael's response to him.

Nevertheless, despite the strenuous debates, auteurism has prevailed in appreciable measure. How? Corliss answers that, as auteurism was introduced to the United States, more elite and academic critics did not "get" the appeal of Sarris' often jokey prose style and entertaining word play. Moreover, Sarris' base at *Village Voice*—a "popular" (non-academic) and "hip" publication—meant that auteurism's impact was partly off the radar screen of more established nay-sayers. More substantively, Corliss characterizes Sarris' interventions as a "thoughtful and well-timed challenge" to "social realist" criticism that measured a film in terms of its plausibility and that previously prevailed as reigning critical paradigm (1985: 594).

However, even while delivering the heated fusillade, Kael overlooks one of the easiest targets to criticize in Sarris' formulation (or that of any auteurist). In particular, film production is highly collaborative almost as a matter of definition. Rarely is the filmmaker working alone. A material reality of collaboration necessarily complicates auteurist assumptions. With few exceptions for films that achieve any notable distribution, a director is "immersed in material contingencies, surrounded by a Babel of voices and the buzz of technicians, cameras, and lights" (Stam 2000a: 4). Indeed, the *mise-en-scène* on the set presents stark contrast with the poet, diligent at work, reinforced only with cigarettes and a coffee pot!

Corliss similarly posits that, "The director *is* right in the middle of things" (original emphasis; 1985: 594). "At the very least," Corliss adds, the director is "on the sound stage while the director of photography is lighting the set that the art director has designed and, later, while the actors are speaking the lines that the screenwriter wrote" (1985: 594). In other words, as an advocate of what he playfully calls the *"politique des collaborateurs"* (1985: 597), Corliss points out that between shouted imperatives of "Action!" and "Cut!," a great deal occurs beyond the director's remit—up to and including the final cut of the film, by the film editor. In this vein, contemporary credit sequences may extend as long as ten minutes and employ as many as 169 stunt performers as in *Bourne Ultimatum* (Paul Greengrass 2007) (French 2007). Ridley Scott further testifies to the crowded milieu in which he directs: "'My crews average anywhere between 400 and 500 people . . . It's like walking into an army camp every morning. You have to go right "Right" [he claps his hands], and everybody moves. You've got to embrace the manpower and embrace your department heads'" (quoted in Moss 2007: 7). Hence, Corliss' efforts to shift attention from the unitary impact of the director are counsel well taken.

While some practical concerns weigh against auteurism— namely, as noted above, film is almost always a collective artistic enterprise—others weigh strongly in favor of it. The industry has constructed directors as stars in their own right, thus giving the concept of auteurism force by endowing the director with a proverbial close-up via promotion. Along with a prominent or sub-culturally valenced director's role in publicity, the filmgoer may experience a film in such terms as "a new Iciar Bollaín," "a forgotten Kubrick," or "an under-the-radar Todd Haynes" in much the way that stars or genres have long shaped and partly organized the viewing experience. In a more affective and experiential register, the auteur theory enables a feeling of "dialogue with the personae imagined to lie 'behind' the films" of a favorite auteur (Stam 2000a: 6).

While practical considerations such as promotion have buttressed auteur approaches, they have not been unequivocally celebrated. Although the alpha and omega of globally metastasizing market-oriented economics are not within the world of film, Janet Staiger draws a continuity between the generally prevailing egoistic individualism of market-enabling neoliberalism and the film industry. She writes, "Neoliberal economic theory supports using individuated authorship within its marketing and promotion"— even as the corporate holders of copyright realize the main benefits of the "individual" artist (Staiger 2003: 42). Bear in mind that auteurism originated as a "rebel yell" from the *Cahiers* group that proclaimed the merits of commercial film when steered by directors only partly bridled by the studio constraint. In the present, however, auteur film largely stands in distinction to the "high concept" studio production by emphasizing a more "personal" and "idiosyncratic" directorial vision.

Beyond the commercially cashiered motives for niche promotion of auteurism, considered above, Staiger also traces the outlines of a progressive political project within auteurism. As she phrases it, "forgetting authorship and individuals takes away a history necessary for social activism and utopic imaginings" (2003: 30). This line of thinking reinvigorates an individual subject with politicized decisions to address and with agency at his or her disposal about what to do in word and in deed. Reclaiming the agency of individual subjects may also strike against a potentially immobilizing emphasis on discourse that extends to the horizon. This concept of the individual acknowledges that we are not monads: Rather, it asks, with one life (that we know of) vested within each of us, what do we do with it? And, further upstream, with regard to questions of agency in film: How do we approach an auteur's corpus with the necessary caution surrounding the potent tension between individual and supra-individual influences?

Notes on the Auteur Theory in 2009: A Model and Method

While discussion of film authorship presents a method and a trope that inaugurates the process of unpacking and examining films, it need not be the final word. Other categories announce themselves as candidate (albeit non-mutually exclusive) nexuses of analyses of films: for example, genre, or appeals to national cinemas with their particular tendencies, political economies, and historical vectors. These other candidate categories are, however, decomposing to some extent and being reconfigured as categories. John Cawelti (1985) presciently envisions a future of generic recombination while galloping increases in international co-production beg questions about national film identity. More specifically, where genre is concerned, a film such as *Big Lebowski* (Joel Coen 1998) rewires the generic DNA of the comedy, "buddy film," film noir and detective genres. Where production is concerned, transnational films such as *The Lord of the Rings* trilogy have become part of the landscape; in the trilogy's case, with U.S. and German finance, a Kiwi director and crew shooting on location in their native New Zealand, and a cast composed of nationalities from all over the English-speaking world.

In light of these and other salient considerations that present potential alliances with auteur analysis, what should one demand of a rigorous auteurism? Writing eleven years after Sarris' auteurist plea, Buscombe provides a useful answer. He posits that, "What is needed now is a theory of the cinema that locates directors in a total situation rather than one which assumes that their development has only an internal dynamic" (2001: 32). He elaborates what this charge may mean:

> First, there is the examination of the effects of the cinema on society . . . Second is the effect of society on the cinema; in other words the operation of ideology, economics, technology, *etc.* Lastly . . . the effects of films on other films. (1981: 32)

In this spirit, the auteur theory that I apply to Almodóvar, von Trier, and Winterbottom consists of the following elements. First, I assume that a director has a stylistic signature, a look and manner with formal elements that is, in one way or another, often recognizable across films. Second, I posit that the directors present thematic motifs across their films. Informed by common sense and observation, these motifs can be extracted by mobilizing the insights available from theories of ideology, gender, formalism/realism and psychoanalysis. An approach to film that fashions an elaborate, extra-textural framework is also attentive to national and international contexts with the attendant tensions that these imprint onto the celluloid; namely, the political economy of film, patterns of collaboration, funding streams, sociopolitical climate, and critical response. Serious pursuit of a "thick" description of context advances auteur investigations beyond Sarris' author-reductionist formulations.

Reading Strategies

In considering thematic motifs, analysis of structuralist binaries are not new with respect to their intersection with auteur theory. In one case, Peter Wollen's account of Howard Hawks' corpus of films offers analysis of "systematic (binary) oppositions" that form a "lexicon of motifs" (1985: 562), an approach that is indebted to the structuralism of Claude Lévi- Strauss (2001). In Wollen's interpretation, Hawksian oppositions typically revolve around gender. In turn, the binaries themselves are not "innocent" but recirculate the terms of materially grounded power in the society that summons given binaries into play.

Each person—auteur included—may be construed as at once an individual and also as a subject of his or her time and place; as at once idiosyncratic and typical, in other words. Hence, the film-maker channels important submerged aspects of the culture(s) that have been insinuated into him or her. In this vein, consider the romantic paradigm of "the artist," in which he or she is con-strued as being in conflict with society and as crafting messages in defiant opposition to the status quo. Now, however, consider a countervailing view: That prominent artists *worship and aggran-dize their societies*, albeit with telling slippages that make for riv-eting art in betraying a measure of the dystopia submerged within their cultures. On this view, the director is situated as the "indi-vidual through which a dominant cultural discourse is arranged into celluloid" as "the historically constituted . . . locus of social, psychological and cultural discourses and practices" (Staiger 2003: 48, 49). At the same time, culture and the people who dwell within it are diverse and not monolithic. Subjects do not tell the same story in the same way as their co-enculturated peers even if they are similarly anchored in resonant common reference points. Robin Wood phrases the idea like this:

> The cinema that I am interested in is not one that attempts to eliminate the basic structures and conflicts of our culture, but one in which they are dramatized, made visible; to dramatize something inevitably repro-ducing it, but not inertly. Many films *merely* reproduce, and thereby rein-force, but there are also many—the interesting ones, the complex ones, the distinguished ones—that, in reproducing the social and psychic structures of our culture, also subject them to criticism. (1998: 23)

Thus, I assay to capture the tensions (continuities and slip-pages) between the auteurs and the societies of which they are a part.

Auteur studies have taken steps toward Buscombe's prognosis, cited above, and this partly accounts for auteur theory's durability. As David Bordwell (1989) observes, auteurists have dramatically widened their methodological remit and routinely engage with symptomatic readings of films. In turn, symptomatic readings may assume various forms (demystification, against-the-grain, structuralist, psychoanalytic, gendered) that go beyond explicating what the film says at face value or implies at first blush. Questions of whether images (of, e.g., minority groups) are presumed as "positive" and "negative" give way to elaborating how the tensions that films channel are deeply implicated in the logics/illogics of the society that they represent. Instead of asking "Are African-American subjects portrayed positively?" the line of inquiry locks onto the materially grounded fissures in society that are partly obscured by a circumscribed focus on calibrating "positive" versus "negative" representation. On this view, social conditions of inequality and chauvinism transpose analysis of the mechanisms of the class-divided society into problematization of more readily observable issues (such as degree of pigmentation and its subsequent representation in images). Symptomatic reading assays to tease out distortions, repressions, and transpositions that condition what films say—including the body of films that compose the auteur's curriculum vitae. In light of these considerations, the recognized auteur's corpus is of interest as a particularly revealing exemplar of the unresolved tensions of a given time and place.

What I'm Not Talking About

In her extensive survey of tendencies within auteurism, Staiger critically discusses the concept of "psychological unity" between artist and the works produced. This view posits unity that "'binds the artist's thought and behavior to the finished work'" (2003: 31). Hence, depressed Ian Curtis is assumed to perform depressed songs while fronting Joy Division. Curtis notwithstanding, reading the tea leaves of an artist's state of mind off the work and its devices is flat and overly fastidious. As Foucault (2001) emphasizes in his discussion of the author function, different egos are in play in the act of authorship. The "I" who composes the preface of the book and thanks his or her department head is understood as distinct from the ("same") author who presents the formal mathematical proofs that comprise most of the book's contents. Similarly, the author of the fictional work may indulge his or her fantasies, albeit in the proverbial "hall of mirrors" with respect to the real subject who is behind the work. Reading the psyche off of the work is particularly vexed with filmmakers given the already noted collaboration-intensive character of film. More concretely, does it mean anything of moment that notably melancholic Lars von Trier has directed a comedy—or that he did so before his May 2007 retirement from film due to ongoing depression? Or that an apparently "nice guy" such as Robert Rodriguez—so generous in sharing himself and his craft to fans and interested audiences (Rodriguez 1996)—makes extremely violent and even anti-social films?

The doctrine of unity also has the unwanted consequence of easing the assumption of an essentializing 1:1 correspondence between a director's identity and the films made. On the assumption of correspondence, a woman (or a gay or a Catalan) filmmaker is "speaking for his or her people" and/or making "women's" (or "gay" or "Catalan") films. Essentializing and reductionist assumptions may underwrite stereotype and caricature, if unwittingly, in reducing the film to the director's identity without acknowledging any possibility of slippage between them.

Moreover, what a director says in testimony about or interpretation of his or her own films should be taken as "useful evidence"—and not as "final word." While a director may undoubtedly furnish useful information on production histories of films, his or her accounts may be inflected with everyday myopia, run-of-the-mill memory lapses, idealizations and/or vendettas toward collaborators. In this vein, Roman Polanski (1984) devotes passages of his autobiography to personal attacks on actress Faye Dunaway, co-star of *Chinatown*. Upon seeing the film, it is apparent that Polanski's verbal assault exaggerates (if not invents) any failings Dunaway may have as an actress apparently in the service of the director's score settling. If one is committed to the view that part of what is expressed in the film is in some measure supra-individual and embedded within the culturally circumscribed time-and-place, a director's remarks require careful interpretation (much like the films themselves!).

By contrast with thrashing through a psychological Rorschach projected on screen, what Staiger (2003) calls the "biographical legend" of the director may be useful in coming at auteur films with thick contextualization. To invoke biographical legend does not posit a chain of causality between the director's psychological cast of mind, at one end of the chain, and a resultant film at the other. Rather, biographical legend refers to perceptions that surround a director's reputation that impact on how films are anticipated and received. Even before a contemporary subject has seen his or her first Hitchcock film, one has been prepared to expect bravura suspense and an ambiance of dense ambiguity. These are expectations that cannot be readily parsed from the experience of watching. On this view, a director's biographical legend may be construed as roughly analogous to an actor/actress's "star image" that complicates or underscores reception of particular performances by its resonance with the previous corpus of work.

However, the legend should itself be subject to scrutiny and interpretation, not taken as given. To take one salient example: Interpretations of Pedro Almodóvar's films are to an appreciable degree enveloped within the biographical legend that the director's life has run in parallel with a whole generation of Spaniards. Marvin D'Lugo traffics in this legend when he asserts unconditional equivalence between Almodóvar (born 1949) and his generation in Spain that was liberated from Right-wing dictatorship as young adults. He posits, "The clichéd equation between Almodóvar and Spain or Almodóvar and Spanish cinema . . . is valid" (2006: 4). As D'Lugo observes, the director was an "internal immigrant" from peripheral Extremadura to Madrid, like millions of Spaniards who exited the countryside for the city during the mid-twentieth century. Thus, Almodóvar is a typical twenty-first century urban Spaniard with roots in *la España profunda* of the periphery. Nonetheless, D'Lugo's unqualified investment in the legend also misses what is also particular about Almodóvar's films and not pan-Spanish (with respect to, e.g., gay and punk sub-culture)—and what may also be less celebratory to both the individual and national legend.

To return to the opening epigram: *What difference does it make who is speaking?* On one hand, discernible patterns arise in the corpus of films associated with a given director of note. Consistencies across Hitchcock's long career suggest a world that revolves around repeated themes (e.g., the transfer of guilt through complicit knowledge). These themes are encased within a recognizable stylistic signature that endow the adjective "Hitchcockian" with force for questioning or extending the logics of prevailing social paradigms (of, e.g., gender, class, the Other). On the other hand, an ultra-individualistic concept of auteurism effaces too much to pass muster, including the mode of film production in global terms that was discussed in the previous chapter. Thus, one task of the following chapters is to "thread the needle" between analyzing the particularities of the directors while being scrupulously attentive to the broader frame of the social-political milieu that (informally) nominated them as film artists of significance.

SECTION II
PEDRO ALMODÓVAR

CHAPTER 4

"It Was Almost Impossible to Dream That..."

"'It is a surprise that I'm making movies . . . because in my case it was almost impossible to dream of that. I was not born in the right place in the right family in the right town in the right language or in the right moment to make movies'"
—Pedro Almodóvar (quoted in Willoquet-Maricondi 2004: vii)

Despite modest origins in a nation that functioned to the specifications of a third world police state at the time of his birth and early life, Almodóvar has been hailed as "the most acclaimed European director in a generation" (D'Lugo 2006: 1). He is perceived to be "an ambassador for Spanish cinema" (Acevedo-Muñoz 2007: 1)—indeed, as an emissary for all of Spain. Paul Julian Smith anoints Almodóvar as "the one true auteur to emerge in the 1980s" although his greatest success was to be realized, temporally, further upstream (2000: 5). Moreover, Smith characterizes Almodóvar as presenting a "dream director" for English-language academicians for being "equally exploitable for courses on gender, ethnic, or lesbian and gay studies" during the era of high post-modern inflected identity politics within the academy (2000: 5). In the *Reconfiguring Spain* anthology, Marsha Kinder comments that Almodóvar "runs like a thread" through the English language text "even though only one essay is devoted exclusively to his work" (Kinder 1997: 3). By 1997, even before his most high-profile successes, Almodóvar and his films are internationally recognized emblems of the new "hyperliberated Socialist Spain" (Kinder 1997: 3).[1]

Born in 1949 in Castile-La Mancha (Internet Movie DataBase 2008b), Almodóvar's family moved to the peripheral and traditionally poor region of Extremadura in the 1950s.[2] He characterizes his upbringing as "'very García Lorca, very folkloric'" surrounded by strong women (mother, sisters), talking and sewing on sun-drenched patios (2006: 12). His father, Antonio, was a muleteer who delivered wine and was barely literate (Mackenzie 2004). In a poignant anecdote that illuminates how relatively "backward" Spain was at the time for a Western European nation, Almodóvar recounts going "'with a tin can full of glowing pieces of cheap charcoal . . . to keep warm'" at the village's improvised cinema; "'My conception of cinema is still that it's something that gives me warmth, that comforts me, like that tin can'" (quoted in Smith 2000: 177). Almodóvar moved again to Madrid as a teenager in the late 1960s, against his father's stiff objections. In time, the young Almodóvar found a niche as a Telefonica public sector functionary during the working day—and, nocturnally, as a nascent cultural force. Along with performing music and writing novels during Madrid's *La movida* arts upsurge, the budding filmmaker made short films on 8mm with titles such as *Folle . . . Folle . . . Fólleme, Tim*, i.e., *Fuck . . . Fuck . . . Fuck Me, Tim*. Almodóvar exhibited his early film efforts at house parties with running commentaries and his own "live dubbing" of all the characters' dialogue (D'Lugo 2006: 16).

In his book-length study, Marvin D'Lugo (2006) catalogues a variety of influences that he finds in Almodóvar's corpus; the eclectic array includes film noir, Italian neo-realism, Hollywood films, and French New Wave. Beyond the influences from the big screen, D'Lugo places considerable emphasis on the impact of twentieth-century folkloric Spain, and some of its attendant kitsch, on the filmmaker: Melodrama, the bullfight, popular songs, advice columns, soap operas on the radio are all posited as having left a footprint.

Table 4.1. Almodóvar's Feature Films

Volver (2006)
La mala educación (2004) (*Bad Education*)
Hable con ella (2002) (*Talk to Her*)
Todo sobre mi madre (1999) (*All About My Mother*)
Carne trémula (1997) (*Live Flesh*)
La flor de mi secreto (1995) (*The Flower of My Secret*)
Kika (1993)
Tacones lejanos (1991) (*High Heels*)
¡Átame! (1990) (*Tie Me Up! Tie Me Down!*)

Table 4.1. Almodóvar's Feature Films (continued)

Mujeres al borde de un ataque de nervios (1988) (*Women on the Verge of a Nervous Breakdown*)
La ley del deseo (1987) (*Law of Desire*)
Matador (1986)
¿Qué he hecho yo para merecer esto? (1984) (*What Have I Done to Deserve This?*)
Entre tinieblas (1983) (*Dark Habits*)
Laberinto de pasiones (1982) (*Labyrinth of Passion*)
Pepi, Luci, Bom y otras chicas del montón (1980) (*Pepi, Luci, Bom and Other Girls on the Heap*)

During a large swath of Almodóvar's career, reception to the director's work within Spain was hostile in many quarters; particularly with respect to Spanish commentators taken with "the cinema of quality." In turn, the "cinema of quality" was promoted with an eye toward raising Spain's cultural profile in the decade following the dictatorship's demise. During the 1980s, the ruling Center-Left Partido Socialista Obrero Español (PSOE)'s policy was to make fewer films of ostensibly higher quality with government subsidies upfront for preferred film projects. Under the "The Miró Decrees," named for PSOE's Directora General de Cinematografia Pilar Miró, film production dipped from 146 Spanish releases in 1982 to 44 films in 1994 (Jordan and Morgan-Tamosunas 1998: 2). While the subsidies were "extraordinarily generous" (Hooper 1995: 337), many of the resultant films were "safe, middlebrow Art House films" (Jordan and Morgan-Tamosunas 1998: 2). Almodóvar launched his career going against this grain with scabrous films that delighted in poking fingers in the eye of authority and celebrating bad taste with some of the resultant flak that this engenders.

Despite the often contentious reception toward Almodóvar within Spain, English language accounts of the Almodóvar corpus often slip toward hagiography (although his films have been criticized outside Spain as well [e.g., Jordan 2000]). One contentious aspect of Almodóvar's corpus of films concerns gender relations. In interviews, Almodóvar is frequently sentimental about women whom he regards as having "'more facets'" than men while harboring "'greater mystery inside'" with "'nuances and a sensitivity that is more authentic'" (Willoquet-Maricondi 2004: x). It follows that Almodóvar has been criticized for at once being an idealizer of women (Matthews 2006)—*and*, conversely, as grossly insensitive toward at least some of his female screen creations (Jordan and Morgan-Tamosunas 1998). The gender theme is of sufficient moment that I will discuss it in detail later. The profile of the intrinsically important gender issue is raised further by Spain's women having borne the lash of fascism with greater intensity than their male counterparts in the Franco era, during which repression of women has been described as "extraordinarily severe" (Hooper 1995: 165). In the Right-wing fugue of Franquista rule, a married woman could not open a bank account, enter into a contract, or take a long journey without her husband's permission—and even a battered wife leaving the home to live with relatives could be charged with the "crime" of "desertion" (Hooper 1995: 167). In turn, women are construed as having driven Spain's recent movement into the forefront of the world's contemporary liberal societies.

As consistently emphasized throughout this volume, films do not spontaneously self-generate or fall from the sky fully formed; they are embedded within a political economy out of which they are produced. As is the case with most any young filmmaker, particularly outside Hollywood's auspices, Almodóvar's early projects were racked with financial compromises. For *Dark Habits*, for example, Almodóvar was yoked to the lead actress, Cristina S. Pascual; she was married to the production company head although Almodóvar felt she was regrettably miscast. Hence, Almodóvar rewrote the script on the fly to shift emphasis from Pacual's Yolanda onto Julieta Serrano as Mother Superior (Smith 2000: 44). Concerning the early struggles to raise funds, the director recollects, "'With my first five films I had the impression of having had five children with five different fathers and of always fighting with each one of them, since my films belonged to them, from a financial point of view, but also on an artistic level, that is, on the level of a conception'" (quoted in D'Lugo 2006: 53). By 1987, Almodóvar established a production company, El Deseo, SA, in tandem with his brother Agustín for the purpose of assuming greater command over projects. The company has been demonstrably successful as, by the turn of the millennium, three of the top five grossing films in Spain's history were El Deseo productions (Smith 2000: 4). During the 1990s, Almodóvar also entered into co-productions with Ciby 2000 "a mainstream French company" starting with 1991's *High Heels* (D'Lugo 2006: 68). The collaboration has proven fruitful as Ciby has given Almodóvar a free hand with its finance and does not even look at the films until they are being subtitled into French. Moreover, it has enabled larger than usual budgets for Spanish-language films that has permitted Almodóvar to minister lovingly to set designs and to heavily rehearsing his cast.

Whereas his early films are typically construed as hedonistic and defiantly apolitical, Almodóvar has long identified himself as at once independent of political parties and as decisively on the left. Along with making notably more polished films in stylistic terms, across his career Almodóvar has also insinuated more politics into them; most notably, the recording of Manuel Fraga Iribarne's announcement of the "State of Emergency" ("*Estado de Excepción*") in 1970 during the opening sequence of *Live Flesh*. Beyond the films, Almodóvar has used his elevated position as an artist of international acclaim to articulate strongly worded criticism of the Hollywood industry's use of ratings as a form of "soft" censorship (D'Lugo 2006: 75). More recently, Almodóvar voiced fierce opposition toward the government's support of the 2003 invasion of Iraq and thus channelled the disgust across the spectrum of Spanish society at President José María Aznar's dubious project.

This chapter will unfold by grounding Almodóvarian cinema in a theory of ideology that is indebted to Louis Althusser (1994). The theory, in turn, furnishes an abstract framework that shepherds textural details toward the claim that a large share of Almodóvar's corpus presents everyday struggle against dominant ideology and its institutional bases. Stylistic signature and thematic motifs are of the moment given the theory of the auteur detailed earlier in this volume. Thereafter, I examine stylistic and thematic tendencies in the corpus of 16 feature films since 1980. After detailing significant stylistic continuities and discontinuities in Almodóvar's corpus, I focus on the construction of church and state (i.e., police) in the films—respectively, representatives of the Althusserian Ideological State Apparatuses (ISAs) and Repressive State Apparatuses (RSAs). Chapter 5 follows with extensive discussion of the family ISA in Almodóvar's cinematic world and then re-frames discussion onto the question of whether the corpus of films is woman-friendly—and how/why. Chapter 6 highlights three more recent films as it applies the analyses rehearsed earlier in section II and completes the account of this signature Spanish artist.

Almodóvar and the ISAs

Despite the checkered career of Louis Althusser and his theoretical constructs, preeminent contemporary scholar of ideology Terry Eagleton posits Althusser's "Ideology and the Ideological State Apparatuses" as "perhaps the key text . . . for our time" on the topic (1994: 87). Althusser (1994) emphasizes subjectification and materialism (i.e., matter permeates mind though practice) in formulating ideology. For Althusser, the subject is recruited into living within and embodying a particular subjectivity via practices and everyday rituals in institutional milieu. The worshipper who stands up in church, the student handing in work on time, the laborer training a new colleague: Each reproduces ideology in material practice, summoned and reinforced by the seductions (and sanctions) of ideology in motion while doing so. Given these emphases, how may Althusserian ideology intersect with a discussion of Almodóvar?

Without doubt, all films traffic in ideology just as all films must necessarily marshal mise-en-scene. However, some films ply the mise-en-scene trade with more brio or in ways that generate more tension and interest; and so it is, similarly, for ideology that is "always already" on screen although it may be channeled in more or less striking ways. Almodóvar's films present greater than usual interest for an ideological critique since, firstly, many of the narratives assume a critical posture toward the inner workings of what Althusser (1994) calls the "Ideological State Apparatuses" (ISAs). In particular, the Althusserian ISAs of The Family, The Church, and The Culture Industries—including mass media—are central to Almodóvar's films. The Althusserian Repressive State Apparatuses (RSAs)—that is, the police and the carceral system—are similarly important facets of several films in the corpus. The pattern of attention toward the RSAs starts with the debut film, *Pepi, Luci, Bom, and Other Women on the Heap*. The film presents scene after scene of uninhibited post-Franco liberation of a sort proscribed on Franco-era screens via tight censorship (Smith 2000). In turn, the clownishly menacing figure of the policeman achieves a partial counter-revolutionary pushback in the face of "New Spain" by reclaiming his wife through sadistic, misogynistic beatings.

Despite the salience of the ISAs and RSAs to Almodóvar's films, it is also evident that Althusserian ideological critique is not a natural "fit" with textural analyses—although some scholars have tried it to stitch one around the other (Goss 2002)! This is because Althusser, and others who follow in his tradition, emphasize ideology as being shot through practices that are enacted in institutional settings that tend to reproduce ruling authority in an embodied, "hands-on" fashion (with correspondingly less concern with concepts such as consciousness). In this view, the subject who goes to the workplace does not necessarily understand and/or believe the market doctrines that circumscribe his or her life; nor is he or she a sold believer in the "meritocracy" that ostensibly drives market relations. In fact, the laborer undoubtedly holds, with varying degrees of regularity and intensity, that he or she is exploited. However, the same worker may sufficiently (and provisionally) renew "belief" to desert the bed, advance beyond the workplace gate, participate in the corporal disciplines of the workplace, and even become engrossed in the game of making more profit for his employers to alleviate workplace boredom prior to cashing the next pay check; all the while, behaving "as if" nothing was awry in the regime of market relations.

Despite the emphasis on ideological reproduction (even if that reproduction is often enacted with gritted teeth), Althusserian ideology has several things to offer an effort to unpack Almodóvar. First, the ISAs that play a prominent role in Almodóvar's films are understood on an Althusserian view to be "relatively autonomous" from ruling authority. That is, while an institution and its subjects may tend to reproduce ruling ideology, there are no guarantees that they will do so. For this reason, battles are joined within the family, the school, and the mass media; these are some of the institutions that constitute the central stakes in what practices steer society toward what ends. Significantly, Althusser argues that to hold formal state power is an empty charade without having decisively impacted the prevailing currents in the ISAs.

Even given relative autonomy between ruling ideology and particular institutions, the ISAs generally reproduce ruling ideology *but not necessarily*, and it is here where shifts in the terms of social life occur and cascade laterally and upward. Almodóvar's films present enormous contestation within the ISAs, notably in the family. While families are understood to have the lead role in the construction of the gendered subject, Almodóvar's films invent and present nontraditional (and, in some cases, more female-friendly) familial forms, as will be discussed later. In this view,

Almodóvar often (but not always!) dwells on the practice of ideology as it departs from clockwork functioning and reproduction. Althusser's "bad subjects" regularly hurl wrenches into the works or alter the institutions from the inside, as Almodóvar's creations often do in their interventions into the ISAs.

Almodóvarian Style

Across 16 feature films, from 1980 to 2006, Almodóvar's corpus exhibits a notable transition away from the broad slapstick and cinema of rude shocks in the early films. In early Almodóvar, characters urinate on others and defecate on themselves. By contrast, later works are characterized by understated visual wit. Several shots in *Volver*, Almodóvar's most recent release as of 2008, dwell on the wind farms that garnish the landscape of Castile–La Mancha (the vast region south and east of Madrid); a twenty-first-century revisioning of Quixote's windmills. Almodóvar's films are also laden with audiences to spectacles on stage within the films' mise-en-scene. However, in the register of style and taste, Almodóvar's career trajectory has been marked by migration from staging punk-inspired stage gigs for bohemian/grungy audiences (*Pepi, Luci, Bom . . . , Labyrinth of Passion*) to rarified experimental dance performances before well-mannered aesthetes in *Talk to Her*.

Production values have also appreciated across the decades. Commenting in the early 1980s, Almodóvar assayed to present his film's technical slips as an "advantage" of sorts, as French New Wavers had 20 years earlier: "when a film has one defect, people say it's badly made; but when it has many, they say it has invented a new style" (quoted in Smith 2000: 14). Smith charts Almodóvar's shift from "eccentric framing and contempt for continuity" to "glossy professionalism" (2000: 3)—a "perfect evolution" for the smoothness with which it has been achieved (Acevedo-Muñoz 2007: 7). Nevertheless, by the most recent film, *Volver*, Almodóvar's command of the medium is still tempered by playful moments of artistic "risk": A high-angle shot of Raimunda at the dish sink seems merely to flatter her breathtaking cleavage. It also—and more conventionally—externalizes and foreshadows aggression toward her husband Paco. That is, the other prominent element of the shot is the knife she is washing that is later used to kill Paco.

Stylistic consistencies in Almodóvar's films stand alongside marked changes—an observation that may be explained in part by frequent collaboration with other supporting artists. In front of the camera, several actors have become part of an Almodóvar repertory including, most famously, Carmen Maura and Antonio Banderas. Cecilia Roth, Chus Lampreave, Marisa Paredes, and Victoria Abril have made multiple appearances beginning in the 1980s along with, more recently, Penélope Cruz and Javier Camara. On the other side of the camera lenses, José Sancedo has cut all 16 of Almodóvar's feature-length films as editor while Alberto Iglesias has composed musical scores on the six most recent releases. Almodóvar's early films featured cameos by the director. His brother, producer Agustín, and mother, Francisca Caballero, were also cast several times in the earlier films.

A large corpus of auteur films will generate repeated curiosities in style. In Almodóvar's case, these include many shots through windows (e.g., the final shot of *Dark Habits*) or shots that implicate mirrors (the spousal confrontation in *Flower of My Secret*); a penchant for the striking high-angle shots that embed the character(s) tightly within a physical environment (Pepa in the flickering light of the film projected toward the screen in *Women on the Verge of a Nervous Breakdown*); dramatic long takes (Lola and Ricky sing and bond in the car at the end of *Tie Me Up! Tie Me Down!*); and shots that are taken from the POV of an inanimate object (the washing machine in *What Have I Done to Deserve This?*). Sex scenes are de rigueur and range from the crude(ly staged) andro-agression of the cop on multiple occasions in *Pepi, Luci, Bom . . .* to the shimmering warmth of slow-motion erotica during the Victor-Elena love scene in *Live Flesh*. Almodóvar's opening credit sequences have been notable exercises in style and often merge imagery from fashion publications with the punk cut-and-paste aesthetic (*Women on the Verge . . .*, *Bad Education*, *Kika*) as well as borrowing from a comic book look (*Pepi, Luci, Bom . . .*). Along with a signature style in the opening credits, closing images have also exhibited patterns. Several early films close with shots of optimistic movement toward modernity and the future suggested by cars and highways (*Pepi, Luci, Bom . . .* , *Tie Me Up! . . .*, *Kika*) as well as an airplane in flight (*Labyrinth of Passion*). Later films have prominently featured doors that close in the final shots (*All*

About My Mother, *Bad Education*, *Volver*), a clear form of end bracketing.

The often artful use of sound in Almodóvar's films demands comment. While sound is crucial in Almodóvar's corpus, it was also noticeably unpolished at the outset with "audible reverb" in *Pepi, Luci, Bom . . .* (Acevedo-Muñoz 2007: 22). Along with heavy use of non-diegetic music, musical numbers staged within the world of the film are instanced in almost all of Almodóvar's efforts. The musical genres thusly referenced range from the live punk inflected performances in *Pepi, Luci, Bom . . .* and *Labyrinth of Passion*; to acoustic performance at the pool of a bourgeoisie house party in *Talk to Her*; to Zahara, the nostalgia-drenched Sara Montes impersonator, in *Bad Education*. Particularly in the early films, the numbers often erupt suddenly.

Dark Habits, the third film in Almodóvar's corpus, anticipates later stylistic turns with respect to music. In a clever use of sound and montage, Yolanda enters Mother Superior's office accompanied by the torchy song "Encadenados" ("Chained"). The pair mouth the lines with studied falseness that thumbs its nose at the illusion that they are singing in their own voices (the voice is, indeed, male) as they perform for each other's gaze; and even as there is no source for the song in the mise-en-scene (e.g., radio or record player) that, following the women's lip-synching of it, fades from the soundtrack as phantasmically as it arose. A similar technique that eschews pretenses of realism informs Raimunda's lip-synched performance in *Volver*. That is, while Raimunda is ostensibly singing "live" for the audience gathered in the restaurant, the moment is "double-coded" since the audience in front of the screen can readily ascertain that the song is lip-synched by actress Penélope Cruz. This particular technique that winkingly celebrates falseness may be indebted to Spanish television that has long featured lip-synched musical performances in "song and dance"–oriented programming that endures to the present in heavy rotation.

Almodóvar's frequent use of sound bridges (in which the sound for a scene either follows or precedes the cut to the visuals) is not just flashy style. In Almodóvar's hands, sound bridges cue interconnections between plotlines. VOs, another Almodóvar staple in the use of sound, are similarly not mere stylistic flourish. VOs furnish the audience with crucial plot information and privileged access to the interior world of the characters. The technique frequently occurs when characters read from the important prop presented by another character's letter or diary. A striking use of VO with regard to a letter occurs in *Law of Desire* in which a series of four characters give voice to the letter's content as they come into contact with it (i.e., Pablo as he writes it; Ada, Antonio and Juan as they read it, although only the latter was meant to do so). Moreover, the Almodóvar corpus presents several VOs of letters and diaries composed by characters who are deceased by the time that the VO occurs (as in *Dark Habits*, *Talk to Her*, and *Bad Education*). The technique speaks to the spectral impact of the deceased as their voices continue to mystify/influence/haunt still living characters.

Cutting strategies (editing) are also used to noteworthy effect in Almodóvar's corpus. The pattern of using cuts to emphasize contrast is evident in the debut *Pepi, Luci, Bom* . . . when the cop/husband's unreconstructed *machista* soliloquy to his wife in the private home cuts to a raucous outdoor punk music performance that presents Madrid's bohemian *la movida* of the 1980s in full flower. In this sequence of scenes, "New" (post-Franco) Spain decisively answers the "Old." Along with making a political point about tensions between the liberal and the revanchist within Spain's trajectory, cross-cutting is also used to implicate characters in each other's storylines. Cuts between Diego and María during the opening sequence of *Matador* signify strong parallels between the two characters (although they do not meet, face-to-face, until about halfway through the film). In *Bad Education*, dark humor informs cuts between the older women rhapsodizing about *chorizo* (ham) at one end of the phone line in Galicia—and the contrasting tawdry scene of drug addiction and blackmail in Valencia at the other end. In this moment, Almodóvar's film also suggests misgivings about the New Spain (albeit, a New Spain where prior *Franquista* traumas echo into the 1977 setting) while celebrating rustic traditionalism.

Genuinely funny slapstick parodies of commercials are cut into some earlier films (*Pepi, Luci, Bom* . . ., *Women on the Verge* . . ., and *Tie Me Up!* . . .). The commercials present stylistic "excess" although they are not mere eye-candy as they channel criticism of Spain's rising commercialism and its attendant rictus-smile hype. The narrative/editing technique of flashback also gains in prominence over the course of Almodóvar's career. Although campy flashbacks briefly fill in Sexi's psychohistory in *Labyrinth of Passion*, the earlier films in the corpus tend toward characters "devoid of 'backstories'" (Smith 2000: 19). By contrast, jig-sawed use of the flashback technique in *Bad Education* and *Talk to Her* enables more subtle calibrations of the characters' constitution as they are refracted through a mosaic of experiences and telling vignettes.[3]

As in many films (including those of notable auteurs Orson Welles and Alfred Hitchcock), props assume substantial importance in Almodóvar's universe. Plots are often driven forward by props (e.g., the script of *The Visit* that Juan stole from his dead brother in *Bad Education*). Moreover, props are often "MacGuffins" in a film. That is, the MacGuffin is in itself something largely unimportant—but it is invested with enormous psychic significance by the characters who, in turn, engage in elaborate quests that pivot on the MacGuffin and that drive the narrative forward (Truffaut 1967). "Rosebud" in *Citizen Kane* (Orson Welles 1941) or the elusive ceramic bird in *The Maltese Falcon* (John Huston 1941) exemplify MacGuffins that set the plot in motion and drive the characters toward a quest—even if these props are in themselves largely trivial, notwithstanding all that has been invested in them psychically.

Variation on the narrative conceit of a MacGuffin may be taken to include characters who loom over the others within the narrative as spectral presences, rarely if ever seen. In *Women on the Verge . . .* , Iván is hardly onscreen in the first hour (aside from a fantasy sequence) and is mainly encountered on answering machines. However, *Bad Education*, may present the clearest instance of the spectral "character as MacGuffin" in Almodóvar's corpus. Ignacio drives and obsesses the other characters in the world of the film (namely, Enrique, Juan, Father Manolo Berenguer). However, Ignacio is never seen alive but *only* in flashback and in the loosely based-on-fact visioning of his script of *The Visit*.

One stylistic difference between Almodóvar's early and later films implicates heightened skill in fashioning a fully integrated narrative. On this view, the early Almodóvar is an accomplished "scene-smith" (or "sequence-smith") who betrays some difficulty in cobbling together film-length narrative. The early Almodóvar films often take up subplots and characters to abruptly drop them or drive into a narrative cul-de-sac. As such, the early films at times give off something like the feel of "variety show" television vignettes that are characterized by rapid-fire shifts from comedic skits to song and dance numbers, with new characters entering and exiting. One noteworthy example: The "General Erections" (*Erecciones generales*) scene in *Pepi, Luci, Bom . . .* is like a skit in the middle of the film in which judges (one played by Almodóvar) measure the size of contestants' penises in order to find a winner (who is promptly fellated). Other films in the 1980s gobsmack the spectator through abrupt *volte-faces* with respect to narrative tone and genre conventions. For example, *Matador* u-turns brusquely from obsessive parallel love stories into a serial killer investigation that is, in turn, further garnished with a supernatural storyline when Ángel—*suddenly*—exhibits clairvoyant powers.

Almodóvarian narrative structure is often characterized by outlandish coincidences. Chance meetings frequently presage characters who later become deeply implicated in each other's affairs. In *Talk to Her*, Marco and Benigno sit next to each other at the *Café Müller* performance. By further coincidence, they later meet again in the hospital and discover that both have love interests in comas. A close relationship between the two men is thus initiated. Even given the measure of poetic licence understood to be in play for any given film, the coincidences in Almodóvar's corpus often strain against plausibility. The later films more readily enable suspension of disbelief in deference to the filmmaker's more seamlessly stitched conceits. Nevertheless, the earlier films should not be dismissed, despite their flaws, since they present audacious touches that anticipate a director who later takes fuller command of the filmmaking toolkit.

Keeping It Real

Almodóvar comments that, "'Even when you decide where to place the camera, you're manipulating reality'" (quoted in Smith 2000: 172). As noted, the use of sound is one of the key stylistic channels in which Almodóvar plays with, and regularly rejects, realism. At the same time, mediated construction of artifice and falseness are at least implicitly theorized within the films; for example, porn star Paul Bazzo appears unable to differentiate between his screen roles and daily life, Nicholas uses his murder sprees as material for the novels he writes, and the precocious reality television entrepreneur Andrea Caracortada recycles life's tawdry indignities into tele-entertainment (all in *Kika*). Similarly, characters discuss and, at times, celebrate falseness. In *Pepi, Luci, Bom* . . . , Pepi embraces artifice. In discussing her intention to make a film of Luci's and Bom's lives, she observes that filmmakers stage rain on the set so as not to damage the camera; a simulation that is better, on this view, for the purposes of transmitting narrative elements with verisimilitude. Twenty-six years later in Almodóvar's corpus, "inside jokes" about departures from realism pepper *Volver*. Irene asks Raimunda if she has had cosmetic surgery on her breasts. Roused-to-indignation, Raimunda denies it (although Cruz, the actress playing Raimunda, has undergone breast enhancement, according to Spain's *prensa rosa* celebrity press [*¡Qué Me Dices!* 2006]). Positing that "The ass is very important," Almodóvar acknowledges his insistence that Cruz don prosthetic buttocks enhancement to play the part to the fleshy specifications of *la latina típica* (Canadian Broadcast Company 2006). These flourishes square with the themes articulated in Agrado's (Althusser-inflected) on-stage monologue in *All About My Mother*. Accounting for her many cosmetic surgeries, Agrado comments, "you are more authentic the more you resemble what you've dreamed of being."

Agrado's statement both assumes Althusserian ideology that posits subjects as immersed in material practice and an affective relation to the external world—*and turns it on its head*. Althusser (1994) theorizes subjects as irresistibly recruited into ideology via material pulls from institutions and rituals. The interface between style and content is implicated in the rejection of strict realism in Almodóvar's corpus; it also gestures toward possibilities for subjects to enact interventions in their material circumstances and, thus, to re-work their relation to the external world. In other words, when one changes the material base of everyday life, one changes the person (subject)—as Agrado advocates, on one's own terms, in alignment with one's fantasies. Almodóvar's fictional creations are at once constituted within materially grounded institutional settings—notably, the family and its gendered practices—and they regularly reconstitute their material conditions and re-work their subjectivities. On this view, relations between style and content in Almodóvar's corpus run in parallel with the Althusserian subject's fantasized relations of material conditions, thus anticipating a neo-Althusserian vision of subjects recrafting subjectivity from the material ground up.

Thematic Overview

In unpacking the themes embedded within Almodóvar's films, I will emphasize the depictions of, first, the church and state; and, second, the family and gender within Spain (where each film is entirely or almost entirely set). I will also more briefly address a battery of other themes that arise in the director's work across the 1980s, 1990s, and 2000s. These themes include the penchant for media workers and mediation in the films as well as the construction of an array of identities.

Aside from the "hipsters" who often appear in Almodóvar's films (most notably the earlier ones), many Almodóvarian characters are involved in the culture industry ISAs. For example, Pepa and Iván (*Women on the Verge . . .*) work dubbing imported films into Spanish for the peninsula's screens. In other entries in the corpus, Pablo is a prominent film director (*Law of Desire*), Marina is an actress and her sister Lola a production assistant (*Tie Me Up! . . .*), Becky is an actress and her daughter Rebecca a news anchor (*High Heels*), Ramón is a fashion photographer and Andrea a tabloid television entrepreneur (*Kika*), and David is an Olympic athlete who attracts advertising accounts (*Live Flesh*). Writers are prevalent in Almodóvar's fictional worlds as central characters such as Nicholas (*Kika*), Leo (*Flower of My Secret*), and Marco (*Talk to Her*) have all "taken up the quill" in various genres of writing.

Given the prevalence of media workers, it is not surprising that Almodóvar's corpus presents sequences in which a variety of forms of mediation are captured. For example, the opening sequence of *All About My Mother* includes a pedagogical role-playing video, Estéban writing in a diary, a Truman Capote book gifted from mother to son, a film that Manuela and Estéban watch on TV (*All About Eve*) and a play on stage that foreshadow narrative turns (*Streetcar Named Desire*)—all in the opening ten minutes of the film's runtime. In Almodóvar's films, the ubiquity of mass media is often used to introduce important characters, as instanced by Lydia's initial appearance in *Talk to Her* on an intrusive interview program. However, the later films in the corpus incorporate the shifts presented by these mediations more tightly into the narrative—and less self-consciously than in the early films with their frequent, abrupt shifts in tone and substance. Similarly, whereas the earlier films court risks of narrative clutter and even shades of incoherence (e.g., *Matador, Law of Desire*), Almodóvar's narratives are tightly crafted to intricate specifications in later films. For example, a song that Marco recalls in flashback in *Talk to Her* occasions a brief flashback-within-a-flashback. In the same film, an audacious eight-minute silent film-within-the-film channels many of *Talk to Her*'s themes of desire and masochism—while also serving as an ingenious scrim that conceals Benigno's rape of Alicia.

The pattern of mediation and media reference is established early in Almodóvar's corpus of films. For example, *What Have I Done . . .* opens with a camera craning and crew on set as Gloria enters the dojo to clean. *Matador* leads with Diego masturbating to tele-pornography while Almodóvar's subsequent film, *Law of Desire*, crosses over from consumption of pornography to its production; the extended first scene depicts an actor masturbating vigorously in shot while a Foley artist furnishes heavy breathing off the set. *Tie Me Up! . . .* features an extended "backstage" scene with film director Max Espejo steering events. As this partial roster of mass media's implication into Almodóvar's films suggests, the director calls upon both "high" and "low" art forms from, e.g., experimental theatre to pornography. Nonetheless, more vulgar spectacle tends to prevail in the films from the 1980s versus the later films that traffic in more elevated registers. Emphasis on the media industries also unmistakably transmits an assumption on Almodóvar's part that the mass media ISAs are an essential component of Spanish society (i.e., its practices, steering mechanisms and its sense of itself).

Identity Crises?

The "over-representation" of media workers in Almodóvar's world on screen squares with the general emphasis on media and mediation that is characteristic of his corpus of films. Similarly, "subaltern" and "alternative" identities are also accented in displays of "a deeply felt sense of empathy for the marginalized and the misunderstood" (Willoquet-Maricondi 2004: viii). Transsexuals (*Law of Desire, All About My Mother, Bad Education*) and heroin addicts (*Dark Habits, Tie Me Up! . . .*) frequently appear. In another register of distinctive identities, characters with international backgrounds have also long been prominent in Almodóvar's films: The Muslim cabal in *Labyrinth of Passion*, Nicholas the American in *Kika*, Mañuela the Argentine in *All About My Mother* et al., inhabit Almodóvar's version of Madrid well before Spain and its capital became a manifestly diverse attractant for immigration. Moreover, Almodóvar has been cited for channelling gay identity toward the mainstream in part via his nonchalance about placing gay characters front and center. D'Lugo (2006) observes that Almodóvar may be credited with "the groundbreaking treatment of the normalization of gay romantic narratives in Spanish film" (2006: 59) humming the cultural mood music that later enabled legislation for gay marriage in 2005.

In Almodóvar's world, characters are often "doubled" or "tripled" via multiple identities—with their attendant secrets, stage names, impersonators, and doppelgängers. One example will suffice to give force to the claim that Almodóvar harbors a playful posture toward identity. Specifically, in *Bad Education*, Juan pretends to be his dead brother Ignacio while he also insists on being called by the stage name of "Ángel." In the reconstructions of (the "real") Ignacio's script that is based upon his autobiography and that play out in Enrique's mind, Ignacio is also a Sara Montes impersonator who performs under the stage name Zahara. In both the vision of the script in Enrique's mind and the version of it that he directs in the diegesis of *Bad Education*, Juan pretending to be Ignacio while insisting on being called Ángel and imagined as Zahara are played by Gael Garcia Bernal. Although Enrique suspects almost immediately that Juan is not Ignacio, the fluidity of identity is clearly evoked in this character's array of charades and guises.

Beyond any given character, Spain's identity is also at stake in the corpus. Spain's regions have long experienced fraught relations since the "Catholic Kings" Fernando and Isabel assayed to unify central Castile with eastern Aragon in the fifteenth century via their power marriage (Williams 2000). Today, these tense relations manifest themselves in assertive nationalist movements most notably in *Cataluña* and *País Vasco* (Basque Country). Barry Jordan insists, hyperbolically, that, "though we may be able to talk of the Spanish state in political terms, we cannot sensibly talk of a national culture or for that matter a uniform national cinema" (2000: 70). While Jordan posits Spain almost as "other" to itself, Ernesto Acevedo-Muñoz places orientalizing stress on ostensible "stasis" in Spain and its image of itself. He posits Spanish national identity as reducing to "identity crisis" (2007: 1–2) in part occasioned by the reverberating traumas of Francoism. Commenting on *Bad Education*, Acevedo-Muñoz concludes that "the weight of Spain's historical processes, during and after Franco, continues to fatally enclose Almodóvar's characters" (2007: 287). There is no serious question that the Civil War and Franquista rule from 1939 to 1975 are events of extraordinary magnitude that must be kept on board in understanding Spain. However, Acevedo-Muñoz reiterates that Spain still bleeds for its "troubled past under Franco" (2007: 10) to such an extent that he implicitly posits a static Spain—even as the nation has been transformed from the relatively impoverished periphery of Europe to one of the world's ten largest national economies, boasting a Gross Domestic Product of 1.434 trillion USDs (*The Economist* 2007) along with a burgeoning immigrant population. Discussion of Spain should not be locked into a paradigm that arbitrarily takes, for example, 1974 (or 1492 or 1808) as an unquestioned benchmark that eclipses the present.

Nevertheless, Almodóvar's approach to identity largely skirts around the question of Spain's regions, despite the heavy accent on regionalism in Spain's discourse and politics. One means by which Almodóvar seemingly avoids confronting Spain's internal division is to dwell on Spain in relation to other nations. In *Tie Me Up! . . .*, differences in national identity are (confrontationally) evoked between Spaniards and Germans in a barbed parody of a commercial. While young Spaniards tango their youth away, romantically and frivolously, elder Spaniards are depicted in the pseudo commercial selling trinkets by Madrid's Ventas bullring for the lack of earlier foresight in planning for retirement. Young Germans in Nazi armbands are, by contrast, attentive to the bureaucratic rigors of planning for the future, and they spend their golden years disco dancing, however creakily, on their property in sunshine-laden Spain. The pursuit of romance and the arts contrasts with the relatively joyless efficiencies of the Anglo-Saxon culture to which Latin people often contrast themselves. Hence, the pseudo-commercial, a commonplace of Almodóvar's 1980s films, simultaneously expresses both national pride and defensiveness.

A later film, *Live Flesh*, is significant for its more explicit elaboration of paradigm shifts within Spanish politics and identity. The film opens with title cards that quote the "State of Emergency" that Franco's regime imposed in 1970. In the opening sequence of the film, *Franquista* Minister Manuel Fraga Iribarne announces

the law over the radio with sound furnished by the original recording and *not* a voice actor's reconstruction of it. The radio
broadcast in the original voice is a pointed political gesture by
Almodóvar at an active politician; the Minister Fraga who read the
law in 1970 was premier of the Galicia region by the late 1990s. As
the announcement is made in the film, Doña Centro discovers that
Isabel is going into labor. The two women go to the street (devoid
of citizens) to find transport to the hospital. With Doña Centro's
assistance, Isabel gives birth to her son Victor on a city bus that is
empty aside from a going-through-the-motions driver. The ambiance of the city is deserted and run-down, reminders of the police
state backdrop for Fraga's reading of the law.

In the final scene of the film, Victor is a young adult shepherding the pregnant Elena through the bustling and prosperous
streets of Madrid in a car. Surveying the new circumstances as
part of the generation with few (if any) direct recollections of
Franco, Victor observes, "Spain lost its fear a long time ago."
Hence, along with the characters' trajectories, the narrative
movement of *Live Flesh* clearly addresses the nation's vector
across more than 20 heady years of change. Earlier, the same film
references another keynote year for Spain: 1992. It was the year
when Spain's transformation from third world-style police state to
reinvigorated continental and world player was consolidated with
the World Exhibition in Seville and the Olympic Games in Barcelona (at which *Live Flesh*'s David represents Spain in wheelchair
basketball).[4]

In the corpus of films, Almodóvar also presents a "back to the
village" movement that is largely a sentimental construction with
respect to Spanish identity; these plot lines appear, in various
measure, in *What Have I Done . . .* , *Tie Me Up! . . .*, *Flower of My
Secret*, and *Volver*. However, this movement (beyond August vaca-
tions!) does not have worldly concomitants in an increasingly urban Spain. It may be interpreted as Almodóvar's effort to reclaim
la España profunda of the heartland provinces from decades of
Franquista mythology.

On the other hand, Almodóvar addresses a new element of
Spain's identity: namely, immigration, a contentious issue in a nation that was only recently effectively all Latin Iberian. When Sole
and Irene discuss how to conceal the mother's identity while she
works in the hair salon, they casually run through the prominent

immigration waves in Madrid (Dominican? Chinese?) before strategically settling on presenting her as a non-Spanish-speaking
Russian. Along with the nonchalant acceptance of new faces in
Spain, Sole's customers also mobilize their causal prejudices about
Eastern Europeans and map them onto Irene—who is, of course, a
red-blooded Spaniard. The film thus takes a jab against prejudice
in which "knowledge precedes knowing." *Volver* also deals in clear-
eyed fashion with the character of Regina and her place within
contemporary Spain. A South American, Regina toils as a prostitute in the open-air Casa de Campo brothel. Briefly, but with dignity, she laments not having security or legal documents. She
urges Raimunda to hire her to tend bar in the restaurant and thus
endow her with work papers. While brief, these moments present
sensitivity to Spain's rapid demographic reconfiguration and do so
without the cloying pathos or sentimentality of Hollywood at its
most vulgar.

CHAPTER 5

A Dedication

It is supremely delicate to bring up the former dictatorship in Spain, given some unsettled debts from this era and the nation's deservedly intense pride in the magnitude of its reconstitution. In a particularly dramatic illustration, Spanish King Juan Carlos (himself a key figure in the orderly transition to a constitutional republic [Hooper 1995]) made an absolutely sincere and livid public slap-down in November 2007 on Hugo Chávez when the Venezuelan president dismissed the authenticity of Spain's post-Franco renaissance—in glib defiance of all evidence to the contrary. Whereas the previous chapter dwelled on identity in more "personal" terms, this chapter pins down Almodóvar's corpus that has arisen in the post-Franco era as it playfully reworks some of the enduring apparatuses of Spanish society.

Church and State

Upon winning an Academy Award for *All About My Mother* in 1999, Almodóvar used the global platform of the ceremony to make the following statement: "'I would like to dedicate my prize to the democracy in Spain'" (quoted in Jordan 2000: 77). In contrast to Spain's newly minted democratic steering mechanisms, church and state interpenetrated during Franco's lengthy rule. Heavy-handed state censorship also proscribed the following topics on screen, each of which would later be mainstays in Almodóvar's narrative toolkit: "suicide; the use of violence as a means of solving social or human problems; prostitution; sexual perversions; adultery and illicit sexual relations; . . . anything tending to undermine the institution of marriage and family; drug abuse and alcoholism" (Smith 2000: 15). Almodóvar's films collectively thumb their nose at these proscriptions from the recent past; indeed, the debut film *Pepi, Luci, Bom . . .* may be construed as "a string of vignettes devoted almost exclusively to topics banned from cinema screens only a few years earlier" (Smith 2000: 15).

Beyond the close-up on the formerly verboten topics, the decades of repression under state and clerical auspices echo audibly into Almodóvar's films—particularly the earlier ones released within a decade of Franco's death. The pattern begins in the opening scene of Almodóvar's debut, *Pepi, Luci, Bom . . .* The cop—a representative of the state who has no name in the film—enters Pepi's apartment and demands that she remove her marijuana plants. In short order, he rapes her (in an uncomfortably cartoonish depiction of such). The cop continues his depravities throughout the film, finally visiting sexualized spasms of violence onto his estranged wife Luci on a heap of industrial worksite trash. The cop's commentaries express loathing for independent women in favor of traditional wifely behavior and warn about leftist "threats" menacing Spain. Thus, words and deeds position this early Almodóvarian creation as an unreconstructed *Franquista* with all the attendant ugliness—albeit, ugliness leavened with the over-the-top cartoon qualities that tint the early films.

Unflattering depictions of cops abound in subsequent films as well.[1] In *What Have I Done to Deserve This?*, Polo is impotent and hires Cristal the prostitute to pose as his girlfriend for a visit to the psychologist. Later, Polo abuses his position to assay blackmail for free sex in Cristal's apartment/brothel. Within the parameters of his police work, Polo is also clownishly inept and unable to solve the crime that leaves Antonio dead—even after Gloria admits to having killed him. Domínguez in *High Heels* is similarly curious in his personal predilections (e.g., cross-dressing Becky impersonator) and also cannot decode confessions issued by murder culprits when they clash with gumshoe pretensions. The partnered cops in *Kika* are inept as they betray laziness wedded to self-importance. By contrast, when "amateur" non-state agents—Andrea in *Kika*, Enrique in *Bad Education*, Agustina in *Volver*—set out to investigate crimes, they do so with far greater efficacy than the cops in Almodóvar's corpus of films.[2]

Later, in *Live Flesh*, a pair of policemen presents continuities and departures from the generally withering view of the police. On one hand, Sancho is an unreconstructed relic of past abusiveness. He drinks heavily on the beat and intensifies conflict, rather than reduces it, with trigger-happy antics when summoned to Elena's apartment. Sancho is, moreover, riddled with sexual jealousy that drives him to shoot and cripple his own partner, David—and to then frame the innocent tough, Victor, for the shooting. An unreconstructed *machista*, Sancho abuses and finally kills his wife Clara. By contrast, David displays prudence and professionalism as an officer when he damps down tensions in Elena's apartment and disarms Victor, prior to Sancho's disastrous interventions. David leaves the police force after the shooting.

As with the police, the Catholic Church tends to be a bigger presence in Almodóvar's earlier films than in the later entries in the corpus; *Bad Education*, from 2004, is the obvious exception. In later Almodóvar, much of the "sacred" has been discharged to secular authority. For example, hospital functionaries deal with death in part by reassigning organs from the deceased to patients in need (a narrative element from the opening sequences of both *Flower of My Secret* and *All About My Mother*). While it may seem *jejune* to take jabs at the Catholic Church, its ready alliance with *Franquista* authority justifies criticism. Moreover, revelations that the international church hierarchy has covered up for serial pedophile priests warrant further criticism to firmly nail these crimes into the cultural record; even as one is able to acknowledge members of the same church's unfathomable courage, most notably while carrying out the "preferential option for the poor" in 1970s–1980s Latin American terror states (Lernoux 1980).

Almodóvar's third feature is the most closely concerned with the Catholic Church as the vast majority of it is set within a convent. Given its scabrous account of the nuns' lives, *Dark Habits* was banished from the competition at the Venice Film Festival. Nevertheless, *Dark Habits* is not a polemic against Catholicism, nor an "easy parody of one of the pillars of Francoist culture" (D'Lugo 2006: 34)—although it may seem to lean in that direction at first blush.

Early in the film, the Marquesa convenes with the Mother Superior to indicate that she is cutting off the annuity that her now deceased husband had paid to the convent. The Marquesa characterizes the former husband as a fascist, thus dropping a strong hint of the former regime's links to the church. However, the nuns of this convent are not right-wing poster children. In over-the-top fashion, they are deeply implicated in society's habitually flogged "vices" and alternative lifestyles. The nuns drop acid, pursue lesbian affairs, author widely read pornographic novels, and prepare

to traffic drugs in order to generate revenue. One nun is being
sheltered after the Mother Superior lied on her behalf to spare her
a murder conviction. The nuns are also free of pious moralizing
and (for the most part) cynical exploitation of their authority—in
contrast with the unredeemable, predatory men of the cloth in *Bad
Education*. As Almodóvar says about his creations in *Dark Habits*,
"'The paradox of the film is that these women have a religion, but
not a religion inspired by God'" (quoted in D'Lugo 2006: 32).[3]

At the same time, Almodóvar avoids gratuitous swipes at the
nuns even if the ensemble of characters is not idealized. They thrill
to the possibility of their sanctuary being filled with prostitutes,
murderers, and druggies (as it will put wind in the sails of their
project of service) alongside suggestions that they take a dim view
of humanity as fallen. Moreover, Mother Superior milks advantage
from an opportunity to be physically close to the troubled Mercedes
Cora while harboring her in one of the convent's beds—and simultaneously uses Mercedes as a distraction to conceal her obsession,
Yolanda, from the police. Nonetheless, authority external to the
convent is presented in harsher terms. The police force's appearance to apprehend Mercedes is depicted as a heavy-handed intru-
sion. The scene's violence is due to the male cops' brusque entrance
into a surrogate family (matriarchal) sanctuary to forcefully seize
the troubled young woman. The violation is further emphasized in
Mother Superior's gesture of giving Mercedes her shoes while the
cops brutishly haul her away, underscoring sensitivity to the
young woman's vulnerability to the RSAs. The other unsympathetic authority in the film is part of an upper tier of the church
hierarchy; namely, the Mother General. In her brief appearance,
she shoehorns in a racist aside about Africans and takes umbrage
at the sisters' names as well as the bawdy party that they have
celebrated. Finally, the Mother General announces that she will
disband the convent, thereby terminating the experimentation
that she (accurately) senses has seized hold of it to liberal specifications.

Implied criticism of the church initiates the plot of *Tie Me Up!* .
. . . In its opening credit sequence and first scene, Ricky's psychotic
behavior is presented as an efflux of his experience of being raised
as an orphaned ward of the church. The handsome Ricky has for
years been an informal prostitute in the institution with even his
exit punctuated by carnal action with the Mother Superior. Ricky
emerges from the institution insistent on his normalcy. He pro-

ceeds to violently kidnap Marina, the object of his obsession. Both church and family fail Ricky in constituting him as the subject that he becomes—although the final sequence strongly implies that Marina's family will at least attempt a reclamation project with him.

Later in Almodóvar's career, *Bad Education* presents more penetrating criticism of the church. A viscerally terrifying scene depicts Father Manolo's pedophilic "hot pursuit" of the ten-year-old Ignacio (as envisioned/recollected by Enrique while he reads the script written by the then-deceased Ignacio). In contrast with Almodóvar's crass and jokey staging of rape in the opening of *Pepi, Luci, Bom . . .*, the violation in *Bad Education* is wrenching in part for the stylistic command marshaled in staging it. After masturbating each other at the cinema, Ignacio and Enrique are unable to sleep and spontaneously convene in the dormitory bathroom to commiserate. The scene is shot in a low-key lighting scheme, presumably with blue filters that endow it with an eerie gloss. The panoptic Manolo's pursuit of the pair in hiding, as he opens and closes a series of ominously echoing doors, is tensely staged. It suggests the pedophile's white-knuckle drive for control over the ten-year olds. Manolo subsequently convenes Catholic ritual in full regalia in the sacristy, shot in incongruous golden light. The wrenching sequence finishes with a close-up of Manolo's dark robe (that, in turn, functions as a fade to black) as he descends on the pre-adolescent Ignacio. In the next scene, Enrique is on the other side of the fence having been expelled despite Manolo's promise to Ignacio to not separate the pair. Hence, *Bad Education* channels withering criticism of the church's male "rank-and-file" to an extent not observed with respect to *Dark Habits*' ensemble of women. *Bad Education* is also of a piece with D'Lugo's argument that Almodóvar has become more direct in confronting the *Franquista* legacy (2006: 97); previously, the director thumbed his nose at Franco by celebrating *la movida* libertarianism and otherwise ignoring the dictatorship.

The Family ISA

As Almodóvar observes, the family that follows the template of his own (four children, parents married until death), "is a concept that belongs to another age; the family has survived but it has taken on a different shape" (quoted in Willoquet-Maricondi 2004: xiii). The corpus of films back-up this claim that is, in turn, a reasonable characterization of the contemporary scene in Spain. *Law of Desire* captures the radical reordering of tradition in Almodóvar's early work as the family is composed of "a gay male as father; his sibling, now a lesbian transsexual, as mother; and a daughter of a lesbian to complete the new familial trinity" (D'Lugo 2006: 56).

What Have I Done to Deserve This? presents Almodóvar's first feature-length treatment devoted to family life and, at the onset, is more grounded in the traditional family form. The spectator is positioned to be sympathetic to Gloria as a diligent woman burdened with thankless drudgery inside and outside the home. Her life is further damped down by a dead-end husband and haughty children. Her difficult life is made more poignant for the contrast with the foils who dwell in her building: The prostitute Cristal (who makes the "oldest profession" appear to be glamorous, showbiz style fun) and the relatively wealthy, if sour, single mother Juani. *What Have I Done . . .* also anticipates later processes of decay of family life in Almodóvar's world on screen. Gloria seizes the opportunity to gift her son Miguel to the lecherous dentist who is better able to materially support his precocious acquisitiveness. Having accumulated savings on a drug deal, Toni exits the family's cement block barrio of Madrid to work the land of the grandmother's pueblo. After the *machista* husband Antonio slaps her hard and draws blood, Gloria kills him with a quintessentially Spanish hambone in the kitchen. However, finally being alone in the apartment at the end of the film does not bring liberation to Gloria but gestures toward suicide. Her savior turns out to be Miguel who suddenly returns home with a stated project to be the "man of the house," an ambiguous claim, given his father's *machista* precedent, but one that nonetheless occasions joyful tears on Gloria's part. Thus, the film evidences push-and-pull between several contradictory moments in its posture toward traditional family life.

Almodóvar's feature releases have all been post-Franco. As Marsha Kinder (1987) suggests, the films indirectly express a desire to jettison the abusive national patriarch through a cinematic effacement of fathers (and, to some extent, parents in general). In the debut film, *Pepi, Luci, Bom . . .*, Pepi's father is reduced to a voice on the phone that demands she get a real job, which Pepi does, albeit by developing the menstruating doll. In another 1980s film, Carlos of *Women on the Verge . . .* is raised by his grandparents while his mother is institutionalized and his father is preoccupied with an endless cascade of philandering. Ricky of *Tie Me Up! . . .* is an orphan raised mainly in institutional settings. What little recollection he has of his parents revolves around a photo that "confirms" to him that they existed. Upon returning to his *pueblo* in Extremadura, Ricky discovers only deserted rubble as stand-in for the family that he barely knew. More recently, in *Live Flesh*, Victor's mother is a prostitute with whom he had limited contact during her short life while the question of patrimony is not even raised. In another variation on the theme, *Talk to Her*'s Benigno has a mother who never appears on screen and whose physical condition demands constant care. His father is characterized as absent from his life when the psychologist asks about him. It bears consideration that the pattern of missing fathers may also be construed through a more traditionalist set of spectacles: On this view, a lack of guiding parental (especially patriarchal) authority generates problems for these deracinated, even troubled characters.

Alongside phantom fathers, a series of abusive patriarchs in the corpus of films may be taken as symptomatic gestures toward the national traumas of the "national father" of the Franco period. Almodóvarian fathers are often monstrous figures as patriarchal rape/incest is a repeated narrative element. Salient examples include the psychotic and incestuous dry cleaner in *Labyrinth of Passion* while the doctor in the same film and Paco in *Volver* present variations on this theme. In particular, the doctor believes that he is having carnal relations with his daughter Sexi at the end of the film (it is Queti, surgically transformed to double for Sexi) and Paula is actually Paco's stepdaughter. The unseen father in *Law of Desire* is sordid even by Almodóvarian standards. Tina tells her amnesic brother that their father molested her when she was still a boy, encouraged the sex change operation—and then abandoned her in Morocco. Even given this stiff competition, Nicholas in *Kika* is arguably the most dubious instance of the father species in the corpus of films. He is an assertive sexual rival to his stepson—and a serial killer in addition to being an incorrigible serial philanderer.

By contrast with the track record of family patriarchs in Almodóvar's corpus of films, the construction of mothers offers a more generally affirmative, if mixed, portrait. Àngel's chilly and aggressive Opus Dei mother in *Matador*, on screen briefly, is offset across Almodóvar's corpus by models of maternal sacrifice and/or warmth such as Gloria (*What Have I Done . . .*) and Raimunda (*Volver*). In a variation on the theme, Becky in *High Heels* is initially overbearing and self-centered. However, her dying gesture is to assume the guilt for her daughter Rebecca's murder rap, selflessness driven by the advent of awareness of the daughter's sacrifices and resentments. Moreover, when family is presented as being an organic and pro-social force in the Almodóvarian corpus, it is heavily accented with matriarchy. Instances include Leo's journey in *The Flower of My Secret*. She returns to her pueblo following a series of personal shocks in Madrid and is immersed in a patio of supportive women. The sequence is keynoted by the mother's speech at Leo's bed in which she posits, in rustic metaphors, that women without their familial support (most especially from other women) are like "cows who have lost their bells." Surrogate families that form in Almodóvar's films appear set to thrive when they are female-friendly, as when the widowed Marquesa recruits Yolanda and Sister Alley Rat into her home at the conclusion of *Dark Habits*.

Contrasts between the female-affirmative and androcentric visions of family arise in *Tie Me Up!* . . . . The film presents a sphere of sisterly concern and support between Lola and Marina. For his part, Ricky yearns for a traditionalist restoration of the family with its base in marriage and children. While marriage with children is a reasonable objective in itself, Ricky's method of imposing his desired project conforms to right-wing masculinist specifications. Coercion and kidnapping are his means. Marina and Lola later go (literally) far out of their way to agree to the terms Ricky seeks to impose via his paroxysms of violence. In doing so, Marina and Lola may be falling back on the strength of their own family life to absorb the deeply troubled Ricky. In this vein, the narrative may be further (and generously) interpreted as claiming Ricky from the wilderness and inserting him into the regime of female powers of secular socialization by the end of the film. Nonetheless, the closing is unsettling for the affirmation of Ricky's androbrutishness in the service of tradition that enthrones the male's quest to get what he wants, whatever his flaws may be.

Beyond adult foibles in Almodóvar's corpus, family life is often trauma-laden as it impacts on child characters. One may pull together these striking narrative threads (including several referenced earlier) as follows: Becky in *High Heels* murders her

stepfather to advance her mother's career in the face of the husband's unswerving *machista* demands while Queti (*Labyrinth of
Passion*) is raped by her father, on screen with sadomasochistic
relish. Ada (*Law of Desire*) is neglected by her self-indulgent
mother and largely raised by Tina. In turn, Tina, a transsexual,
was molested by a priest when she was a male child in addition to
being her father's sex object. Further examples: Ricky (*Tie Me Up!
. . .*) is orphaned at age three and Victor (*Live Flesh*) is raised by a
largely absent prostitute (dialogue testifies to these off-screen
events). The prepubescent Ignacio (*Bad Education*) is molested by
a priest. In *Volver*, Raimunda is raped by her father (off-screen
and decades earlier) while her early teen daughter Paula kills her
stepfather attempting the same (also off-screen, but in the present
of the film's narrative). These ineffably painful childhood traumas,
typically at the hands of parental (patriarchal) and church authority, speak to a deeply suspicious posture toward these traditionally
valorized founts of authority.

Bent Gender-Bender?

A central question that was rehearsed earlier is whether
Almodóvar is the "woman's director" that received opinion holds
him to be. The question is thus begged: What constitutes a "pro-
woman," gyno-affirmative posture in a film? In sketching an answer, common sense is one touchstone. That is, if something gives
pause for looking discomforting or misogynist, it likely is in some
measure.

However, even given the value of common sense, films are often
slippery signifying systems and can look different in various registers with regard to, for example, explicit versus implicit meaning,
or narrative elements versus visual spectacle. In this vein, Janey
Place (1978) is attentive to the tensions and paradoxes that surround the woman in film noir. In the classic instances of noir on
which Place concentrates, the femme fatale is often punished
within the narrative in reply to her castrating transgressions
against male order. At the same time, the femme fatale is the most
arresting spectacle on screen and easily eclipses the good and duti-
ful woman who restores the man's masculinity. Place concludes
that noir is at once male fantasy art *and* a sharp reminder of the
disruptive incipient power of the woman that—traditionally—must
be addressed, policed, and cabined.

Attentive to such tensions, I draw on a raft of gender theory as it intersects with film to claim that woman-friendly cinema presents some identifiable elements. On this view, asking whether women are being presented "positively"—as "pleasant," or as the head of the company—is too pat and one-dimensional as a metric or analysis (see Gough-Yates [2003: Chapter 1] for discussion in the context of women's magazines). In particular, I posit that the woman-empowering film enacts:

(1) Examination of the determinations of the gendered situation as it coalesces through the interpenetrating practical spheres of tradition and socio-economic status. Such examination implicates analysis of contrasting (binarized) versions of femininity and masculinity within the world of the film. It also works against white-knuckle enthronement of androgenic tradition as unquestioned template of social life (discussed at length by Ryan and Kellner [1988]).

(2) Recruitment into the characters' situations via identification strategies that are, in turn, embedded in formal technique (Wood 2002). Close-ups, reaction shots, VOs, dream sequences, flashbacks, shared knowledge between the characters and the audience: All present strategies that strongly tend toward recruiting audience identification with a given character that may also support the considerations raised in (1).

(3) Denial of idealization, pandering, and sentimentality that ring false and entomb social tensions in "soft focus" gestures. While strict adherence to a doctrine of "realism" is not demanded, facile caricature tends to blunt analysis and recirculate dominant tropes.

(4) Discretion and care for the characters' dignity, even if they are fictional creations. For example, an explicit (and/or "burlesque") rape scene readily begs questions of what kind of spectacle the filmmakers are constructing. Other forms of gratuitous humiliation toward characters beg similar questions.

As noted, received opinion positions Almodóvar as a woman's director—even to the extent of inspiring criticisms of the director as a gyno-idealizer (Matthews 2006). By contrast, Jordan and Morgan-Tamosunas (1998) enact a more measured appraisal. They argue that Almodóvar's films have been characterized by a de-essentializing, "deconstructive approach" to gender—while, at the same time, the films often present "rounded and sensitive characterization of his female protagonists" (1998: 115). Nevertheless, Jordan and Morgan-Tamosunas are attentive to what they take as the director's significant moments of extended slippage from "his self-declared pro-feminist position" (1998: 115). Among other parts of the corpus, they criticize Almodóvar's defence of *Tie Me Up!* . . . on the grounds that Marina finally makes a "choice" to be with her captor Ricky: "His audiences inhabit a world in which the repression of women . . . is too deeply entrenched to be entirely free from misogynistic interpretation," thus they find Almodóvar's defence of his creation Marina to be "naïve" (1998: 116).[4]

By contrast, Paul Julian Smith is more certain of Almodóvar as a pro-woman filmmaker. Smith opens his argument by positing that Almodóvar has long been allocated less respect for making films construed as "zany" and laden with "kitsch." Smith interprets this discourse as an implicit downgrading of "a register coded as 'feminine' and for those men who identify themselves with women's concerns" (2000: 2). In this view, to be referred to as a "woman's director" is "an often backhanded compliment" (2000: 2). However, as Smith also acknowledges, Almodóvar's position has been further vexed by readings of his films as either gyno-fetishization or, conversely, as having humiliated some of his female creations for the screen. Smith pirouettes to recast the debate as one that hinges on "cross-cultural incomprehension." In this view, "Spanish libertarianism" with respect to artistic expression (including its implication in sexually explicit themes) clashes with the United States' Anglo-Saxon "regulative pragmatism" manifested in, for example, industry standards that would commercially hinder *Tie Me Up!* . . . with an "X" rating for U.S. exhibition (Smith 2000: 5). Putting aside the question of which culture is actually more "libertarian" with regard to commerce and its regulation: Via the economic-libertarianism-versus-regulation trope that he sketches, Smith dodges the fundamental issue of content. If one *begins* by granting the right of artistic expression, the question of gender is reframed as whether such expression has been used toward the widely assumed woman-friendly terms in *Tie Me Up!* . . . and other films in Almodóvar's corpus.

In placing these interpretive bets, Smith suggests that commentators from non-Latin cultures should not "interfere" (even symbolically) with the "natives" and their "peculiar" ways. However, Spanish people demonstrably do not share this view of their own culture and its movement through time. The former (teeth-gritting) acceptance of *machista* has been substantially turned back across three decades. In recent years, confrontation with Latin *machista* has gained in strength from film narratives (Icíar Bollían's tour-de-force, critically decorated treatment of domestic abuse, *Te Doy Mis Ojos* [2003]) and newly implemented laws on domestic battering that have teeth with respect to enforcement (e.g., courts devoted to the issue [Fuchs 2005]). Along with reactions against retrograde gender activity, change in the progressive register is evident as well; as of April 2008, the majority of Spanish President José Luis Rodriguez Zapatero's cabinet is female (Keeley 2008).

Moreover, Almodóvar's alleged idealization of women does not hold to the extent that Peter Matthews (2006) claims. Consider one traditional and unflattering trope of womanhood as "raw" and pre-acculturated (that may also be taken as undermining dignity/privacy, even for fictional creations). Almodóvar often depicts bodily secretions—and women in particular as authors of them. Examples include the receptionist loosing thunderous flatulence and defecating on herself in graphic detail in *Labyrinth of Passion*. In *Pepi, Luci, Bom* . . . , Bom urinates on Luci (to Luci's rapturous pleasure) and Pepi designs a doll that menstruates. *Pepi, Luci, Bom* . . . also features advertisements for panties that double as adult diapers and flatulence filters (and also, when crisis arises, as a dildo). Raimunda urinates in shot and simultaneously recognizes the signature of her mother's flatulence in *Volver*, and the sister tandem of Marina and Lola both squat on the toilet to urinate in *Tie Me Up!* . . .; they are joined by *Dark Habit*'s Yolanda in being photographed in this manner. Leo (*Flower of My Secret*), Mother Superior, and Yolanda (*Dark Habits*) throw up. In another variation on the theme, Andrea in *Kika* is the (seemingly satisfied) recipient of secretions as Paul Bazzo's masturbatory load arcs from the balcony several stories above the street onto her face. However offhand it may be, the secretion motif recirculates the trope of woman as identified with her body and secretions, a primitivization that suggests that she is at least partly athwart of culture for being girdled within biology and bodily function.

Nonetheless, in appraising Almodóvar's corpus it is important to notice that the construction of maleness is also problematicized and not taken as "given." One manifestation of the problematicization of male subjectivity occurs through depictions of its obsessiveness. In Almodóvar's world, obsession is usually associated with male characters—and it occasions stalker behaviour and violent crimes in pursuit of the man's traditional sense of privilege to possess the object of his desires. Antonio in *Law of Desire* is perhaps the paradigm case of obsession as he kills Juan, his rival for Pablo, and then dates Pablo's transsexual sister Tina solely in an effort to get closer to his obsession. Other instances of obsessed male characters include Victor in *Live Flesh*, Ricky in *Tie Me Up! . . .*, and Benigno in *Talk to Her*. Lucía is a clear exception as, in *Women on the Verge . . .* , this obsessed woman attempts premeditated murder of Iván to "settle" jealous accounts; she is also a more quickly sketched character than the obsessed men.

Off-Key Notes

In making a survey, textural evidence complicates assertions that Almodóvar's films are necessarily or monolithically pro-woman. However, before considering the debut film *Pepi, Luci, Bom . . .* in this vein, cautions are in order. It is a first feature by an autodidact filmmaker who never expected to be making films at all. Without doubt, no one foresaw that *Pepi, Luci, Bom . . .* would be subject to academic examination, in multiple languages, in the decades that followed its release. On this view, one can be too sadistically "picky" to academic specifications with a film's content— even if it is a reasonable response to find the gendered characterizations of the cop and Luci to be troubling creations.

The first scene of the first Almodóvar film depicts a rape, albeit one that is presented as burlesque. Thereafter, the plot is peppered with flourishes that may readily be read as woman-unfriendly, particularly with respect to Luci. An apparently timid housewife with a dull existence married to a cop, she discovers edgy lesbianism with the teenage punk Bom. Later, Luci expresses disdain toward her husband for treating her as a mother-figure rather than doling out the dog treatment that she masochistically prefers. When Luci's husband attempts to arrest her after she has gone AWOL with her punk friends, she mocks his lack of manliness in hiding behind his badge rather than acting like a *really* aggrieved man. Her husband responds on cue, calling her a whore, throwing her violently onto a heap of industrial waste and violating her (a scene that is awkwardly staged and uncomfortable to watch). In the penultimate scene of the film, a battered and bruised Luci strokes her husband's hand from her hospital bed and extols his forcefulness that she claims all but killed her—with hopes for a great deal more. Luci also denounces Bom for not being as bad as she thinks she is, while characterizing herself as more of a slut than Bom would ever comprehend.

These features of the plotline are sufficient to account for a queasy reaction to *Pepi, Luci, Bom . . .* 's gendered aspects. However, as Dick Hebdige (1988) has argued in his study of punk style—a style that the early Almodóvar calls upon—one can be too literal in one's reading of signs with regard to sub-cultural expression. From this perspective, *Pepi, Luci, Bom . . .* may be taken as patently offensive to gender sensibilities as a means of lampooning tastes and defiantly fashioning vulgarities as one might spray-paint graffiti. Moreover, if one assumes that subjects are constructed in vivo to socially prescribed specifications, rather than being born "as is," the cop's misogyny and Luci's masochism may reciprocally summon each other into being, fictional correlates to everyday subject formation. On this view, the considerable vestiges of Francoism did not perish (monolithically, indivisibly) in the dictator's deathbed five years earlier. A middle-aged woman such as Luci may not know any subject position but subservience coupled with an effort to gain pleasure where it can be found (in exaggerated form, in this fictional rendering). Alternatively, in a more prosaic register, *Pepi, Luci, Bom . . .* may strain the predictable joke that the mousy housewife is more transgressive than the ostentatiously and self-consciously punk characters—even as Luci's "transgression" assumes the form of celebrating intensified *machista* practice.

Although response to the film was by no means monolithic (Smith 2000: 97), Almodóvar's reputation as a woman's director was minted in part on *Women on the Verge . . . .* Thus, a close look at the film is warranted through the gendered lens. Following a credit sequence that features pastiches of images from women's magazines from the mid-twentieth century, Almodóvar introduces the central character of Pepa and her lover Iván. He is an aging playboy, roughly old enough to be father to the late 30s-ish Pepa. Iván's narcissistic sense of entitlement is expressed with wit in his first appearance on screen (that, given its expressionistic qualities and pre-wakeup timeframe, may be taken as Pepa's dream). He appears in a close-up of his mouth, pampered with breath spray, before he speaks into the microphone that signifies the authority of his address. A medium tracking shot follows the well-groomed Iván as he strolls through a series of representations of female types with whom he may liaison (including an African woman, a Usonian in cheerleader garb, and a Northern European). Following Pepa's dream sequence, Iván is largely absent as he repeatedly misses Pepa's frantic phone calls and movements through Madrid. When Iván is within the film's diegesis, he presents as practiced in being disingenuous (e.g., cheesy sentimentalized messages on Pepa's answering machine) and cowardly (ducking down in a phone booth to avoid Pepa).

While Iván presents as a character who has jetted straight from adolescence into middle-aged adultery, the protagonist Pepa is of intrinsically greater narrative interest as she changes appreciably during the 90-minute runtime. At the outset, she is desperate to talk to Iván who has dumped her—via a message on her answering machine (!), although he does not realize that he has impregnated her. By the close of the film, Pepa discovers her incipient female possibilities. When she finally encounters Iván face to face at Barajas airport, she saves him from his ex-wife Lucía. She is a deranged foil to Pepa's emergent independence who intends to kill Iván out of sexual jealousy. After short-circuiting Lucía's murder attempt with a baggage cart as projectile, Pepa confirms that Iván is a dead-end. Pepa places him in pitiless close-up while he attempts to sneak away via airplane with the new girlfriend and simultaneously serves up tired, disingenuous platitudes. While Pepa does not say a word about the pregnancy to Iván, significantly, she returns to her apartment and tells Marisa that she will be having a baby; clearly, aging playboy Iván will have no part in the life of the child. Smith (2000) observes that Marisa and Pepa—together in the film's closing freeze frame—have achieved the landmarks of first orgasm and incipient parenthood, respectively, with their men vetted from the scene.

The titular women of *Women on the Verge . . .* are not, however, idealized or sentimentalized—thus avoiding a disconcerting sense of falseness in the film's gender politics. Indeed, Candela fulfills stereotypical specifications as she is moved to emotive speeches by hormones and relationship-driven histrionics—and is clearly annoying to Pepa. Enacting a different trope, Paulina Morales is initially identified by Pepa as an "*abogada feminista*"—feminist lawyer—and thus suited to help Candela with her problems. However, when Pepa talks face-to-face with Paulina, the lawyer is catty and aggressive. Unbeknownst to Pepa at this time, the uptight Paulina is Iván's new paramour. Thus, Paulina acts out insecurity and aggression cross-hatched with her elevated professional class standing that alienates her from other women even

as she may mouth "feminism." The title *Women on the Verge* . . .
also channels a chimerical position. The "women" of the title are
indeed privileged as dramatic personae. And while some of the
film's content is stereotypical—with regard to the "nervous break-
downs"—Pepa hurtles out of this orbit and looks poised to land on
her feet. The role is a significant part of what makes Carmen
Maura an enduring feminist icon in Spain.

Ties that Bind

By contrast with *Women on the Verge* . . . , *Tie Me Up!* . . . stands
out as a film that defies Almodóvar's image as a "woman's director." I will dwell on it in part to strive toward a more comprehensive portrait of the director's corpus that is attentive to its
contradictory elements and alive to the female-friendly film crite-
ria discussed earlier.

Two contrasting men are situated at the heart of *Tie Me Up!* . .
. . The first is the aging director Max Espejo who directs Marina in
a horror film. The second is 23-year-old Ricky who kidnaps Marina. Both engage in male obsessiveness and quests for control
that characterize a raft of Almodóvarian men (as noted above). In
the case of the 60-something Max (played by screen legend Fran-
cisco Rabal), these characteristics are leavened with humor that
qualifies what would be creepy behavior from a more virile man. In
one sequence, Max calls Marina to make an appeal for love. On her
answering machine, he summons the pastoral trope of the aging
bullfighter who is carried by his fans from the bullring to the balcony of his home to make a farewell address to the throng gathered
below. Following this poignant play to Latin sentimentality, delivered with a touch of class, Max engages with a more recent and
tawdry "tradition" that speaks to his desires. On VCR, he watches
Marina being penetrated from behind in a scene from her previous
career in porn. For her part, Marina coolly thwarts the wheel-chair
bound director's advances and denies him a glance up her skirt,
pointedly shielding her *culo* from his gaze by clapping a pillow
against it.

While Max presents the aged male lecher in retreat, practiced
in summoning a veneer of class (even if it often slips), Ricky is a
clearly menacing figure. The opening sequence of Ricky's departure from the institution gives clues to his psychohistory of being
(ab)used sexually by a cloister of nuns. Thereafter, he breaks into

Marina's dressing room and pockets, among other items, a pair of handcuffs (foreshadowing). The next spatial transgression occurs at the door to Marina's house when he answers her resistance to his entry with a vicious head-butt and punch; acts that go far beyond boorish chauvinistic conduct that tacitly understands its limits (as is the case with Max). When Marina gains consciousness, Ricky "explains" that she did not previously pay attention to him; thus, he "had to" ("*tenía que*") kidnap her. His stated quest is to demonstrate that, in the future he intends to impose on her, he will be a good husband to her and father to their children. He emphasizes that he is 23 and has no one and nothing in the world but the paltry sum of 50,000 pesetas (i.e., a few hundred USDs). Via these forceful means, Ricky announces his project to impose normalcy to the conventional template of the intact nuclear family. While he evidences anomie and ostensibly "touching" awkwardness as to "how" to conduct himself as captor, the fact remains that it is an enactment of false imprisonment with sexual motives.

Marina initially resists this bid to possess her. However, over the course of about two days, she is turned around. By the final reel, Marina actively and amorously seeks out her former captor. The shift occurs across a series of vignettes. Early in her captivity, Marina denounces Ricky from her position on the toilet, eventually calling him a clown. Nonetheless, Ricky's project of "breaking" Marina's resistance begins to gain traction. To secure painkillers for her toothache, they prepare themselves before the bathroom mirror (to Ricky's stated pleasure, in behaving as a couple grooming in parallel) and walk hand-cuffed to the residence of Marina's doctor. The doctor immediately sees them as a couple, endowing Ricky's desires with external social confirmation. In short order, the doctor fails to comprehend the meaning of Marina's whispers about being kidnapped. The visual spectacle of coupledom renders the (truthful) content of Marina's whispers as incomprehensible—even to another woman. Ricky also retrieves and parades the doctor's children in the salon, thereby furnishing a literalization of his stated desire to be a father for Marina's gaze.

Marina has been sequestered and isolated from her work and family, bonds with the outside world that the monadic Ricky does not have. Nevertheless, Marina quickly becomes accustomed to being isolated and moves her behavior more and more into alignment with a script composed by the forceful male's expectations and fantasy. In short order, she expresses no modesty toward her captor about being seen disrobing. When Ricky's attempt to secure pain-killers for Marina in nocturnal Madrid prompts a thrashing from a drug dealer whom he had cheated earlier, Marina construes *him* as victim and tends his wounds with tenderness that quickly erupts into a passionate sexual encounter. Complications arise, however, as there is the "danger" that Marina's concerned sister Lola will discover the pair. As Lola closes in, Ricky is enraged and accuses Marina—the woman whom he is kidnapping—of having tricked and wronged him. He quickly calls upon a misogynist trope to garnish the anger, denigrating her as a whore. Marina not only resists calling out to her sister who is within shouting distance but addresses Ricky in the imperative:, "Tie me up!", she pleads (*"¡Atame!"*), during the effort to evade her sister. She becomes, in other words, an accomplice in her own kidnapping.

Despite the precautions, Lola discovers her bound sister after Ricky has fled in a hail of *machista* insults. In a scene that follows, alone with her sister, Marina recounts *his* story to Lola with palpable breathlessness—23 years old, 50,000 pesetas, alone—and tenderly handles artifacts that remind her of him. The sisters subsequently drive from Madrid to the periphery of Spain, Extremadura, in search of Ricky. After finding him among the ruins of the parental home, Marina reunites with him. Upon learning that Ricky has handyman skills and can sing during an extended take on the trio in the car, the previously protective Lola affirms that Ricky can be absorbed into the family as Marina's love interest. Both women thus acquiesce to Ricky's traditionalist assertions of what their relations should be.

According to Jordan and Morgan-Tamosunas (1998), Almodóvar has defended the seemingly retrograde gender politics of the film on the grounds that Marina has exercised a choice. One may grant that few people are able to formulate important decisions without external pressures of one sort or another. Nonetheless, Ricky's kidnapping of Marina goes beyond the pale in constraining choice; even if—or especially *because*—the captive "learns to love" the captor. *Tie Me Up . . .* furnishes evidence against an unqualified equation between Almodóvar and "the woman's film" given its robust reproduction of the trope of submissive female masochism eagerly embraced. Moreover, the closing sequence—a privileged narrative moment of most any film—is not imposed as a narrative deus ex machina. The pairing of Ricky and

Marina is endemic within the story arc that traces her shift from rebellion against, to participation in, extending her own captivity. Moreover, this narrative appears long after critiques of rampant masculinism animated Spanish society.

Shock ("Chic") of the New: Men on the Verge

Jordan and Morgan-Tamosunas (1998) posit the formation of "New Spanish Woman" and "New Spanish Man," on-screen and off-, following the Franco era. Carmen Maura has emblematized "New Spanish Womanhood" by playing parts that were in various measures educated, liberal, middle-class, single and/or separated, sexually active, and generally assertive. In line with these characteristics, the New Spanish Woman is conjured within an acting style that is more nonchalant and less beholden to overblown melodramatics. And New Spanish Man? In contrast with "garlic-chewing, ball-scratching, muscle-flexing" *machista* who once ran roughshod over the Iberian domestic space (Jordan and Morgan-Tamosunas 1998: 142), New Spanish Man participates in the new gender deal that pivots on enhanced egalitarianism. Although these new figures have palpably emerged following the Franco era, they do not present a monolithic tendency—either onscreen or more broadly in social life where recalcitrant tendencies still gain nourishment.

An entry from the latter half of Almodóvar's corpus, *Live Flesh* presents an illuminating site in examining the director's depiction of men and their relations (with each other and with women). That is, in *Live Flesh*, the New Spanish Man and Woman arrive with noteworthy tensions. Male pride, and the paradoxical vulnerability that underwrites it, is a central feature of the film. Victor embarks on his quest for Elena in large measure due to her insult about his sexual performance during their first haphazard encounter (offscreen). Years later, Elena's husband David has his ego deflated when she reports that Victor appeared at her father's funeral. Although David and the marginalized Victor apparently had only met once, five years earlier, the appearance at the funeral is sufficient for paroxysms of anger and suspicion on David's part. In turn, he enacts surveillance on Victor's ramshackle home with a camera.

Despite the easily injured ego and suspiciousness, David fits the New Man template. He is willing to tell the truth to his wife about even awkward matters and she does the same for him. Victor is a more ambiguous entry into New Manhood. Talented and caring as a social worker with troubled children, Victor knowingly instrumentalizes Clara as his sex instructor. Moreover, the sex lessons are enacted in pursuit of his stated quest with its egoistic, woman-unfriendly currents (if unconventionally so). In particular, his stated quest is to make vigorous love to Elena—and then leave her begging for more that he will, in turn, deny her.

Masculinist conflict plays out as a rapid series of pirouettes between affiliation and aggression. David invades Victor's home and punches him—significantly—in the genitalia. The pair's immediate joint response is to turn to the television and cheer a *fútbol* goal being scored, in a parodic version of male bonding over sport. Subtle threats follow immediately thereafter, verbally from David and silently in Victor's case as he demonstrates his physical vigor by executing a series of "seal-claps." Thus, the encounter features manly stare-downs—but with a measure of New Man tempering of aggression, garnished with an undercurrent of mutual respect.

In the final sequence of *Live Flesh*, Victor has supplanted David as Elena's love interest. However, David treads the enlightened New Man route and takes his defeat with grace. He visits friends in Miami and, via a letter in VO, states that he now realizes that Elena never laughed around him. It is an acknowledgment that Elena's commitment to David pivoted more on duty (and a sense of guilt for being an indirect cause of his being injured) than on ripe, spontaneous love. David, the New Man, answers his colossal setback with reflection rather than on insisting on his privileges as a husband and member of the male gender.

While the rough-around-the-edges Victor is far less the New Man, drunken cop Sancho is an unreconstructed holdover from the epoch when *machista* ran rampant. When Clara voices her wish for a divorce, Sancho physically attacks her in response. Self-pity is evident as he insists that the physical blow that he authored hurts *himself* more than her; and, similarly, in stating that he has always been subservient and crawling toward Clara—after he fatally shot her.

As compared with *Live Flesh*, *Bad Education*'s masculine ensemble presents less in the way of contrast between "old" and "new" gendered tendencies. The men who populate the film range from damaged (Ignacio) to despicable and predatory (Manolo Berenguer, Juan) to compromised (Enrique). Ignacio trades on his troubled past of abuse visited upon him by the pederast priest to formulate a blackmail scheme. A jaded heroin addict by the time of the blackmail attempt, the desperate Ignacio steals his elderly aunt's pension to subsidize the habit. Following his pedophile activity in the Catholic boarding school in Extremadura, Father Manolo Berenguer exchanges his catechism and collar for the quasi-"cool" middle-class respectability of being a book editor, married with children. He is thunderstruck with attraction upon seeing Juan doing pushups in his underwear and contrives to furnish him with material (e.g., tuition for acting classes) in a quid pro quo for sex. Juan's super-8mm films of Berenguer in the throes of sexually driven torment manifest the middle-aged man's unattractiveness and raw desperation; the shots underscore that bare-knuckled opportunist Juan is not on board for love of a man old enough to be his father. Together, in turn, they plot to murder Igancio.

Juan's amorality may meet and exceed Berenguer's more seasoned version, as he later impersonates the brother whom he killed in an elaborate ruse driven by ruthless professional advancement. Juan's campaign for himself is furthered by acting as Enrique's boyfriend, although shots of them having sex manifest Juan's discomfort. Enrique is plainly the most sympathetic character in this menagerie—although he too is compromised by the vortex of events. According to the closing title card, Enrique successfully pursues his directing career into the future. Nonetheless, Enrique is complicit in Ignacio's murder after the fact via the guilty knowledge about it that Berenguer brings. None of these male protagonists—damaged, criminal or compromised—is cut from New Man cloth. The implications of such verisimilitude do not placate all commentators. Citing *Bad Education*'s array of male characters, Matthews (2006) argues that it all comes back to what he construes as Almodóvar's idealization of women; it makes for trite cinema, in Matthews' polemical appraisal, in comparison with the director's more gripping and unvarnished treatment of men.

CHAPTER 6
Three Films in Close-Up

Almodóvar's career trajectory presents noticeable slack in the middle. Following the early successes with bawdy cinematic libertarianism, the 1990s opened for Almodóvar with critically and artistically awkward feints between the filmmaker that was and the filmmaker to be. *High Heels* (1991) and *Kika* (1993) are arguably the least noted entries in Almodóvar's corpus. The director appeared to be careening toward the status of a spent force, overstaying his welcome, before the more assured *Flower of My Secret* (1995) and *Live Flesh* (1997) heralded artistic renaissance. The final chapter of this section analyzes three more recent films that have been released since Almodóvar turned 50 years old. The films were integral to (re)establishing Almodóvar as a filmmaker reaching the top of his game (as, e.g., Luis Buñuel and Alfred Hitchcock are often posited to have also done after age 50). I elaborate lines of analysis that have been pursued earlier while staying attentive to the particular accents in the full artistic hand that these three films play. In particular, I will analyze *All About My Mother*, *Talk to Her*, and *Volver*, addressing them in the chronological order of release.

All About My Mother

Released in 1999, the film inaugurates the later period of Almodóvar's career after an often awkward decade following 1988's *Women on the Verge* . . . The film has been characterized as the most heavily awarded film in history (D'Lugo 2006: 105), an honor that is partly driven by the hothouse proliferation of international film festivals, but that is typical of Spain as a nation that has long "punched above its weight" in international artistic circles.

The film features many previously discussed Almodóvarian tendencies. An emphasis on outsiders is evident as the *protagoni-*

sta, Mañuela, is not Spanish but Argentine. Other principal characters include a transsexual prostitute (Agrado), an unsympathetic junky (Nina), a lesbian actress with a fondness for drink (Huma Roja), an HIV-positive nun (Sister Rosa), and a transsexual with a talent for impregnating (Estéban/Lola). The previously noted doubling and tripling of characters is also in play. Besides the transsexuals' "double lives," the film also features three Estébans: Estéban/Lola is followed by two sons named Estéban by Mañuela and Sister Rosa.

Other elements of *All About My Mother* are in register with thematic motifs examined earlier; in particular, gender and the family. *All About My Mother* is readily characterized as a woman-oriented film since the ensemble of central characters is overwhelmingly female (i.e., Mañuela, Agrado, Huma Roja, Nina, Rosa, and Rosa's mother). The male characters are, by contrast, limited to Estéban, Estéban/Lola, and Rosa's father. Mañuela's son Estéban is accidentally killed by a taxi about ten minutes into the runtime of the film. While only on screen briefly, Esteban's death occasions the bereaved Mañuela's trip to A Coruña and later, for most of the film, to Barcelona. In turn, shifting settings present Almodóvar's recent penchant for setting extended sequences outside the geographical/political center of Spain in Madrid (notably, *Bad Education* with sequences in Galicia, Extremadura, and Valencia).

Beyond Manuela's son Estéban, the other two men of narrative interest are similarly little evident on screen. Transsexual Estéban/Lola is a genetic male who is characterized by Mañuela as a farrago of the worst in stereotypical male *machista* and female connivance—and the character is discoursed upon for much of the film. Despite prominence in the dialogue, Estéban/Lola only appears in two short scenes at the end of the film before perishing off-screen due to AIDS. The brevity on screen is belied by narrative impact as the impregnator of both Mañuela and, almost 20 years later, Sister Rosa. However important as progenitor, Estéban/Lola's presence in the children's lives is nonetheless nil. Similarly, Rosa's father, ostensibly the patriarch of a bourgeoisie family, is a zombified shell of a man. An Alzheimer's case who has largely been jettisoned to the care of the family dog by his chilly wife, he does not recognize his daughter the last time that he sees her. In other words, while the men have a vast impact on events in the narrative, it is simultaneously blunted by death or debilitating illness in each case.

While the women characters are front and center, they are not fitted for halos of idealization. Mañuela, as a single mom and subsequently as bereaved parent, is a nexus of considerable audience sympathy. In her own gender critique during an angry outburst, Mañuela posits women as "assholes" for what she appraises to be a self-defeating female tendency to collaborate in setting traps with the unworthy men who careen through their lives. In addition to the sympathy that the character of Mañuela is designed to prompt, the audience has privileged knowledge of all of her actions. The audience can, therefore, see the manipulative and partly self-interested agenda that she pursues, more so than the characters with whom she co-exists in the film. In particular, Mañuela insinuates herself into Huma Roja's life and thus realizes the charged experience of replaying her past by once again acting in *A Streetcar Named Desire*. In turn, Sister Rosa seeks Mañuela out and casts the older woman as a surrogate for, and a bridge to, her own uptight and judgmental mother.

Along with the conflicted relations among the flawed women, the bad woman straight from central casting circulates among them. Nina is drug-addicted, histrionic, self-centered, jealous, suspicious—and never softens up. Her relationship with Huma is as dysfunctional and disorderly as a male-female mis-pairing (including physical battering, off-screen). Nina is jettisoned by Almodóvar's closing sequence while the fulfilled ensemble of women gather in Huma's dressing room. Nina's belligerent pursuit of her own interests does not finally perturb the others (in contrast with, e.g., a classic femme fatale who sets off narrative shock waves that cascade through the film's closing).

Where the family is concerned, *All About My Mother* visions it as a tense, even vicious battleground within the ostensibly tightly knit environs of Southern European culture. Mañuela is a single working mother who has raised a seemingly well-rounded young man with artistic inclinations. When the attractive Mañuela bounds onto teenage Esteban's bed in order to gift a Truman Capote book to him, the scene is underwritten with a dreamy Oedipal tension given the absence of the father (as noted, a frequent absence in Almodóvar's world). However, via posthumous VOs from his diary, the audience learns that Estéban harbored deep resentments toward his mother for keeping secrets from him. Principal among the secrets was that, across his 18-year life, Estéban never met nor knew who his father was. In another of *All About My Mother*'s families, Sister Rosa characterizes the dog as her best familial relationship, ahead of her judgmental mother and husk of a father.

Surrogate families encounter greater success. Scandalized by the circumstances of Estéban's birth to Rosa and Estéban/Lola, Rosa's mother gives the nod for Mañuela to adopt her daughter's baby (in addendum to Mañuela having informally adopted Rosa when she was ill). The final scene of the film stitches the relationships up to the happiest of specifications as each of the characters gets what she aspires to and/or "deserves": The sympathetic older women Huma and Agrado have paired up, Mañuela is a fulfilled adoptive mother to an AIDS-free miracle baby, while the nasty Nina has returned to the pueblo to have a baby derided as "ugly" (and apparently cashiered her lesbianism in a script for further unhappiness). Although the final scene comes perilously close to courting sentimentality, the unfolding of the film's paradigm generally resists such.

Talk to Her

In gendered terms, *Talk to Her* may seem at first blush to address two male-female relationships. Parallels between the two male-female pairings are also evident as the woman of each dyad is in a coma for most of the runtime. However, the relationship between the men is central by the end of the film. Indeed, Lydia is only on screen as a conscious and functional character in the flashbacks that largely constitute (or complicate) the film's jig-sawed narrative structure, before she perishes in a coma. Thus, Lydia may be taken as a variation on the Almodóvarian narrative device of the spectral presence.

The Marco-Lydia pairing is about ten years senior to Benigno and Alicia. A starker contrast is, however, that while Marco and Lydia are middle-aged boyfriend and girlfriend to generally conventional (if tense) specifications, Benigno's love affair with Alicia plays out largely in his own mind. They had met but twice, briefly and non-romantically, before the advent of her coma. Benigno and Marco initially appear to present striking contrasts despite the similarity of their involvement with women in comas. However, some parallels between them speak to common themes in their situation as male subjects.

The character of Benigno is rendered to fetishistic, obsessive, and masochistic specifications (Goss 2008). Along with the male obsessiveness that is frequently observed in the Almodóvar corpus, Benigno can also claim ancestry in a long line of Almodóvarian characters without fathers. Moreover, his mother is an invalid whose voice is heard summoning him one time from off-screen. Shortly thereafter, she passes away (also off-screen).

Prior to the accident that puts Alicia in a coma, Benigno invades her room at home and steals a hairclip. It is a fetishistic gesture proximal to control that grasps hold of a "trophy" that stands in for the (unattainable) whole woman. Following Alicia's descent into the coma, Benigno's fetishism is directed toward her drastically truncated existence. Masochism is also in play since Benigno has positioned Alicia as lodestar and center of his universe. In Gaylyn Studlar's conceptualization, the masochist continuously replays the primordial drama in which the pre-Oedipal mother stars:

> The female reflects the fantasy of the desiring infant who regards the mother as both sacred and profane, loving and rejecting, frustratingly mobile yet the essence of rhythmic stability and stillness. In the masochist's suspension of the final 'gratification' of death, the obsessive return to the separation from the oral mother must be reenacted continuously . . . . . Masochistic repetition sustains the paradoxical pain/pleasure structure of the perversion's psychodynamics . . . (2000: 210)

On this view, the masochistic male retains the idealized concept of the omnipotent mother. Moreover, he returns, over and over, to this maternal image of "first source of love and object desire, first environment and agent of control"; indeed, "the oral mother of masochism assumes all symbolic functions" as Alicia does for Benigno (Studlar 2000: 210). Alicia even furnishes Benigno's spectorial tastes in dance and silent film. She is, however, beyond reach due to her medical condition. Hence, Alicia furnishes the essence of stability for the fixated masochist Benigno. In turn, across his years of devotion to her, he inserts her into his matrix of ambivalent desire that orients toward the unattainable, mysterious and ineffable.

The film that Benigno sees at Madrid's filmoteca, *Amante Menguante* (*Shrinking Lover*), awakens the suppressed conflicts in this man-child. The black-and-white, silent (title-carded) film-within-a-film climaxes when Alfredo shrinks to the size of a finger and enters Amparo's vagina—never to emerge again. Benigno's rape of Alicia occurs off-screen during his account of the (to him) shattering narrative of *Shrinking Lover* that is cut into *Talk to Her*. In theoretical terms, the masochist's move from fetishism and ever-thwarted desire—the infinite loop of pleasing/painful reenactments of the "moment of separation" from the omnipotent pre-Oedipal mother—to the realization of desire may occasion disaster (Studlar 2000: 210). So it is with Benigno. His step from continual deferral and suspension of gratification into attainment of his desire via rape of an unconscious, non-consenting woman occasions his incarceration and subsequent suicide.

Benigno's constant fussing and devotion to Alicia may well have saved her as she teetered liminally between life and death. Moreover, one may take the sex act as having metaphorically awakened "sleeping beauty," an inference that the sequence of causal narrative events invites. At the same time, the much-discussed fluidity of identity in Almodóvar's world complicates spectator response in this case. To wit, rape may readily be construed as a violent assertion of traditionalist androgenic social power in an act of terror (i.e., it is perpetrated against one woman, but signals violent threat toward the whole group). In this instance, however, the perpetrator Benigno is a highly feminized male. A nurse by vocation, he embodies devotion to the work of caring in his professional conduct. Almodóvar's name for his creation, translated into English, is "benign." Although he can hardly fathom "adult love," Benigno exhibits vast sensitivity when he is able to sense distance in Marco's relationship to Lydia—even as she is unconscious. Finally, Almodóvar's discreteness in not showing Benigno's crime invites the audience to, in this case, reevaluate the passion that underwrites what is otherwise indefensible penetration for having been enacted without consent. Whereas in the first scene of his first film, Almodóvar bluntly stages a rape in the center of the frame for laughs (albeit very awkwardly), the questions that *Talk to Her* begs are far more troubling. Even if one quite appropriately condemns Benigno's violation of Alicia, one can acknowledge that the film expresses a discomforting thesis about the proximity of ostensibly uplifting passionate love to the desire to enact unilateral control.

While Marco is clearly a more worldly man than Benigno—he writes travel books—he too has a girlfriend in a coma. Beyond this shared happenstance, Marco is also sad, lonely, and painfully cognizant of his circumstances to a far greater extent than Benigno. The parallels are expressed in the two men's first appearance in the film. It is a two-shot of them during which Marco cries as audience to the performance of *Café Müller*. Each attends alone, in coincidently adjacent seats. Moreover, the film drops heavy hints that, like Benigno, Marco is in love with Alicia. After Marco is informed, retroactively, by Niño de Valencia that Lydia had already dumped him before her coma, he "cruises" the hospital to Alicia's room for a new possibility in the hospital's love circuit. Marco also bequeaths the travel books that he authored to Benigno to enable the "talk to her" doctrine via reading to Alicia. Later, Marco's visceral anger at Benigno's stated desire to wed the coma-stricken Alicia is informed by the unquestioned proposition that an unconscious person cannot enter such a contract—but with further shadings of sexual jealousy in the subtext of Marco's outburst.

In the final sequence of the film, Marco goes further in "becoming" a doppelgänger to Benigno. Marco moves into Benigno's former apartment, stands at the window as Benigno had done to gaze upon Alicia across the street in the dance studio—and Alicia is phantasmically present, having regained consciousness. The final scene at the dance performance is laden with further clues to an incipient pairing between Marco and Alicia. Romantic lighting bathes them both as Marco glances back at her, two rows behind, to her obvious delight. A title card announces "Marco y Alicia," and the scene cuts to romantic, dance-mediated pairings that are moving rhythmically into the privacy of backstage.

The two men are not so different even if Marco negotiates the obstacles of his own complexes and the world he inhabits with more skill than the fixated and masochistic Benigno. As for the women in the film, being encased in comas is no posture of empowerment and has its creepy moments; namely, shots of unmoving, passive female bodies acted upon by hospital staff. In a similar register that is unfavorable to the female characters, Almodóvar mints a grimly funny implication when Lydia in effect "breaks up" with Marco long after she has descended into a coma. The sequence raises the androgenic trope of the woman's deep-seated treachery that is not interrupted by "merely" descending into unconsciousness. In a narrative event that evokes a similarly traditionalist trope, Lydia's coma is caused in the first place by her masochistic decision to stand in the path of the charging bull.

Volver

Volver's heart is in the pueblo of rural Castile y La Mancha, the zone in which Almodóvar was born and originally lived. It is the pueblo to which the characters appear poised to return in the closing sequence (hence, one reason for the film's title since "volver" is "to return" in Spanish). Due to the fact the men of the village tend to die before the women do (much like Spain itself), the graying, elderly pueblo appears in some shots to be entirely populated by women. Hence, along with its significations as bluff, heartland Spain (*la España profunda*), the pueblo is revisioned as a matriarchy. Moreover, although elderly and frail Aunt Paula passes away early in the narrative, a wave of much younger women appears ready to settle into the pueblo by the end of the film. Raimunda and her teen daughter Paula's commitment to renew their roots augurs rural-accented rejuvenation—albeit, of a sort not much observed outside the frame of the film as Spain has become an increasingly urban society over the decades.

Beyond the gyno-empowering mise-en-scene, men in the world of *Volver* are the origin of most of the problems between the women, even though men are spectral presences or seen only fleetingly. Indeed, the only male character of note is Raimunda's dead-end husband Paco, who appears in a brief sequence early in the film. The intoxicated Paco absorbs a *fútbol* match from the couch and petitions Raimunda to serve him (yet another) beer in the first shot in which he appears. In short order, Paco reports that he has lost his job. En route to the bedroom at the end of the boozy night, he peeks through the crack in the hallway door at early adolescent Paula while she disrobes, voyeurism of which she is agonizingly aware. After arriving in bed, Paco's bid for sex is turned down by an exhausted Raimunda. The spurned patriarch rolls over and begins masturbating furiously while the mortified Raimunda gazes off-screen. Paco apotheosizes the useless, creepy male in the brief sequence. However, Paco's most egregious actions occur off-screen when, while again drunk, he attempts to molest his daughter. In response, Paula fatally knifes him. With the man removed from the scene, Raimunda opportunistically and successfully rewires the material base of her life; in Althusserian fashion, she sponta-neously seizes the chance to self-employ as a restaurateur, annul-ling her previous subjectivity and its double duty as housewife and dead-end manual laborer at Barajas airport. Self-employment brings empowerment and an enhanced quality of life.

As noted, men are the origin of many of the long-standing toxic deposits of secrecy and misunderstanding between *Volver*'s ensem-ble of women; secrecy extends up to Sole concealing the charged fact that their mother Irene is alive from her sister Raimunda for most of the drama. However, *Volver*'s most embedded secret con-cerns Irene's husband/Raimunda's father. As is often the case in Almodóvar's corpus, a character who registers a tremendous im-pact on the others is dead or off-screen for all (or almost all) of the film. In *Volver*, this spectral character is once again the patriarch who passed away several years earlier but whose actions continue to reverberate. Irene's daughters Sole and Raimunda experience surprise in learning that her relationship to her husband was tense and troubled due to his constant philandering. They later learn another secret: Irene set fire to the hut in which her husband carried on an affair with Agustina's mother, killing them both. Thereafter, Irene laid low in the pueblo, pretending to be dead, never venturing out the door of Aunt Paula's house while the eld-erly woman to whom she ministered was alive.

Another seismic revelation concerning the father: He raped Raimunda. Although Paula only learns for certain after Paco's death that he was not her biological father, the teen is not told the full story of her origins. The father's crimes of rape and incest in turn spun off into Raimunda's resentment of Irene for what she took to be her mother's obliviousness to the patriarch's crimes and for not protecting her from his predations. Reconciliation among the women is achieved, little by little, as wrenching secrets of past abuses are addressed and the shame of complicity in silence is in-terrupted. In the film's closing scene the formerly estranged mother and daughter exchange their vows: The mother's "I'll see you every day. Between us, we'll manage" is answered with the daughter's "I need you, Mom. I don't know how I lived all these years without you."

Concerning the "why" behind the secrecy, Agustina presents an interesting figure in *Volver*—as well as darkness at the margins of the seemingly sentimentalized ending. On one hand, Agustina insists throughout the film on knowing the truth about the fate of her disappeared mother. On the other hand, she is tactful toward others' vulnerabilities in a manner that tempers her pursuit of the truth. Agustina has connected the dots and is all but certain that Irene is alive and that it was her own "disappeared" mother who died in the fire. However, even when bribed on a tabloid television program with a junket to Houston for cancer therapy, Agustina subordinates her quest for truth to the sensibilities of the other people affected in the series of tragedies (Raimunda, Sole, and Irene whom she presumes to be alive). Irene returns the debt for maintaining the secrecy over her passion-driven crimes by volunteering to be the cancer-stricken Agustina's caretaker. Thus, a mutually agreed form of justice is administered without the intervention of the RSAs.

Marvin D'Lugo (2006) interprets *Volver*'s immediate predecessor, *Bad Education*, as an assertive gesture against complacency and reminder to Spaniards of the living memory proximity of the Franco regime. In register with this interpretation, *Bad Education* betrays Enrique's complicitous silence, after-the-fact, in Juan and Manolo Berenguer's collaboration to murder Ignacio. Despite *Volver*'s glow of matriarchal breakthrough and moments of comedy, a similar brooding darkness circulates within it. Specifically, a central theme of *Volver* is silence about the crimes of the patriarch that have damaged the delicate geometry of the characters' relationships in the decades that follow.

The blocked channels of communication in the film may be understood as parallel to Spain's "Pact of Silence" that followed Franco's death. General amnesty, and not Truth Commission investigation, was implemented on the theory that Spain could move forward without further acrimony. On one hand, the strategy has proved almost flawless in practice as, in the course of a generation, Spain is now firmly lodged at the center of Europe's project as a progressive, dynamic, and confident nation. Spain is cited as a model for "how to emerge from darkness into democracy" as there has been "no other contemporary example where the success had been so complete" (Elms 1992: 2). However, as journalist and long-time observer of Spain Giles Tremlett comments, "the line separating regime collaborators from opponents runs not between people but through them" (Tremlett 2007b: 24). As successful as public silence has been in shepherding Spain toward its current status, the willful repression of the "Pact of Silence" also prompted conditions for symptoms against forgetting such as *Volver*, thirty years after the dictator expired in his bed. The repression has also prompted more formal, albeit belated, gestures. Given that it was defeated in the Civil War's Rightist rising, the political Left gave up more in the post-Franco arrangement to cashier claims to truth settling. Hence, to better settle the accounts, grass roots groups in the new millennium are devoted to exhuming Civil War era graves in order to recognize victims of the conflagration (Tremlett 2007c). In 2007, the year following *Volver*'s release, the ruling Socialist government (headed by the grandson of a victim of the Rightist rising) controversially introduced the "Law of Historical Memory" to answer back at the silence.

SECTION III
LARS VON TRIER

CHAPTER 7

"Agent Provoc-Auteur"

According to Astrid Söderbergh-Widding (1998), the "Golden Age" of Danish cinema was both brief and long ago. She periodizes it as roughly 1910–1915; hence, the importance of Lars von Trier, both within Denmark and internationally. Von Trier has registered the most significant impact of any recent Danish director and only Carl Theodor Dreyer (1889–1968) compares in stature during Denmark's screen history. The recent *The Danish Directors: Dialogues on a Contemporary National Cinema* (Hjort and Bondebjerg 2001), features only one director on its cover despite the volume's more inclusive title. It is von Trier, in full shot, posed beside a globe, a flesh and blood emblem of Denmark's recent film ascendance. According to the Internet Movie DataBase, von Trier's sum of awards is a cool, rounded 100 as of June 2008 (57 wins, 43 further nominations)(Internet Move DataBase 2008a).

Von Trier's impact is somewhat chimerical in having been a vocal critic of his European film elders whom he construes as living off reputations forged decades earlier and having clotted the screens for too long. He singles out fellow Nord Ingmar Bergman (Tapper 2003). At the same time, von Trier (born 1956) has been a highly enabling figure for his peers via substantial collaborations with other Danish filmmakers. In this vein, von Trier co-authored the Dogme95 manifesto with a junior Danish cineaste, Thomas Vinterberg (born 1969). Von Trier also collaborated with the script for the Vinterberg-directed *Dear Wendy* (2005). At the other end of the age continuum, von Trier has paid homage to experimental documentarian Jørgen Leth (born 1937), who represents an earlier generation of Danish filmmakers. Von Trier's collaborative film with Leth, *The Five Obstructions* (2003), is part Dogme95-type stylistic experiment and partly a document of their friendship. Von Trier has also been a leading international figure for championing enhanced access for aspiring filmmakers via new technology. Digital video in particular circumvents a filmmaker's need for costly film stock. In a techno-determinist mode, von Trier has speculated that film may become an as yet unrecognizable hybrid of film and video in the future (Smith 2003).

In characterizing von Trier's impact, Caroline Bainbridge (2007) posits him as an "avuncular" figure. In Bainbridge's appraisal,

> His reputation as an evolving *auteur* whose impact on twenty-first-century cinema is to be measured not only in terms of his cinematic output but also in terms of his influence on the new formations unfolding across the industry. Increasingly von Trier characterizes his work with reference to his collaborative ventures in filmmaking, some of which are at the level of production rather than direction. (2007: 101)

With approval, Bainbridge anoints von Trier as an *"agent provoc-auteur"* (Bainbridge 2007: 22, original emphasis).

Other appellations have been applied to von Trier and all have not been so kindly or aggrandizing. The director has been called "confrontational," "self-promoting," "arrogant," "testy," and "misogynist" and has been characterized as "a manipulator" and even the "anti-Christ" (Lumholdt 2003: ix). Von Trier has himself been a name-caller on occasion as he characterized Roman Polanski as "a midget" when the jury that he chaired at the Cannes Film Festival did not recognize von Trier's *Europa* with the *Palme d'Or* in 1991 (Lumholdt 2003: ix). No stranger to the outrageous statement, in the course of one interview, von Trier described himself as an "American woman" and his mother as "The slut!" (Nicodemus 2005: 5). In the register of idiosyncrasy with more serious overtones, von Trier is a noted phobic whose long roster of fears includes trains, airplanes, hospitals, crowds, and restaurants. Given these fears, von Trier seldom leaves the Nordic world and has even missed the Cannes festival due to his phobias (Lumholdt 2003). In May 2007, von Trier announced that he would not direct further films due to intensifying depression (Burke 2007). It remains to be seen whether retirement will endure or whether he will devote himself completely to non-directorial film activities.

Von Trier grew up outside Copenhagen in a wealthy and cultured family that scorned religion and middle-brow sentimentality. He was a Danish television performer by the age of 11 (Hoffmann

Table 7.1
Von Trier's Feature Films

Direktøren for det hele (2006) (*The Boss of It All*)
Manderlay (2005)
Dogville (2003)
De Fem benspænd (2003) (*The Five Obstructions*)
(segment "The Perfect Human: Avedøre, Denmark")
Dancer in the Dark (2000)
Idioterne (1998) (The Idiots)
Breaking the Waves (1996)
Europa (1991)
Epidemic (1987)
Forbrydelsens element (1984) (*The Element of Crime*)

2003) and used his earnings from television to precociously make super-8mm films as a teen during the 1970s. In 1979, he enrolled in the National Film School of Denmark. Von Trier's graduation film, *Images of Relief/Befrielsesbilleder* in 1982, was highly provocative as it stressed Danish collaboration with the Nazis 40 years earlier. Von Trier defended himself against the resultant criticism by observing that his mother, a communist, was active in the resistance to Nazi occupation of Denmark. Von Trier also posits that the Right-wing hysteria of the 1930s is integral to understanding the Europe of previous generations—as well as its present (Tapper 2003). Von Trier's relationship with the Holocaust and the Other is highly charged for having grown up believing himself to be Jewish in post-Holocaust Northern Europe. However, on her deathbed in 1989, his mother informed the 33-year-old von Trier that he in fact was not Jewish—and that his biological father was someone whom he had never met and *not* the man who had brought him up (Koplev 2003).

Where influences on his filmmaking are concerned, von Trier often cites Carl Theodor Dreyer. His regard for his Danish forebear is such that von Trier employed Dreyer's cinematographer Henning Bendtsen on *The Word/Ordet* (1955) to work on his film *Europa* in 1991. Von Trier also wears a tuxedo that was originally purchased by Dreyer in the 1920s (Af Geijerstam 2003). In addition to the influence of his fellow Dane, Andrei Tarkovsky and Stanley Kubrick have also impacted von Trier. The influence is noticeable in the palpable perfectionism that characterizes von Trier's early work. Alfred Hitchcock is another evident influence for the early shadings of perfectionism as well as in the heavy and expressionist reliance on back projection (most notably in *Europa*).

Von Trier's signature as filmmaker underwent a radical shift from the formalist tradition of a puppeteer-style filmmaker to a looser and more free-wheeling signature from the mid-1990s onward. This is part-and-parcel to a career that has not been a continuous upward arc but has been characterized by starts and stops. Given the uneven response to his films, von Trier has done extended work in television programming as well as commercials (Bainbridge 2007: 63–80; Hammond 2003; Tapper 2003). While *The Element of Crime* was generally well received, von Trier's sophomore effort, *Epidemic*, was a flop. The film attracted a paltry 4,929 viewers in Denmark (Lumholdt 2003: xiii). *Epidemic* also prompted walkouts when exhibited at the Cannes Film Festival. Nevertheless, the film is regarded in retrospect as a key work in anticipating the von Trier who would subsequently pioneer with Dogme95 and proto-Dogme experimentation in *Breaking the Waves*. Moreover, in composing this chapter, I found myself referring back to *Epidemic* for explanatory purposes, far out of proportion to the film's initial impact. Von Trier's third feature was *Europa* and it fared modestly at the box office as well with 31,000 spectators in Denmark (Lumholdt 2003: xiv). However, it garnered more positive critical appraisal as well as a "Technical Grand Prize" in the high-profile international forum of Cannes. *Europa* was the third leg of von Trier's "European Trilogy" (or "E-Trilogy") and also signaled his last attempt at highly formalized filmmaking.

Along with Thomas Vinterberg, von Trier composed the famed Dogme Manifesto in 1995 in "around an hour over some wine" (Roman 200: 138) while humorously minting overblown terminology for their concept (i.e., "Dogme," "Vow of Chastity"). The jokiness presents jarring juxtaposition to the attention and acclaim that has since been devoted to Dogme. The concept was to set down rules for Dogme filmmaking that would compel the filmmaker to take a fresher, "back-to-basics" approach to handling the material. The rules present a tight girdle within which to work. For example, the vow demands, "1. Shooting must be done on location. Props and sets must not be brought in . . ."; and "2. The sound must never be produced apart from the images or vice versa . . ." (von Trier and Vinterberg 1995: 1), hence no non-diegetic music or voice-over (hereafter, VO). Lighting set-ups are also *verboten*. As restrictive as the commandments are, also notice how much is retained in the filmmaker's toolkit: Scripts, rehearsals, and most forms of editing are intact. Despite the tough remit, many filmmakers across the globe have been eager to attempt its regimen and 201 films were registered on the Dogme95 Web page by July 4, 2007 ("DogmeFilms" 2007).

The authors of the manifesto have since shifted away from working within its dictates. Vinterberg made one Dogme certified film (1998's stunning *The Celebration/ Festen*), which was also the inaugural Dogme film. Von Trier's one Dogme effort, *The Idiots*, was also released in 1998 although several von Trier films have been Dogme-esque in parts of the stylistic palette. Spin-offs from Dogme95 can be readily detected in the discussions on camera between von Trier and Jørgen Leth as they hash out new restrictions for the elder director to work under in *The Five Obstructions*. Some of the restrictions imposed in *The Five Obstructions* are quite severe, even by Dogme standards, such as one that dictates that no shot last longer than half a second.

The attention that Dogme has generated testifies to von Trier's prominence as flagship of Danish film in a moment when the diminutive Nordic nation garnered a more sustained close-up from the international film community. Along with Dogme95, von Trier has been innovative in the "ABBA-ization" (!) of film. In particular his English-language films with international casts present not only international collaboration but a nascent "genre": the "English language international film" (Smith 2003).[1]

In an interview with von Trier, Katja Nicodemus leads off with an unconventional question. The query is, "Lars von Trier, who in your opinion has the power in the interview situation, the interviewer or the interviewee?" (Nicodemus 2005: 1). It is a perceptive question for von Trier since power is a central concern in his films; that is, power and its dark shadow, sadism (Freud: " . . . an instinct for mastery which easily passes over into cruelty" [1991: 378]). In turn, von Trier's reply recounts an often rehearsed part of his autobiography. To wit,

> I come from a family of communist nudists. I was allowed to do or not do
> what I liked. My parents were not interested in whether I went to school

or got drunk on white wine. After a childhood like that, you search for restrictions in your own life. (Nicodemus 2005: 1)

Power exercised by one person over another (or others) that
shades, or even explodes, into sadism is central to several films in
von Trier's corpus. The most notable instances are *Europa*, *Breaking the Waves*, *Dogville*, and *Manderlay*.

The issue of power has implicated the method by which the
films are made. This is apparent in von Trier's one Dogme95 effort,
The Idiots, that submitted to the rigors of the Dogme prescription.
The Five Obstructions is clearer still on this question of power; von
Trier prescribes restrictions on Leth that condition the senior
filmmaker's series of remakes of his classic 1967 short film, *The
Perfect Human/Det Perfekte Menneske*. These moments of power
take on a sadistic edge when von Trier instructs (demands) that
Leth create a version of *The Perfect Human* in the location that the
elder friend regards as the worst place on earth. In the resulting
short film, Leth is clad in a tuxedo (like the original *Perfect Human*) and sits down to an elegant meal in the middle of the street
in the red-light district of Bombay (Mumbai), India. Hard-scrabble
people look on from arm's length behind a transparent plastic
sheet; discomfort and sadism all around, including (in attenuated
form) for the spectator who witnesses this "in your face" representation of global class inequality staged for the camera.

The Other is also of the moment in von Trier's corpus. It is, of
course, a long-standing concern in the Occident, part of the efflux
of histories of conquest and domination that echo into present-day
challenges of multiculturalism. For the psychodynamic tradition,
the sorting out of self and other is the basis of psychic life (complicated by vexing Others, real and imagined, within psychic life).
Edward W. Said elaborates in interrogating the terms by which
the Other is summoned into being as the fundamental invention
that consolidates group identity (i.e., in opposition to that Other).
Said directs his challenges to the longstanding habit of constructing an Other toward anthropological accounts (1979), the literary
culture that a colonizing order secretes (1994), and contemporary
news (1997).

Von Trier's corpus is laden with films in which the Other is of
the moment: *The Element of Crime*, *Europa*, *Breaking the Waves*,
The Idiots, *Dancer in the Dark*, *Dogville*, and *Manderlay* all fit the
scheme with abiding interest in the situation of the Other. This

body of films is also characterized by deep pessimism to classically conservative specifications about the relation of Others to a community. As will be seen, this is particularly so in the frequent occasions when the Other is conflated into the von Triersian figure of the idealist outsider.

In the analysis that follows, I will begin by characterizing von Trier's stylistic signature, charting its profound change of course away from stunning formalism that began in the mid-1990s with *Breaking the Waves*. Turning to themes, I discuss von Triersian trances and, in greater detail, the "failed idealist" plotline and argue that it is located at the heart of all of von Trier's features. Indeed, the recurring failed idealist presents an unusual degree of dedication to a thematic motif even for an auteur. Thereafter, chapter 8 enacts a long take on von Trier's presentation of the United States to which he has devoted several films; these films, in turn, elaborate a critical discourse about the media-omnipresent global hegemon. Chapter 8 concludes with extended discussion of *Manderlay*, a film that I appraise as having missed the high standards of its predecessors and as compatible with right-wing cynicism on racial issues.

A Style-ista

Von Trier's early stylistic flourishes are those of a virtuoso. These flourishes include using the camera to pan from one scene into another in elliptically transporting *The Element of Crime*'s Fisher from the edge of the whorehouse to its front yard without an apparent cut or craning between sex and suicide on different floors of the troubled Hartmann family home in *Europa* to, in effect, crosscut without cutting. Style is at times used to comment on filmic conventions as when the camera cranes upward at the end of *Dancer in the Dark*. The mobile framing refers, ironically, to Selma's repeated comment on the cloying happiness of the penultimate song in classic movie musicals; it also symbolically evokes Selma's ascending soul following her execution.

Von Trier often utilizes different film stocks to heighten effects. Two of his films have been shot in black-and-white stock (*Epidemic* and *Europa*, although the latter features a couple of shots in color for effect). The damp and dank world of *The Element of Crime* is filmed in a burnt orange-yellow scheme that suggests fire in contrast with the ubiquitous water (i.e., basic elements in tandem, suggestive of apocalypse). In *Dancer in the Dark*, the escapist musical numbers are shot in crisp, saturated colors, evocative of the Technicolor musical, in contrast with the drearily muddy color scheme of the rust-belt town and penitentiary. Similarly, in one shot following the psychic's entrance into the dinner party in *Epidemic*, a change in film stock from grainy fast to slower stock signifies the moment in which the script that Lars and Niels have written crosses into the diegesis of the film; shortly thereafter, the epidemic breaks out in Copenhagen.

Third-person voice over is prominent in several of von Trier's films. It is not only a stylized use of sound; the VOs fill in significant narrative ellipses and furnish omniscient (often sardonic) commentary. Neither *Dogville* nor *Manderlay* would be the same film without John Hurt's frequent interventions as narrator that often prevail over the almost inaudible dialogue onscreen. These VOs are unabashedly judgmental as well as omniscient in, for example, characterizing Bill Henson as "dumb and he knows it" in *Dogville*. The same importance holds in *Europa* for which Max von Sydow furnished third-person VOs. Von Trier personally delivers VOs that are accompanied by his reflection in the window in *The Boss of It All* although these are brief and make a stab at whimsy (for example, dismissing the film at the beginning as being a comedy, thus of little importance). By contrast with von Trier's preference for VO that is external to the diegesis of the characters' world, Pedro Almodóvar depends on first-person VO (albeit, at times from characters who are deceased by that point in the narrative but continue to speak through diaries and letters). First-person VOs are nonetheless prevalent in von Trier's *The Element of Crime* although they mainly consist of prompts by the hypnotist to elicit further miserablist recollections from Fisher who otherwise says very little.

Some of von Trier's stylistic interventions are so old that they lay claim to the sheen of newness. In this vein, *Dancer in the Dark* opens with a musical overture accompanied by abstracted shapes changing form and color on screen. Along with pre-signifying Selma's problems with vision, the overture is a stylistic move that evokes epics such as Stanley Kubrick's lone studio-produced film, *Spartacus* (1960). Similarly, the title cards that punctuate each of the chapters in *Dogville* and *Manderlay* evoke silent film era title cards. Von Trier first deploys title cards to divide chapters of

Breaking the Waves although these are garnished with popular rock music (e.g., Jethro Tull's "Cross-Eyed Mary," Elton John's "Your Song") and undulating movement within the image. The title cards also channel a sensibility of self-consciousness of the film as film. For instance in *Dogville*, a title card reads, "Chapter NINE: In which Dogville receives the long-awaited visit and the film ends," thereby dispensing with pretences of illusionism (original emphasis). In this manner, the film gives stylistic salute to the French New Wave (in particular, Jean-Luc Godard's frequent use of title cards in, e.g., *Masculin, Féminin* [1966]).

Von Trier's early films were very carefully staged for the camera with long scripts and hundreds of storyboard drawings. The effort shows in the final look of the film. *Europa*'s investment in style generates a beautifully realized film despite the sheer bleakness of the gutted world that it presents. Rosalind Galt writes that *Europa* featured, "a technologically sophisticated form of matte effect (that) combines several superimposed and/or back-projected images in a single frame" (2006: 213). The resultant multiply-layered images varied framing of its constituent shots (to place jarring close-ups and medium shots in the same image), film gauges (16 and 35 mm), stocks (color and black-and-white) and lenses (wide angle and telephoto). Von Trier claims that shots were composed of as many as seven images layered together in this manner. The earlier film, *The Element of Crime*, is similarly startling in its visual look that appears indebted to Ridley Scott's visionary *Blade Runner* (1982) that was released two years earlier (albeit to little initial acclaim, with minimal cinematic distribution). *The Element of Crime* is staged almost entirely at night or indoors behind windows that are besmirched so as to defeat all but jagged shards of dingy light.

Aside from the opening shots in arid Egypt, *The Element of Crime*'s Europe is in perpetual drizzle (also evocative of *Blade Runner*). A dreary ambiance of water-logged, paint-peeling decay is evident. While less attention is devoted to *mise-en-scene* in later films, decay is still part of their look. In *Dancer in the Dark*, even the relatively "well off" Houstons live one step from poverty in a deprived, rust-laden environment. The austerity of *Dogville* is partly conjured through its restrained, neo-*Waiting for Godot* "theater-in-the-void" look of few props and buildings without walls. While the *mise-en-scene* is less fulsome in these later films, it is effectively submerged into the storylines that examine the deep-seated impact of socio-economic class on deprived people.

Where narrative is concerned, foreshadowing is also frequently in evidence in scripts that von Trier crafts and films. For example, in *The Element of Crime*, Fisher pockets a talisman that is the Lotto murderer's calling card—a hint of what is to follow. The childhood "Tweetie the bird" story that Grace discusses with her father upon discovering the plantation in *Manderlay* also presents foreshadowing. In particular, it augurs her subsequent failures to "do good" by the plantation residents (and while the device is clear enough, in this case, it is trite and heavyhanded).

Change Afoot. Along with the continuity that auteur theory stresses, change is also a striking feature of von Trier's corpus. In particular, von Trier's stylistic signature is of interest in part for the profound shift that it has exhibited during the course of his career. In particular, von Trier has enacted a startling trajectory from the formalist perfectionism of the E-trilogy to becoming a looser and more improvised filmmaker. As a result of the extensive storyboarding, von Trier's early films present strikingly composed images staged for the camera. For example, *The Element of Crime*'s Fisher floats lugubriously on his back on a raft while tossing blank pages into the water, captured in a high-angle shot. The carefully constructed, poetic image signifies a stymied police investigation. Other disturbing images are carefully constructed for the camera in von Trier's cinema. In *Epidemic*, Mesmer's girlfriend comes to consciousness in a chilling, longitudinally staged image of her coffin—after she has been accidentally buried alive.

Epidemic foreshadows the director who would go on to pioneer a stripped-down Dogme95—and, within the same film, indulges the staunch formalist who fashions tightly controlled works to specifications evocative of Kubrick. In particular, *Epidemic*'s scenes that occur in contemporaneous Denmark anticipate Dogme95 and are shot in a casual, haphazard style on grainy fast stock. One scene depicts the characters Lars and Niels (played by Lars von Trier and Niels Vørsel) as they discuss the techniques they intend to use in the script they are writing (e.g., strains of Wagner for the appearance of the killer bacteria). In other words, they let the "wires show" with respect to the cinema machine they are preparing to mobilize, rather than assaying to elicit awe at virtuoso technique that is out of sight and "behind" the image. How-ever, in the scenes in which Lars envisions the film that he is scripting with Niels in his own head, the look changes to a glossier slow film stock with far greater tonal variations. Moreover, in these sequences of *Epidemic*, the visual style is distinctly different as the images are artfully composed and more cinematic tricks are in evidence. For example, overexposed blinding light from the win-dows in the chamber where the doctors convene suggest the holo-caust outside while making their white lab coats glow ominously.

A paradigm change in acting is implicated in von Trier's larger stylistic shift. In the early films, von Trier elicits performances that are stilted and mannered. Michael Elphick's portrayal of *The Element of Crime*'s Fisher stands out as particularly lugubrious. At this time, actress Kirsten Rolffes described the young von Trier as a "very sweet boy" who "hasn't the first idea about actors" since "they are hair in the soup" for his elaborate filmmaking schemes (Lumholdt 2003: xv). *Breaking the Waves*, *Dancer in the Dark* and *Manderlay*, by contrast, unbridle the performers and feature wrenching scenes of characters convulsed with emotion and often crying alone. While shooting *Dogville*, takes were often unre-hearsed and as long as 40 minutes. Moreover, the ensemble cast was on the large sound stage for shooting at all times to fill in the background of the transparent town (Refn 2004). As von Trier has worked more closely with actors and actresses, the results prompted an Oscar-nominated performance from previously un-known Emily Watson (*Breaking the Waves*). Internationally ac-claimed pop singer and novice actress Björk also garnered an Oscar nomination in 2000 for the poignant and emotive lead per-formance in *Dancer in the Dark*.

Sleepwalking

In surveying across the corpus of 11 feature films since 1984 with an eye toward motifs, it is apparent that, in almost all of von Trier's films, important characters split into an "alternative" state of consciousness that could be called a trance. In J. A. Brook's or-thodox Freudian account, the dissociated subject assumes the most drastic form that splitting may take. Specifically, the dissociated subject is characterized as having split "psychic groups" (i.e., "ac-tual," not metaphoric, fracturing of the ego). Grounded in deep-seated trauma against which it is a defense mechanism, dissociation is theorized as manifest in "sleep-like hypnoid states, fugues, and absences, and in extreme cases complete multiple personalities" (Brook 1989: 3). As with any defense, splitting is often "incomplete" in its "attempts at detachment" from a reality deemed too troubling for direct confrontation (1989: 7). Hence, a split subject commonly exhibits "oscillation between acknowledging and denying" the split and its traumatic origins (1989: 8). As a rule, what is denied paradoxically presents itself conspicuously as the blank or gap that calls attention to an effort at effacement ([In]famous example: Richard Nixon's Oval Office tapes and their 18 minutes of erasure).

Why the prevalence of trances in von Trier's corpus? The emphasis on them implies that identities are not stably consolidated since society as presently constituted is unsuitable for sustaining psychically integrated people. As noted, the emphasis on the split subject and trances may also be interpreted as a clue to reverberating, deep-seated trauma. While small, prosperous Denmark at the edge of Europe does not have the blood-soaked recent history of Rwanda or Burma, the director's frequent references to WWII suggest the enduring impact of Euro-fascism and the Holocaust on the generation that was born shortly afterwards.

Trances arise in von Trier's films across the 1980s, 90s, and 00s. Indeed, the montage of Egypt that opens von Trier's feature debut, *The Element of Crime*, is accompanied by a VO from a hypnotist who is inducing a trance in the protagonist Fisher. The film is punctuated with further VOs as the hypnotist urges Fisher to go deeper into Europe and further into his recollections of it. Hence, the film may be construed as an extended trance mediated via Fisher to which the audience bears witness. Fisher's headaches and several surrealistic scenes (e.g., floating through a tunnel and encountering police colleagues) suggest that the viewer is gaining privileged access to the protagonist's troubled mind—further slips from reality within the overarching trance that the mysterious man in Cairo induces. Similarly, *Europa* opens with VO performed by Max von Sydow that tells the protagonist Leopold what he will do. Among the commands that this unseen hypnotist makes that are subsequently carried out are commands to wake up, fall in love with that woman, and to die. Indeed, during the course of the film, Leopold is led and manipulated so much by the other characters that he may as well be a somnambulist. His uncle in the film is a somnambulist of a more literal sort, often via drink-induced means.

Trances become von Trier, playing himself, in *Epidemic*. The film's plot centers on von Trier and Niels Vørsel (also playing himself) as they attempt a new script for the producer on short notice when the computer eats their previous project. Von Trier exits from diegetic situations, as cued by the camera shots and editing, into quasi-hallucinatory states to ponder sequences of the new script on an epidemic. A trance-like "exit" occurs, for example, while Lars sits in the bathtub, hearing ominous sound effects in an aural point-of-view from the water tap while a guest in the salon discourses on vine diseases. In such moments, von Trier's character appears to find ominous signs in everyday life, necessitating escape into a trance that in turn prompts artistic output.

The closing sequence of *Epidemic* is even more explicit in its presentation of trances. Lars and Niels present producer Claes Kastholm Hansen with their script at a formal dinner party and he is unimpressed. A hypnotist and a psychic arrive at the dinner party and the psychic is asked to "channel" the script. She detaches from the immediate milieu with increasing agitation and horror—describing screams, crosses painted on houses, rats, the contagion of panic—before hyperventilating and crying hysterically. The monologue lasts almost ten minutes and presents exceptionally emotive acting, particularly in contrast with the mannered stiltedness in von Trier's previous film, *The Element of Crime*. The twist is that the trance induced by "entering" the script becomes realized in the diegesis of *Epidemic*. The psychic pulls her hands away from her neck to reveal gigantic, blood- and pus-laden boils as she is herself a victim of the incipient epidemic that engulfs the dinner party—and the entire continent of Europe!

Other films in the corpus similarly feature trances. John Hurt's VOs in *Dogville* reference the tormented Grace's mental exits during the serial nighttime violations that the men of the town inflict upon her. In *The Boss of It All*, Kristoffer behaves like a "Manchurian Candidate" upon hearing the name of his theatrical hero Gambini. Thereafter, he immediately signs the company over to Finnur. The almost zombified Kristoffer proceeds to make the meeting room into a theater, emerging from behind the window curtains for a performance for the executives, oblivious to the workers (whom he had previously championed) as they pack their boxes and exit the building for having been outsourced and off-shored. Bess' frequent exchanges with god in *Breaking the Waves* have a trance-like quality for being removed from what is materially going on around her as she consults the non-ethereal "father." Selma's song-and-dance numbers in *Dancer in the Dark* erupt in her head (and on-screen) when she is bored (e.g., at the factory) or under great strain (e.g., in court, on death row); they are also trance-like exits from the diegesis of the film that are elaborately staged for the camera.

Split subjectivity arises in *Europa* in which werewolves are referenced. Katharina Hartmann is wife to the flawed Usonian idealist Leopold, by day, while her father subordinates the family business to the U.S. occupation. By night, she splits and acts as a "Werewolf." That is, as a member of the recalcitrant Nazi group, she writes threatening anonymous letters to her father and participates in espionage during the postwar campaign against the United States and its collaborators. The werewolf allusion at once references the legend's metaphor of "split subjectivity" and the Rightist terror groups that were covertly active during the end-game of the Reich (Galt 2006: 208).

Given that almost all of the films in the corpus feature characters who detach and send themselves into trances, what interpretation may apply to them? Most straightforwardly, the prevalence of trances may be taken as a device to dramatize characters having become detached from the "normal" self in order to cope with and live through difficult moments. However, in a more symptomatic vein, the trances may also signify a widespread, deeply traumatic split in the subject's experience of industrial society. On this view, alienation from the self that is mediated by trances and split subjectivity is a means by which to cope with the vertiginous shocks of the modern—with von Trier's particular Danish accents on the same.

Idealists Defrocked

A central recurring motif in von Trier's corpus is that the protagonist is an idealist who enters a situation to which he or she is an outsider. Although the protagonist is animated by manifestly high ideals, he or she presents character flaws that, in turn, occasion betrayal of the ideals—and of other people and/or the community. Catastrophe follows. Arguably, this is the storyline of *all* of von

Trier's feature films, in an unusual degree of dedication to a thematic motif even within the assumptions of auteur theory. Caroline Bainbridge anticipates this approach to von Trier's corpus that hinges on the disasters occasioned by the failed idealist (2007: 47). However, she does not develop this thematic motif as I will assay to do below.

The implications of the repeated "failed idealist" storyline may cut both ways, politically, in signifying a distrust of "utopias" imposed by "idealists" whatever their political persuasion (Left or Right). The scattered, washed bones of utopia betrayed are found everywhere across the globe in the course of the twentieth century. At the same time, the repeated depiction of idealism in von Trier's films as a portal into unfathomable danger seems to weigh more heavily against even mild progressivism. The pattern presents a classically conservative endorsement of the status quo that is tampered with at vast peril. In this regard, von Trier's films are open to the critique of being cynical about the possibilities of not only utopia—but also reform and incremental betterment, in reply to even a manifestly unjust or unsatisfactory status quo. In this view, von Trier's fictional worlds suck the oxygen out of struggles for social betterment.

Nevertheless, von Trier consistently avoids one common (Right-inflected) storyline: the "hero paradigm." Michael Ryan and Douglas Kellner (1988) elaborate this storyline and its variations in which the individual (masculinist) hero, necessarily rugged and initially encumbered by weaklings and convention, clubs these obstacles down by the final reel. Von Trier unswervingly eschews these hints of conservative triumphalism in his corpus of films. However, the strict persistence with which the von Triersian protagonist fails and occasions wider disaster may also be read as conservative—albeit, a classical conservatism that is suspicious of even the most carefully measured pace of change.

The failed idealist thematic motif in von Trier's films differs, for example, from Luis Buñuel's *Viridiana* (1961) that wades into similar depths. In Buñuel's film, the title character leaves the nunnery after her uncle's suicide and initiates a selfless project of charity for homeless beggars on the uncle's former estate. Although her devotion is high-minded in its motivations and thoroughly self-effacing, the thankless beggars trash the project at the first opportunity and attempt forceful violation of Viridiana herself. The flaw in her project is its very perfection wedded, Buñuel implies, to the otherwise intelligent and selfless Viridiana's sentimentality and naiveté about the dark currents of human nature (de la Colina and Pérez Turrent 1992). By the end of the film, she is in a state of mute shock, her ideals shattered as she takes shelter with her practical and narcissistic cousin Jorge. Nonetheless, despite the harshness of its critique, Viridiana's romanticized folly mainly brings ruin on to herself. Von Trier ups the ante in presenting his figure of the idealist as flawed by more than Viridiana's "excess of virtue" while the von Triersian idealist's designs are often unmitigated disaster for the larger group.[2]

Moreover, in *Epidemic*, this theme is explicitly discussed. Von Trier (playing himself) and Niels Vørsel (his scriptwriting collaborator, also playing himself), hash out the plot of the film-within-a-film. On the walls of the apartment, they paint a storyline in order to further brainstorm a script about a plague. The storyline that they devise concerns the young idealist Doctor Mesmer (also played by von Trier in the scenes that dramatize their script), who leaves the walled city for the apocalyptic world of disease that lies beyond it.[3] However, Mesmer is actually carrying the seeds of disaster with him rather than righting the situation in the outside world (although the storyline is muddled, notwithstanding assertions in the script that Mesmer worsens matters). Moreover, the creation of the fictional Mesmer coincides with the plague vector in Europe that erupts within the diegesis of *Epidemic*.

Another moment in this thematic motif concerns the community that the Outsider assays to penetrate and change. The community is often characterized by stasis and defensiveness about its backwardness while it acutely feels the threat presented by the encroachment from the outside world. In *Dogville*, Grace is an encroachment in herself—and she is also followed by the thrusts of the police and finally the gangsters into the village (who, in turn, annihilate it). *Manderlay* follows the pattern as Grace is an interloper on the plantation. In turn, other pressures exerted from outside turn up by the gates of the plantation (e.g., Hector). Perhaps the most interesting case in this respect is the quasi-commune in *The Idiots*. Stoffer runs the group out of his Uncle Svend's house that is on the market to be sold. Hence, during the scenes when people outside the commune show up (Svend, a potential buyer and her husband, and a representative of the local government), the "idiots" take measures to repel the interlopers and retain their arrangement. However, when Josephine's father comes to the property, alone and deadly serious about reclaiming his daughter, the resultant shock to the group is such that it dissolves quickly afterward.

In von Trier's debut feature, *The Element of Crime*, Fisher occupies the role of idealist outsider. He has been exiled from Europe for 15 years, hence the dilapidated, failing continent to which he returns is strange and unfamiliar. Fisher's mentor, Osborne, was also an idealist who wrote the book from which the film takes its title. In it, Osborne lays down a method by which to investigate crime that pivots on reconstructing the criminal's mindset to anticipate the next move—a game of chess, in other words, but with higher stakes. The method is implied to be rational, effective and humane in the service of the community's safety. Moreover, the method contrasts with what the audience sees of the current chief, Kramer, and his preference for black-booted policing methods. Indeed, Kramer dismisses the idea that information guides police work as being "old fashioned."

Fisher is distressed to see that his mentor Osborne is gracelessly aged and marginalized—his book is no longer used in training the police—and that he appears to have lost his mind. An outsider without allies, Fisher is nonetheless determined to demonstrate that the humane idealist Osborne's method is effective and that it trumps the crude techniques of Kramer. Thus, as the investigation proceeds, an increasingly disturbed Fisher rejects his lover Kim's pleas to turn his findings and the investigation over to Kramer. Fisher assays to reconstruct serial killer Harry Gray's pattern of behavior and movement. Toward this end, he instructs Kim to, "Call me Harry." However, Fisher's fragile (and split) sense of who he is within a decaying Europe becomes sufficiently perturbed that he goes beyond reconstructing Gray's movements for the purpose of trapping him. Fisher decisively "splits" into Gray and commits the final serial murder (of the child whom he was ostensibly protecting). Following the murder, Kramer leads Fisher to the sight of Osborne's suicide. Kramer points to the final defeat of the idealist and his pupil by explaining that Osborne had similarly succumbed to becoming Harry Gray. Osborne continued the "geography of murder" that Gray had inaugurated—and passed it on to

Fisher to discover, reconstruct, and enact in a chain of idealism gone berserk.

The final leg of the E-Trilogy replays the pattern of a well-meaning outsider who holds—and finally cashiers—high ideals. Leopold Kessler arrives in Germany in the immediate post-WWII epoch with missionary zeal to assist in reconstruction. A pacificist who did not participate in the organized mass-violence of WWII, Leopold is also an outsider since he is a Usonian, one generation removed from the family's origins in Germany. Throughout the film, the idealistic Leopold who yearns to assist Germany's peaceful reconstruction is constantly out of his depth and manipulated from all angles. By the end, he is married to an unreconstructed Nazi to whom he has misplaced allegiance due to his love (or "love" as the unseen hypnotist cues Leopold to fall into it). At the same time, Leopold is used by Colonel Harris as a means of surveillance and infiltration of the Werewolf underworld. The cynical Usonian colonel not only acts against the recalcitrant Nazi Werewolf terror group, but he also clears the path for the United States to place the former Nazi industrial base under U.S. management. With breathtaking amorality, Harris bribes a Jew to participate in the exoneration of now-favored wartime Nazi industrialist Max Hartmann, thusly easing the takeover of German infrastructure with U.S. management grafted to the top of the flowchart. By the end of the film, Leopold's head is hopelessly spun around as to whether he should engage in a terrorist act against innocent civilians and blow up the train and the bridge. The sincere young man of high ideals who seeks only the satisfaction of doing good has snapped.

There are other entries and variations in von Trier's menagerie of idealists who seek to do right for the community—and who harden into cynics and/or destroy the community they had assayed to protect. A brief survey: Kristoffer in the The Boss of It All is initially motivated to save the high-tech company for its workers upon learning of Ravn's plot to sell the company to Finnur while pretending to be acting on instructions from "the boss" in North America—a boss who does not exist and whom Ravn has invented to avoid flack for unpopular decisions. However, when Kristoffer's vanity is stoked by a fleeting and coincidental reference to his theatrical hero Gambini, he goes into a trance of thespian showiness—and signs away the company that he had previously saved for its employees.

In *The Idiots*, Stoffer similarly sets up an alternative commune-like arrangement in his bourgeoisie uncle's home while it is for sale. Within the commune, middle class standards are mocked and social misfits take refuge. The home is presented as a beachhead toward security for vulnerable people like Josephine (breaking away from being heavily medicated) and the abused/browbeaten wife Karen. Despite the pro-social dimensions of the commune project, Stoffer is jaded in word and in deed. Concerning words, he makes beyond-the-pale tasteless comments about people with low cognitive functioning. Where deeds are concerned, he puts his compatriots in uncomfortable (or worse) situations. In this vein, Stoffer abandons Jeppe in a biker bar where he is taken to the bathroom by the bikers. It is a tensely staged situation in which it is unclear whether the bikers mean to help or molest him (it is in any event exceptionally awkward), while Jeppe is compelled to remain "in character" or risk being battered for playing a sick joke. Giving space to gentle misfits, even transiently, seems epiphenomenal to Stoffer's misanthropy. Hence, the film produces a variation on the von Triersian idealist who intends to help and brings instead copious misery; paradoxically, Stoffer's hardened cynicism brings a measure of fulfillment to the denizens of the commune (perhaps inadvertently and, in any event, transiently).

Dog Days

Dogville is another entry in von Trier's corpus that prominently features idealists who are compromised and who, in turn, visit catastrophe on the community. In this case, along with continuities, there are variations on the thematic motif. To start with, the film presents two central characters who may be construed as functioning within the role of idealist; namely, Tom and Grace. Both are presented initially as idealists with significant character flaws that will, in turn, compromise the idealistic project. Tom's failings are more obvious: he is shallow and intellectually lazy despite his pretenses. Moreover, in the closing chapter, he makes a decision to cashier his fellow idealist when she threatens his self-importance by smoking out the emptiness of his posturing.[4] By contrast, Grace presents a more ambiguous case. While Grace is far cleverer than Tom, her relationship to her ideals is more complicated as she seems to vacillate between idealism and practical exigencies. As a vulnerable outsider, she may be playing along with Tom's project in order to secure Malthusian safety. However, following the be-trayal by Tom, she dispenses with even the appearance of idealism and embraces the seductions of her father's offer of raw power and authority.

As the scion of the one wealthy person in the town, Tom is privileged and performs no discernable labor in contrast with the other residents. He walks the streets, ponders, and periodically calls upon his sense of entitlement to convene meetings at the church that functions as the nexus of the village's civic life. As the film opens, Tom has summoned the village to hear his charge for "moral re-armament." The presentation goes over badly since his thoughts are ill fashioned and garnished with hectoring appeals. "He thinks he is a philosopher," the castrating Liz comments, as unrest ripples through the audience. However, Grace's escape from the gangsters into the village furnishes the possibility of "illustra-tion" (Tom's term) of moral re-armament for the villagers via the act of "receiving." To wit, will the village receive Grace the out-sider?

However, Tom also exhibits a characteristic of other idealists in the corpus of von Trier's films as his frustrated sexuality makes him easily manipulated. It may also present a metaphor for the weaknesses inscribed within the larger idealistic project. Specifi-cally, Tom's moralistic crusade is complicated by his amorous feel-ings for Grace (and by the villagers' awareness of, and über-puritanical response to the same). Tom exhibits principle (or deep repression) in not taking advantage of Grace when the other males of the village do—although he also does nothing to halt the serial depravities visited upon her despite his privileged situation.

At first blush, recruiting help for the vulnerable (if shadily am-biguous) Grace may seem to constitute a laudable impulse. Tom's project with Grace as "illustration" is, however, flawed in the first instance since the contract is highly asymmetrical and made under duress (see Pateman 1988 on contract theory). While Grace needs cover to evade the gangsters *and* law enforcement, the villagers do not need her *per se*; hence her campaign to contrive her worth to the hard-scrabble village. Grace the outsider is indebted and all parties are always acutely aware of this circumstance. She is en-snared in a matrix of intensifying vulnerability to the whims of increasingly petty and vengeful people acting out their frustrations on her. Within this precarious framework, Grace performs labor for all of the other villagers in Dogville. Her idealism is expressed in diligent work and, more so, efforts to coax the villagers into overcoming self-imposed obstacles.

Grace's flaws with respect to her "fit" to the village of Dogville are cued by her costume. Specifically, she wears a fur coat and elegant dress that suggest that she has escaped from a cocktail party into the scruffy town during the opening sequence. Tom's introductory account of the village to Grace suggests his mixed feelings about the place while she sees an opportunity to seize upon: "If this is the town that you love, then you really have a strange way of showing it," she says. While the comment is barbed for demanding that Tom live up to his ostensible ideals, it also positions Grace as having appraised an opening to be an even more zealous "booster" of the dead-end town. In the same scene, the VO narration takes note of Grace's approving reaction to the figurines in the window of Ma Ginger's shop, since only days previously she would likely have mocked them as "tasteless." This and other moments call into question whether Grace is as enamored with the town as her behavior may suggests—or simply attempting to insinuate herself into it for the protection it affords. Grace is also cutting in her observations about Tom having "so much going on in his head" and in teasing out his painfully awkward, and nearly aborted, attempt at a declaration of love. The declaration is, in any case, followed by a shot of Grace on the bench alone in apparent amusement at her ability to emotionally turn him any way she pleases.

Alongside self-interested games, many of Grace's interactions with Tom play out in a register of seemingly sincere affection. Her insistence to Tom that they make love only within the context of freedom may indeed be a manipulative put-off that is ensconced in the high-minded veneer of idealistic gesture, but, even if so, the sentiment also channels the truth of their situation and an idealistic yearning for something better. Grace is not free as long as she owes the village a debt that cannot be discharged, one that is renewed each day in the community's ledger for endowing her with a protectorate.

The two flawed idealists finally betray each other as the closing sequence of the film approaches. After Grace's escape plan is foiled, Tom adds further betrayal by placing the blame on Grace for the ten dollars taken from his father. Grace suffers for Tom's selfish maneuver that also presents a dress rehearsal for further betrayals. After the robbery for which Grace is falsely accused, the degradations and depravities that are visited upon her intensify. In turn, Tom arranges a meeting for Grace to explain her grievances to the village. After the meeting, Tom lies to Grace to recruit her into sex by claiming that the villagers asked him to choose them or her. Grace perceptively points out the betrayal he is enacting with her by using the subtle coercion of emotional blackmail, whereas the other villagers had simply been cruder about their desires. Tom is crushed. First, Grace enacts sexual humiliation as even the crisis that Tom has concocted to get sex from Grace has been trumped by the high card of idealism that she plays. Second, Grace recalibrates her view of Tom and decides that he is as tawdry as the rest of Dogville *and* lets him know it. The result is a body blow to Tom's pretensions with the attendant "moral mission" and "situation as philosopher" that he supposes for himself.

After lying about having disposed of the gangsters' calling card, Tom retrieves it and summons them. However, Tom's betrayal of idealism appears minor when compared with that of Grace. Once they are reunited in the back of his enormous staff car, Grace's father seductively presents her with a vision of vengeance as purifying mission. He claims that she is arrogant to not hold the people of Dogville to the standards that she holds herself. When Grace counters meekly that they are doing their best, he counters, "Is their best really good enough?" Moving back and forth between the main street and her father's realm in the back seat, Grace becomes visibly intoxicated with the authority within her grasp.

The degradations dealt onto Grace during most of the second half of the film—degradations that include serial rape—may easily facilitate sadistic desires to see retribution in the final sequence of the film. And retribution is copiously delivered as, e.g., the viperous Vera is forced to witness the execution of her six bratty children. However, from the perspective of von Trier's motifs, what is of further interest is that Grace's ideals are cashiered by her father's rhetorical turns that she willingly invites and abets—tossing out claims for her father to rebut with muscular skill—once a large measure of power is on offer to her. Grace herself executes Tom at close range with her father's gun to underscore that one idealist's betrayal of the other sets a donnybrook into motion.

On one hand, this conclusion defies a made-to-order Hollywood happy ending. It is also chimerical for, on one hand, suggesting a manipulative game on the part of the filmmaker to trigger a thirst for revenge in the audience—and to then serve it up. Alternatively, in a more "enlightened" register, one can read the film as implying that that the Dogville residents are themselves victims of class structure in the first instance, deal out abuse to someone who seems more materially vulnerable—and, via a logic of classism, end up suffering apocalyptically for it, once tables turned and Grace was empowered. However, read in context with von Trier's corpus of films, it presents another variation on the theme that idealism is a dangerous illusion with a catastrophic telos.

Breaking the Mold? In *Breaking the Waves*, Bess is set up as an idealist early in the film. In contrast with Grace, however, the collapse of her idealism occasions disaster mainly for herself. During the first scene, she quietly but firmly confronts the crusty traditionalists of the village in affirming that she will wed the outsider Jan. Subsequently, Bess exhibits ineffable depths of devotion to him via, for example, her stunning emotional explosion when he leaves to resume work on the oil rig. While waiting for his return, Bess makes a suicidal gesture as she runs out to the rock formation by the storming sea. It is a fitting metaphor for the depths of her emotion that is skillfully played by actress Emily Watson. Bess is clearly a romantic with unconditional love, regardless of identity, as her ideal.

Nonetheless, Bess' idealism occasions disaster. Following his crippling and near-fatal injury, Jan instructs her to meet other men and to tell him about their encounters as a means of having vicarious sex with her. While fulfilling these desires, Bess dies of injuries inflicted (off screen) by a pack of hard-core misogynists on a boat. Like Grace in *Dogville*, Bess is burdened and constrained by a debt. Grace's debt is to the tawdry community that harbors her; Bess' debt is to the main object of her idealism, Jan, intensified by guilt at his near fatal accident. Since she had prayed for his return, she holds (superstitiously) that she had caused the accident.

Nevertheless, in portraying Bess' idealism and sacrifice, there is also slippage from the motif of idealism. First, Bess' idealism is in some respects a case of being more severely Scottish Presbyterian than her fellow villagers. That is, while they orient around ritual in practicing the religion, Bess has a more personal relationship with the infinite that is dramatized in several scenes in which she converses with god—alternating between a "male" adult voice for god and her replies in an exaggeratedly childish voice. God is typically severe in his instructions to Bess. Moreover, as Bess is "playing both parts" in the drama with respect to her dialogues with god, the question is begged: Who is speaking for god in Bess' exchanges? The obvious answer is Bess herself, as it is her own (if affected) voice. However, given the strictness and conventionality that generally governs god's replies to Bess, the literal answer that Bess "is speaking" demands interrogation. On this view, it is the voice of internalized, prevailing ideology that speaks through Bess in exerting conventional demands upon her—demands with which she subsequently complies in material terms.

Bess also refers to her imagined interlocutor, god, as "father." This presents another moment in demonstrating her high-fidelity internalization of prevailing ideology. Bess indeed has a literal father. He is coded as a weak and ineffectual figure in his brief appearance on screen at the dinner table. However, in the film, literal weakness is cancelled out via the more abundant force of ideology that (like mythology) is not tempered by literalism or mere fact. The patriarch's power is recuperated in practice by appeals to an omnipotent "Father" whom Bess regularly conjures in church. A flesh and blood male, Jan also occupies this role of patriarchal totem (see Silverman [2000], who prompted this interpretation). As with the god that Bess invents for her exchanges, she assays to scrupulously implement Jan's demands for extramarital relations. Bess carries out Jan's sexual directives in two scenes— albeit, joylessly, to the specifications of duty being executed.

Ideology speaking through the character of Bess also aligns with the traditionalist specifications of the film's conclusion. Following what Bess apparently intends as her mortal sacrifice on Jan's behalf with the psychotic males on the boat, Bess is surprised that Jan has not recovered by the time she is wheeled into the hospital with her soon-to-be-fatal wounds. However, after Bess has died, Jan not only recovers and lives—he rises from the hospital bed and walks as she had intended. In this manner, von Trier's creation of Bess enacts the gender traditionalist trope of female sacrifice for the purpose of male advancement. *Breaking the Waves'* affirmation of Bess' sacrifice is expressed via the closing bells from heaven that celebrate her sacrifice that lands Jan back on his feet—and onto the oil rig with his covey of male buddies. The film's commentary on Bess' sacrifice may thus be taken as approving of the traditional demands that over-determine the final image—a "whimsical" and "romantic" image, particularly if the spectator can be recruited into the ideological assumption that the woman's re-mit is sacrifice.

Bess may be an idealist but the ideals that the character holds are intensely traditional. Her attachment to gendered ideology aligns with tropes of the female in its content (sacrificial, self-effacing love for the male) and in its conduct (emotional to the core). As Slavoj Žižek argues (1995: 327), the subject who is living under the forces of ideology may behave "as if" the ideology is true. That is, a low-wage service worker may behave "as if" the capital-ist ideology of meritocracy is true as, paradoxically, it may make the worker feel more control over his or her situation and pros-pects for the future against day-to-day exploitation. Thus, the "as if" relation "softens" the practical experience of ideology via doubts about it and winks toward what one is *supposed* to internalize as a faithful subject. In the construction of Bess as character, however, there is no "as if." The ideology is internalized, straight and full, such that the idealist is an über-ideologue who literally embodies the sacrificial masochism that ideology demands of her.

Dodo's attempt to confront Bess underlines this interpretation. In particular, Dodo makes a feminist claim in emphasizing that a woman must manage her life carefully and that Bess has surren-dered to Jan and his strategic deployment of the power of his ill-ness. Literally, his illness is brain injury; figuratively, it may be taken as masculinist demands for sex fantasy. Dodo's appeal to Bess while watching out for her friend's interests is ignored since there is no "as if" in Bess' repertoire. At the same time, Bess' deci-sion to ignore Dodo's advice corresponds with a concept of ideology that posits that the ideologized subject does not obey a rational (or even self-interested) calculus (Althusser 1994; Eagleton 1991).

Dr. Richardson is a medical and psychiatric practitioner in *Breaking the Waves*. He also follows the trajectory of the von Trier-sian failed idealist. When he first appears, Dr. Richardson is coded as young, friendly, and a scrupulous professional. When Bess takes up Jan's command for sex outside of marriage, she turns first to

Dr. Richardson. In a scene that presents as a parodic enactment of stripped-down, contemporary courting behavior, Bess arrives at the doctor's apartment. As if following a rote script, she commences to drink heavily, dance to loud music, and finally installs herself naked on his bed. Richardson rejects the overture and insists that he just wants to talk to Bess. While this is professional behavior enacted to non-exploitive specifications, it does not annul the impression of fascination that the doctor holds for the colorful Scottish villager.

Later, Richardson visits Bess' home ostensibly to talk sternly about her unbridled sexual behavior (joyless as that behavior is). Along with idealized and professional conduct, Richardson acts out the male type of the "valent-but-'dissed'-love-interest" who is viscerally pained at the attentions that he sees Bess wantonly direct at other men while ignoring him—the man who regards himself as her principled admirer. In later sequences, Richardson uses his position as doctor/psychiatrist in a vindictive attempt to separate Bess and Jan. It presents a sharp contrast with Richardson's scrupulously professional behavior at the outset. He attempts to have Jan transferred to Glasgow and, more egregious, has the drug- and surgery-addled Jan sign papers to commit Bess to an institution where it is unlikely that she will see Jan again. The doctor appears to mete out punishment due to sexual jealousy and thereby trashes his professional ideals. Richardson's closing testimony before the tribunal channels ambivalence on this score since he at once honors Bess' memory as an idealist who stood up to the village's conventions (albeit, by extending the villagers' severity)—and also backs off under pressure from the tribunal to mouth the conventional view of her presumably disturbed disposition.

These films make arresting cinema with a discomforting critique of human nature that circulates in a different universe from formulaic Hollywood studio sentimentalisms. However, in staging the tragedy of the failed idealist, over and again, von Trier seems not to differentiate between the figure of the "idealist" and the "fanatic." Rather, the corpus of films often rashly collapses one into the other. In this vein, consider that Nobel Peace Laureate David Trimble posits a "'political fanatic'" as "'someone who is more interested in you than himself.'" Trimble explains the apparent paradox:

At first that might seem as an altruist, but look closer and you will see the terrorist. A political fanatic is not someone who wants to perfect himself. No, he wants to perfect you. He wants to perfect you personally, to perfect you politically, to perfect you religiously, or racially, or geographically. He wants to change your mind, your government, your borders... (Trimble 1998: 196)

This conceptual contribution may be kept firmly on board in critiquing not only von Trier's films but everyday political discourse as well.

CHAPTER 8

Old World/New World

The previous chapter traffics in more abstracted concern with the repeated motif of the failed idealist. This chapter's discussion continues and extends what has been argued earlier—but with an added factor with respect to von Trier's visions of the United States and Europe. The "*provoc-autuer*" tends toward a dim view of what he constructs as a static, brooding Europe as well as of the hyperkinetic fanaticism that he depicts in the United States— although the unflattering presentations assume a sharper edge in the U.S. case. This chapter is rounded out with an extended analysis of *Manderlay* in which I argue that von Trier's long-established contrarianism collapses into cynicism.

Continental Decay

Von Trier's first three features constitute the "Europe Trilogy" (or "E-trilogy"). The three legs on which it stands are *The Element of Crime* (1984), *Epidemic* (1987), and *Europa* (1991). All three are set in Europe and present the continent as ensnared in a deep stasis via the somnambulism of tradition—with an ominous primitivism lurking around the edges of its pastoral veneer. Rosalind Galt focuses on *Europa* when she writes that in von Trier's version, Europe is "dark, mysterious, and dangerous" (2006: 196); a stark contrast with its image as a place where life is pampered and a vision that inverts the terms that Europeans have often used to differentiate themselves from Others whom they have dominated. Alongside stultifying malaise wedded to perilous primitivism in von Trier's early films, there are aspects of Europe that are (inevitably) presented in a mainly "positive" register. The research that Lars and Niels perform in the archive in *Epidemic* points to Europe's deeply embedded cultural memory that has been studiously preserved across centuries. In the same film, Niels cheerfully drinking beer in his hospital bed with his friend Lars indexes European—and, specifically, Danish—relaxed geniality. This attitude has indeed been celebrated at length in the Danish genre of *hyggefilm*—"genial films"—that celebrate the pastoral and feature vast quantities of drink and sandwich consumption (Söderbergh-Widding 1998: 18).

Despite the inevitable moments that accent the positive within the familiar, criticism of Europe as dystopia is central. Von Trier's first film, *The Element of Crime*, opens with Fisher, an exiled European in Egypt, being placed in a trance before returning to the continent to investigate a serial killer. The implication that Europe has somehow gone somnambulist—that it has been "hypnotized"—is consistent with von Trier's unflattering presentation of the continent to which the exile returns. The mise-en-scene of *The Element of Crime* presents Europe as having slipped from stasis into absolute decline. Europe is decaying in general and it is inhabited by decaying bodies in particular; for instance, Osborne lodges his head in an eerie plastic bag for breathing therapy. In the next film, *Epidemic*, the motif of bodily decay continues as the psychic is graphically afflicted with the plague while the lead doctor is also in a wheelchair (shades of *Dr. Strangelove* [Stanley Kubrick 1964] or another crazed/fascistic invalid, *Metropolis*' [Fritz Lang 1927] Rotwang). Moreover, *Epidemic*'s team of doctors position to use the plague crisis in order to seize state authority and install themselves as self-appointed elite governance during the crisis; the type of crisis that Michel Foucault (1995) posits that the state may seize upon in the service of a metastasizing infrastructure of power that penetrates further into the subject (without receding back to the former frontiers of such once the crisis has passed).

In *The Element of Crime*, ritualized death and killing are envisioned as the "new normal." Mules pulling applecarts are pushed into the lake to drown while ritualized bunghy jump-style suicide is a "sport" for younger Europeans. At the other end of the lifespan, the disillusioned and (mentally/physically) exhausted rational idealist Osborne hangs himself. The dying culture of Europe as envisioned by von Trier furnishes the backdrop of the Lotto murderer's serialized killing. The serial killer, in turn, follows a calculated pattern of violently murdering female children. This plot element presents a further symptom of a culture reaching a dead end in suppressing its own reproductive possibilities. The mise-en-scene of *The Element of Crime* also includes police chief Kramer's forces as they thuggishly abuse suspects in the background of scenes. A tawdry police state in advanced formation is thusly envisioned.

The Asian Kim (played by the Burmese-British actress Me Me Lai) stands by Osborne's swinging corpse with their baby in the closing sequence of *The Element of Crime*. The brief image presents one of the few references to life or regeneration in the film— and it is coded as extra-European. Moreover, shortly after Fisher encounters Kim, he states his intention to "fuck you back to the Stone Age." The comment condenses a great deal. To start, it implies a desire for a form of sex tourism with a dark-skinned woman that a White Man from even a dying continent feels entitled to enunciate without shame. It also suggests the genocidal-militarist (mainly American-identified) phrase to "bomb them back to the Stone Age" as the decaying West's Eros is presented as saturated with thanatos. At the same time, *The Element of Crime* favorably positions the Occident's traditional Others as contrasting with Europe's slow paroxysms of death. The Near East is valorized via the hypnotist's power over the disoriented European Fisher. The Far East is also valorized via Kim who, while at once presenting the White Man fantasy as a fecund Asian, also regenerates the West in a way that it is depicted as incapable of (perhaps no longer interested in) enacting.

Von Trier's critiques of Europe are insinuated into the other entries in the E-Trilogy. Rosalind Galt praises *Europa* for departing from the pattern of other (mainly U.S.) films about the immediate post-WWII situation that envision fascism as having been as obliterated like the pocked German "moonscapes" that furnish the mise-en-scene. For Galt, von Trier's *Europa* refuses "year zero optimism" by placing it between the "legacy of Nazism, which has still not disappeared" and the cleaving of Europe, including its biggest population/economy in Germany, into two postwar spheres (2006: 191). In Galt's appraisal, *Europa* is significant for the timing of its release in the immediate aftermath of the Autumn 1989 Revolutions and German reunification. She takes the film as establishing a symptomatic correspondence between the missed opportunities for European unity under liberal auspices following WWII (instead, United States and Soviet Empires insinuated themselves deeply) and the Social Democratic Left being outmaneuvered after 1989: "The lost moment of potential in 1989 and 1990 recapitulated a similar missed opportunity in 1945 to 1949" (Galt 2006: 225).

In *Europa*, the uncle is the character who most vigorously enunciates Euro-traditionalist views and functions as the filmmaker's device for criticism of the same. The uncle presents a combination of petty (literal) finger-wagging at Leopold as he assays to position European culture as superior to the New World Usonian upstart. The uncle's pedantry about Europe is undercut by the defensiveness with which he bemoans a lack of respect from Usonians—alongside the disregard he has for the same Euro-traditions when it suits him in his circumscribed domain of "authority" as sleeper car conductor. In sum, the uncle's sanctimonious valorization of meaningless work procedure and open resentment at Leopold's Usonian background, speak to the Old World's injured pride at having been supplanted from the central role in global affairs after WWII. *Europa* is garnished with other sardonic depictions of obedience to ossified rules and ritualistic procedures. The Examiners' pompous and scandalized reaction to Leopold's failure to know arcane trivia that is further reshuffled into trick questions (e.g., a train cleaner *should never be* in possession of the "green card!") is darkly comic as it is cross-cut another plotline; namely, with the hopelessly disoriented Leopold's implication in the terrorist plot to blow up the train on which the same useless examination is taking place.

Epidemic also takes slaps at Europe's cultural bureaucracy. Upon receiving the thin 12-page script from Lars and Niels, the culturecrat Claes is conspicuously unimpressed. He states that the board that runs film in Denmark requires a script of at least 150 pages; it is the kind of high-handed arbitrariness that the less worldly uncle in *Europa* pursues with a vengeance. Claes calls the script's ending "pathetic" and launches into a pedantic description of the role of Danish film for Lars and Niels' edification, an explanation (and perhaps a concept) to which the film effectively gives the raspberry in promptly ignoring his windy insights via a dissolve into the next scene.

Come Together

Although positioned at the edge of Europe in Denmark, von Trier's films have been international in their casting from the start of his career. *The Element of Crime*, for example, was released in 1984 and features players from the United Kingdom (Michael Elphick), Hungary (Janos Hersko), Burma (Me Me Lai), and Denmark (Astrid Henning-Jensen). Galt observes with respect to von Trier's third effort, *Europa*, that "Although Danish in origin, the film was made by Swedish, Danish, German, and French partners, filmed in English and German and shot partly in Poland" (2006: 176). Von Trier's penchant for making films in English also speaks to a self-conscious internationalism with the English language as solvent of difference (for the international casts and, for the audiences). Von Trier's roster of English language films consists of *The Element of Crime*, *Europa*, *Breaking the Waves*, *Dancer in the Dark*, *Dogville*, and *Manderlay*, more than half the corpus, in other words.

Nevertheless, the content of von Trier's films themselves present international/European integration as fraught encounters with Others. Some of this is expressed in the register of humor via comedy in *The Boss of It All*. In this film, Finnur, the overbearing foreign buyer of the tech company, is Icelandic.[1] He communicates with Ravn, stealthily selling the company, via an interpreter and consistently insults Danes as "whores" who are weak for their sentimentality. In the same film, Spencer is the native Anglophone who is not taken seriously and whose spoken Danish is judged by the native speakers to be so poor as to obviate any need to try to communicate with him in the vernacular. Nevertheless, Spencer's earnest and unrequited determination to speak "Dansk" with his co-workers is a running joke.

Von Trier's films address the issue of identity and the Other, as noted above. *Breaking the Waves* is charged with the issue. In this case, the Other is located within Europe itself. In the film's opening sequence, one of the Scottish village elders asks Bess about what good "outsiders" can be said to have brought upon the village, in reference to her imminent marriage to the Scandinavian Jan. For his part, as a tall, fair-skinned (and slightly balding!) man, Stellan Skarsgård's Jan is a Scandinavian straight from central casting. Nonetheless, despite Scandinavia's relative proximity, outsider/Other status defines Jan in the Scottish village from the outset. The audience knows nothing about his back-story beyond his situation as outsider.

Nevertheless, the rural and traditional community that Otherizes Jan simultaneously functions as Other within the gaze that *Breaking the Waves* constructs for the spectator. That is, the spectator is invited to interpret the villagers as Others to a metropolitan subject watching an auteur film. Specifically, the village is presented as fighting a rearguard action against the late twentieth century. Its insular qualities are conveyed via the suspiciousness toward strangers alongside flinty defensiveness about its way of life (e.g., when a village elder snaps that a church bell is not a necessary accoutrement to worship god). The film installs the church as the center of civic life and discourse within it is notably harsh. Bess is excommunicated although the church does endow her with a burial that is punctuated with the priest's uncharitable assertion that she is a sinner and damned to hell.

Within the village, Dr. Richardson is a British islander and also an outsider. However, in contrast with the working-class Scandinavian outsider Jan, Dr. Richardson has a measure of stature by virtue of his work. He is, indeed, entitled to engage in more amused judgments concerning the whimsy of the villagers' beliefs. When Bess tells him that her answered prayers resulted in Jan's accident, he parries with humor about the superstition-laden powers that the villagers presume themselves to possess. Hence, some measure of Richardson's obvious attraction to Bess may be interpreted as an eroticized cathexis toward the Other's "primitivism." However, the closing sequence of the film demonstrates that Richardson understands Bess' Otherness as something more sublime. In front of the tribunal, Richardson posits that Bess' death was occasioned by being "good"; the death was not an efflux of neurotic or psychotic pathology as the tribunal assumes in pithily rejecting Richardson's initially stated appraisal of the matter. While Richardson retreats from this initial statement, the discord over Bess indicates that she is a rebel; a rebel who, paradoxically, is the über-practitioner of the village's severe and superstitious ideologies and in this manner an exceptional "true believer."

Along with local and insular pockets of deprivation such as in *Breaking the Waves*' Scottish village, there are deep wounds of guilt and betrayal beneath the current generalized prosperity in Europe to which von Trier orients. To wit, in the vortex of a war that leveled large swaths of Europe and whose convulsions killed an estimated 30 million people, *Europa*'s Katharina comments on the war of all against all in which betrayal is common currency. Such moments in von Trier's corpus speak to the lessons internalized in Europe about aggression in the international arena and chauvinistic hubris slammed down by hard reality; lessons that the United States has collectively yet to get its head around (despite opportunities to do so: Vietnam, Iraq).

Land of Opportunities

Europe is presented through critical spectacles in von Trier's films, most notably the E-Trilogy that extended from 1984 to 1991. However, the United States is set up in yet more unflattering terms with the later cycle of films that compose the "U-S-A: Land of Opportunities" trilogy. Von Trier's interest in the United States is obvious given that several of his films have been set there: *Dancer in the Dark*, *Dogville*, and *Manderlay* while *Europa*'s protagonist is Usonian.[2] Von Trier also co-scripted the Thomas Vinterberg–directed *Dear Wendy* that is set in the United States and dwells on the nation's weapon pathology. Because of his fear of flying, von Trier has never been in the United States. Nevertheless, with the rise of internationalized mass media, von Trier can claim plausibly (and with a critical accent) that his reference points in life have largely come from the United States:

> America is sitting on our world. I am making films that have to do with America [because] 60% of my life is America. So I am in fact an American, but I can't go there to vote, I can't change anything. I am an American, so that is why I make films about America. (Beltzer 2005: 8)

Thus, an interesting paradox arises that is enabled by U.S. mass media's ready movement across international screens. The vast share of U.S. screen material could be characterized as "sociological propaganda" that inevitably aggrandizes an "American Way of Life" though its sheer visibility, as Jacques Ellul (1965) theorizes. However, in reading the United States' copious media offerings against the grain, one can also assemble a formidable critique of the nation that they represent. The extensive perceptive passages of von Trier's corpus present evidence for this claim.

As Edward W. Said (1979) points out, there is a dubious history of classic anthropologists who have written on cultures that they have never seen first hand and in whose language they cannot communicate. Where von Trier and *Manderlay* are concerned, Jayson Harsin (2006:5) implies in passing that such first-hand knowledge may be indispensable in advance of making a critique. However, von Trier is working off cultural artifacts (films, news, music) that are self-representations and, in fact, have been aggressively inserted into extraterritorial circulation as exports. Putting aside the artistic license that filmmakers are regularly granted in making films about pasts and futures that they have not directly experienced: What, beyond seeing its media output day-in and day-out across one's whole life, would it take for von Trier (or any subject) to "know" the United States? A semester at University of Chicago? A summer job at Burger King? Lifelong residency in Sheboygan?

Fictional films are not a mirror. Nevertheless, one may abstract enough out of the U.S. mass media deluge to cobble together a coherent critique. The spectator may judge if the resultant critique, encased within fiction, resonates truth (about the United States, or small towns, or the broad human condition). *Dogville* in particular captures pious Usonian moralism, missionary certitude embedded within stunted idealism, the relentless defeat of the working class, and the withdrawal of the state beyond its monopoly on the use of force. Less contentiously, one may claim that although von Trier's films are not documentaries, they do present a snapshot of how the United States is critically appraised even in "friendly" Europe with which it shares common tradition as a former colony (of United Kingdom, Spain, France, The Netherlands) and with waves of immigration from all of Europe's nations. Moreover, the ubiquity of U.S. mass media, in addition to the legions of Usonian tourist emissaries on the ground, assures that it cannot be said that the United States and its citizens are "unknown" on their own chosen terms and thus unfair objects to judge and evaluate—even with respect to someone who has not set foot into the country.

The presentation of the United States in von Trier's corpus of films is at times chimerical. *Europa* is perhaps the clearest instance regarding its two major Usonian characters: Leopold, the idealist who comes to Germany to help in its reconstruction and Colonel Harris, who steers the postwar occupation. Leopold is out of his depth from the moment that he arrives, like a gobsmacked tourist who suffers the many indignities of someone who does not grasp what is happening around him. However, by the final sequence of the film, he has cashiered his ideals and blows up the train out of (if nothing else) mounting rage at having being used by everyone else.

In von Trier's construction of the chimera, Usonians are easily manipulated ciphers—and, conversely, Mafia-style Machiavellians. In stark contrast with Leopold, Colonel Harris is an unashamed master manipulator. Steeped in amorality, he is comfortable insinuating himself into the circle around former Nazi industrialist Max Hartmann. Colonel Harris is blasé about the Ravenstein assassination by the Werewolves and also stages the false exoneration of Hartmann via bribed testimony from the Jew (played by von Trier). In contrast with Colonel Harris' easy transactions in the seedy occupation business, the Jew spits as he departs to express disgust at the hideous charade he had just participated in. For his part, Hartmann is sufficiently troubled by the same that he slices himself to death with a razor in the bathtub. In *Europa*, the Usonian is the hopeless chump or the unashamed Machiavellian; as different as they are, neither presents an appealing subjectivity.

Although von Trier is not directing historical documentaries, he is also not taking cheap shots at U.S. behavior in the postwar era by the lights of the historical record. Colonel Harris' bare-knuckled amorality on screen echoes aspects of U.S. behavior on the ground in the immediate postwar theater. During this epoch, the arena of conflict shifted to the Soviet Union and the Cold War. Christopher Simpson (1988) documents extensive deployment of known former Nazis by the United States' scientific and intelligence apparatuses as part of a Cold War retooling.

Other entries in the von Trier corpus refer to the United States, albeit indirectly and with less bite. In *The Boss of It All*, the boss that Ravn invents to provide cover for his unpopular decisions is alleged to be in the United States. This narrative element furnishes an aside on de-regulated, anti-worker U.S. business practice that Ravn spends most of the film assaying to implement in secret. The critique is, however, leavened by comedy. In *Epidemic*, Niels recounts his encounters with the United States via a teenaged "pen pal" in a narratively unmotivated sequence that comes across as a smug and gratuitous. In an odd and discordant moment in the same film, the dying black victim of the plague quotes (without attribution) the infamous racial tirade of Richard Nixon's Secretary of Agriculture Earl Butz.

Corroded Rust Belt

Dancer in the Dark is a more extensive treatment of the United States. The film centers on Selma, an outsider to the United States as an immigrant from communist-era Czechoslovakia, who dwells in a factory town. She works at the factory and steadfastly saves money for an operation for her son, who will lose his eyesight due to a hereditary condition that has already began to abolish her sight. Where her few moments for leisure are concerned, Selma is a devotee of U.S. movie musicals. Like many flesh-and-blood immigrants, she may be characterized as more "Usonian" than even an idealized version of one. She is hard-working, frugal, family-oriented, and worships popular culture. Indeed, she tells Bill Houston that, in Czechoslovakia, her image of the United States was formed in large measure from musicals, a plausible claim within a fictional context (that also echoes von Trier's situation!).

The film also presents a critique of the U.S. legal process and death penalty as most of the last hour of the film is devoted to Selma's trial, incarceration, and execution. Despite "fitting in" with Usonian ideals as a diligent immigrant, Selma also instances the von Triersian motif of being an outsider in debt to the community. During her trial, the prosecutor is able to twist and spin the details of her life story into what the film's audience knows to be false but incriminating contortions. In the prosecutor's account, Selma "committed a callous and well-planned crime" as he connects the circumstantial dots. He asserts a larger disregard for the United States and Selma's debt to it. In his account, Selma "sought refuge in our country" and then inflicted a heinous crime on people "who opened their homes and hearts." Usonian community thus becomes the victim as the prosecutor constructs Selma as an Other who failed to hold up her end of the implicit contract with the nation to which she immigrated. He nails the point down with digs, such as Selma is "a woman who worships Fred Astaire . . . but not his country." In a nod to the 1950s setting of the film, the prosecutor also dwells on her association with communism via below the radar, a xenophobic reference to her Czech origins. During the trial, she is made over as Other and tailored to fit the vestments of a murderous ingrate.

Dancer in the Dark also critiques the United States' practice of the death penalty and the state machinery of its implementation. This is part and parcel to the classist organization of life in the United States that the film depicts. Selma is presented as having had "mailed in" (court-appointed) representation in court who was too inept to parry the prosecutor's aggressive parsing of words and deeds. When an apparently competent lawyer is recruited to try Selma's case on appeal, she adamantly refuses him the money that she has saved for Gene's operation (an operation that would likely have been unnecessary in the first instance with viable public health infrastructure). The sadism of the death penalty—even putting aside the circumstances of Selma's case that should exonerate her—is underscored to the end. Although Selma is about to be killed, one functionary complains indignantly about Kathy's final gesture of handing Gene's glasses to Selma (intended to signify that Gene's sight was saved by Selma's sacrifice). While the bureaucratic machinery of state-sponsored death is presented as hideous, the portrait of the United States is softened by the unaffected kindliness of Brenda, the prison guard. A single mother as well, she is instinctively sympathetic to Selma and willing to step outside the bureaucratic regimen to console her.

Dog's Life

Dogville is perhaps the most significant entry in von Trier's dissection of the United States. It presents a high-impact construction of the microcosmic small village during the 1930s Depression. The biting commentary is set up by *Dogville*'s focus not on the United States' pockets of bedazzling wealth—but on the other side of the nation's ferocious class divide. More importantly, the film considers how pauperization deeply conditions citizens' everyday experience. Primitive infrastructure in the fictional town includes a lack of social services (no school is evident). In Dogville, the dog goes hungry even when there is enough food since, in Chuck's sadistic appraisal, the dog is "meant to be" hungry; classist imperatives are kicked downward until they finally reach their terminal point with the dog (the one sentient creature in town whom Grace later spares).

Given the lack of government buildings, the church functions as civic nexus—thus implying a collapse of private moralism into the steering mechanism of an ostensibly pluralistic state. In turn, the state only appears in its carceral form via the Althusserian Repressive State Apparatus of the police (Althusser 1994). The carceral industry also is referenced via the off-screen construction of a penitentiary outside the poverty-stricken town. Prison construction has indeed been a major "growth industry" in economically depressed zones of the United States in the years leading up to *Dogville*'s production, in synergy with the poverty that drives street crime (Parenti 1999).

Along with being policed but otherwise ignored by the state, repression is inscribed in the "softer" sphere of culture as well. The town is literally transparent with regard to the mise-en-scene with outlines of buildings traced onto the floor and only a couple of props. In lieu of formal governance, discipline keeps the villagers in line via relentless exposure to each other in a dystopian form of "transparency" that is distinct from a well-functioning social democratic order (Foucault 1995). Moreover, a measure of discretion over one's privacy is understood to be a necessary condition for the well-adjusted subject's mental health (Christians et al. 2004). The idealized U.S. "tightly-knit" small town community is thusly stood on its head in von Trier's reworking of the materials.

Repression is also evident in the sexual mores of Dogville that are presented as part of the village's pathologies. When Tom and Grace touch hands at the Fourth of July picnic, the other celebrants look askance and later castigate Tom. While public affection is upsetting to the villagers, Grace is raped by Chuck without any sanction (although what is going on is an "open secret" in the transparent town). In turn, when she is locked into Bill's medieval-looking device to prevent her normal ambulatory movement, the town's men (with the exception of Tom) inflict serialized rape on her. The villagers do not construe it as such since the abuse was the equivalent of a horny "hillbilly with a cow" scenario, according to the sardonic VO. Acts of physical love are not found in Dogville, given repression of even incipient expressions of it, while criminal sexual aggression is wordlessly tolerated in the pious village.

Furthermore, the serialized nocturnal rape of Grace may be taken as a form of "primal crime" that unifies the village in shared guilt and uneasy knowledge of the (otherwise glossed over and unspoken) damage they are capable of doing to fellow humans (Rose 2004). In this view, aggression against the designated outsider is the lubricant of a tense peace among the villagers. The village's women do not rape but are implicated in maintaining silence toward their husbands' depravities. Indeed, they actively harass Grace as the source of problems, thereby cementing the unification of the town against her alien presence in communal collaboration in Otherizing sadism.

In von Trier's construction of it, prevailing market relations have placed the village on the losing side of the class war. Market relations foster an environment *in* which—and a method *through* which—the villagers transfer their deprivations onto someone more vulnerable; hence, the graphic sadism toward Grace in the second half of the film. Initially, the villagers drop hints that emphasize her vulnerability and her "debt" to them—the same villagers who are themselves exposed and vulnerable within the framework of the class system and its array of punitive measures. This perspective is expressed in the stilted idiom of the capitalist market during the town meeting when Grace is assessed with respect to her "cost" to the village. Privately, the concept is expressed more brusquely. Chuck reveals that he has thought of turning Grace in when they first talk tensely and openly. Later, Chuck's obnoxious son, Jason, makes more pointed threats, as the preadolescent child is able to sense the barometric pressure of debt that the community has assessed against Grace. In a prelude to rape, Chuck presses further at her vulnerability and states that the FBI had been searching for her that day.

Grace's envelopment in the head-spinning double bind of being subject to exploitation and overt violation by the villagers, alongside her dependence on them, is made excruciatingly clear. It is, however, the situation of all workers, particularly the working class, under capitalism. Workers are at once exploited but simultaneously ensconced within a disorienting state of dependence on the same class system that exploits their labor and that may expel them from the labor force into outright pauperization. The circumstance is worse for undocumented and non-naturalized workers, an increasingly prevalent phenomenon across industrialized nations, to whom Grace's character may also refer symptomatically (Joiner 2008).

In the character of Ben, one finds a bravura critique of U.S. labor as having had its class consciousness and solidarity largely eviscerated. Ben is a perpetually dirty man with shameful ("open secret") tastes for booze and brothels. Thus, defeat is a way of life.

When he smuggles Grace out of town in his truck for ten dollars, he seizes the opportunity to violate her in the back of the truck. Ben's rationalization for what he is doing is furnished in a capitalist vocabulary that marks its intersection with (mind/body) exploitation. Relying on frequent references to the "freight industry" and its lexicon, Ben the violator states that he is taking a "surcharge" from Grace for carrying "dangerous cargo" (namely, her). Once again, Grace's debt is cast in monetary terms—a conflation of economic and (piously unspoken) sexual exploitation—and then sadistically assessed.

Upon returning to the village, Ben righteously proclaims that "The freight industry cannot take sides!"; it is his cowardly, semantically tortured admission of having sold out Grace. It is also couched in The Man's terms during Ben's fleeting moment of being the deputized exploiter within class relations that have pushed him down into what he is. In itself, such characterizations of fictional people may be interesting (if disturbing) for parallels with those subjects whose minds have been colonized by the terms and experience of exploitation, even down to the lexical level of accounting for one's actions. In this instance, the characterization may be also understood as the type of subject that the market order may regularly produce, particularly in the market-steered United States, as seen from contemporary Europe.[3]

Plus ça change . . .

Dogville skirts at times uncomfortably close to perturbing the delicate membrane between critique of classism and classism itself in casting its gaze on the defects of the Usonian market-oriented order. *Manderlay* breaches such demarcations to an unfortunate effect. Von Trier is, of course, not the first prominent filmmaker to do so. While they praise his unconventional narratives and rejection of the hero paradigm, Michael Ryan and Douglas Kellner (1988) critique Robert Altman's cinema in similar terms. In their appraisal, Altman "does not target the underlying institutions" and their part in an unsatisfactory social reality. Instead his films tend to fault "the very victims of that system" (1988: 273). While von Trier is more attentive to systemic constraints than Altman (e.g., the debt industry), he meets and even raises Altman's jaundiced vision and victim-blaming in *Manderlay*.

Consistent with the corpus, *Manderlay* revolves around the failed idealist and positions Grace as this signature von Triersian figure. I will argue that this particular rendition of the motif is more Right wing and cynical than in von Trier's other versions of it (although, in interviews dealing with the film, von Trier identifies as an off-screen activist against the Danish Right [Nicodemus 2005]). Perhaps for the assumption that proto-Leftism must circulate within the auteur film, if even around its edges, scholars have been relatively muted in teasing out the hoary implications of *Manderlay*. In this vein, Caroline Bainbridge assays to finesse the point with acknowledgment that, "There is much in the film that can be read as reproducing the very racist assumptions that the film simultaneously sets out to expose" (2007: 154). Bainbridge allows that the film's ostensible message about the colonized mind doing the chores of the colonizer is in evidence "(albeit rather clumsily)" in its execution (2007: 155). Jayson Harsin also carefully attaches qualifications in his efforts to partly rehabilitate the film. He argues that one must view it through a Brechtian scrim and account for its strategy of exaggeration: "Otherwise, this turns out to be one of the most ignominiously racist films since *Birth of a Nation*" (2006: 5). It is, in other words, a tall order to rehabilitate *Manderlay*. By contrast, I will pursue an interpretation of *Manderlay* that analyzes its variations on the thematic motif of the failed idealist. This approach also unpacks the contrasts among *Manderlay*'s protagonists as well as the narrative logic that drives the film.

Grace squares with the established pattern through her idealism conjoined to deep-seated personal failings. She is sexually naive almost to the point of childishness, a failing that makes her vulnerable to Timothy's manipulations that, in turn, indirectly set up apocalyptic disaster for her idealistic project at Manderlay. Grace's stubborn insistence on equality is presented as a *flaw* in the film, the germ of the abject failure of her ambitions to bring about "New Times" at Manderlay. While Grace's methods for occasioning equality are undoubtedly lacking, she is simultaneously depicted as behaving in line with her ideals. She demonstrably shares the sacrifice of the African Americans and eats dirt during tough times, follows the general will even when she finds it noxious (meting out capital punishment to Old Wilma with her own hands), and prepares to end her tenure at Manderlay after the harvest has arrived, as she said she would. However, in the world that von Trier constructs at Manderlay, Grace's idealism clashes with a "hard-nosed" reality that African Americans are "not ready" to be other than self-defeating patsies and slaves.

Reading *Manderlay* against the grain of the failed idealist motif yields insights into what disappoints about the film, about where, in other words, it careens from a critical and discomforting piece of contrarian discourse into right-wing polemic. In particular, the father's citation of one racist trope after another in the opening sequence is confirmed, with exclamation marks, by the subsequent narrative in both generalities and specifics. Wilhelm is the conservative black man on the plantation as indicated by his manner, costume (bow tie and suit coat), and "natural" assumption of privilege as authority and spokesperson, the full extent of which is only revealed at the end when he lays claim to the "steady hand" that composed "Mam's Law" that governed the plantation for generations. In the closing sequence, he forcefully voices the view that blacks cannot manage their own affairs and require paternalistic, racialized plantation rule to organize their lives for them down to the minutia—*for their own good*, as Wilhelm indignantly insists. Wilhelm's blueprint for social order pivots on cataloguing the African Americans via a "one" through "seven" scale—a scheme dutifully followed by whites and blacks alike at Manderlay.

With all of these clues at hand, it is straightforward to construe Wilhelm as another version of the von Triersian idealist, in this case, one who pursues retrograde "utopia" driven by tradition with fanatical vengeance. Wilhelm's departure from von Trier's pattern is that his cruel handiwork in constructing a chauvinistic order is that of an insider to the community—thus "organic," and not an alien imposition from outside. Wilhelm's insistence that blacks should be subject to white subjugation and relentlessly inserted into the divisive and contrived status distinctions of Mam's Law makes him an "idealist" with a distinctly Rightist cast.

Furthermore, in contrast with other von Triersian idealists, Wilhelm's backward-looking utopia is presented as having "got it right." The views that Wilhelm expresses at the conclusion of the film check off all of the boxes of the father's opening racist speech. Judgments made by narrative events and outcomes in the film all go against Grace's anti-racist efforts. As Wilhelm offers explanation for the bizarre rigors of the Mam's Law volume that he wrote, a montage of flashbacks underscores that his blueprint was indeed correct while Grace was apparently too self-absorbed to notice. For example, the display of people graded in their essence as "one" through "seven" and presenting themselves in the orchard below Mam's porch for her inspection is defended for enabling the blacks to stand in the shade (backed with a cut to supporting visuals) *as if* there are no other means of finding shade, ones that would not simultaneously reify Mam's authority and the subordinate status of the African Americans with its further pejorative ("one" through "seven") gradations and divisions.

In the closing sequence, Wilhelm claims that the African Americans were "not ready" for a post-slavery existence. In a body slam at Grace's presumed "liberal guilt," Wilhelm also acerbically posits that she must have assumed the African Americans were too "dumb" (Wilhelm's word) to have previously scaled the fence of Manderlay had they really wanted to do so. These two claims do not square with each other, as they pull in contrary directions of expecting too much *and* too little of African Americans. However, von Trier's *Manderlay* allows the Right-winger to effectively get away with having it "both ways," to be correct while positing mutually exclusive notions and, all the while, avoiding interrogation of his fanatical idealism with the rigor that is directed at other von Triersian protagonists across his corpus.

It is an unhappy fact that, under duress, victims have at times abetted their tormentors (e.g., by acquiescence or behaving in conformity to caricatures about themselves). It is also an ugly feature of history that factions within subjugated groups have been recruited into being junior partners in oppression (e.g., local elites abetting the British *Raj* in Colonial India). Von Trier's addendum to these histories of domination is to position the lieutenants in meting out oppression as the intellectual authors of them rather than as opportunists. While the dying Mam's final wish is for the text of Mam's Law to be destroyed, presumably to end the apartheid regime of which she had been figurehead, Wilhelm's project throughout the film is to restore the racist vision that his hand authored.

While von Trier attempts a provocative statement that denies easy pieties with *Manderlay*, intentions are not the final criterion. To paraphrase the father in *Dogville*: Is the resultant film "good enough" to satisfy an ambitious remit? In *Manderlay*, African

Americans fail to thrive even under markedly favorable conditions. Indeed, the regime that Grace implements tilts unfairly toward black interests over those of the former ruling family. A significant flaw in her project is the heavy-handedness of its implementation that kept the guns on which it initially depended out of sight. This presents a useful political critique in positing that means and ends cannot be so easily detached. Where ethical action is concerned, an aphorism is instructive: *Justice is not the destination, it is the path itself.*

However, von Trier's efforts to confront the United States and its ethics collapse into snide caricature of some of its most historically victimized people. In particular, the film suggests that the African Americans are both unable and unwilling to dismantle the status quo even in conditions that, however "imperfect," are at least highly favorable to doing so. Grace's attempts to re-order the culture of Manderlay actually worsen the material situation and are finally met by Wilhelm's demand that the old plantation order be explicitly restored. Given that the reordering of culture fails to alter subjectivities, the film invites the conclusion that something deeper and structural—racial essence itself—accounts for the characters' conditions.

In the opening sequence, Grace obstructs a whipping to be visited on Timothy by the white regime at Manderlay. By the end of the film, however, Grace's conduct has dissolved into that of the apartheid-esque regime. She personally delivers a beating of disfiguring viciousness to Timothy on the same rack. All that occurred across the 130-minute runtime was that a stubborn Grace learned the impossibility of overcoming status quo relations between black and white. A further—and risible—implication is that latent inside an advocate for egalitarianism is the "real" and visceral racist trying to surface. In other words, a film that denies a "happy ending" can be taken as thumbing its nose at classical Hollywood convention (and as part of distinguished tradition of such: e.g., *Casablanca* [Michael Curtiz 1942], *Bonnie and Clyde* [Arthur Penn 1967], *Chinatown* [Roman Polanski 1974]). However, von Trier also denies the possibility of even a modicum of dignity in defeat for Grace's project.

For the spectator, the trials that constitute *Manderlay*'s narrative may seem at first blush to present marked, if uneven, progress: annulling unfair contracts, crafting representative mechanisms, sharing sacrifice in times of desperate want, and finally realizing a harvest. A good deal of this is skillfully constructed and poignantly staged for the camera. For example, it is wrenching to witness Grace as she carries out the execution of Old Wilma. The act collides violently with Grace's own principles, but, at great cost in emotional distress, she faithfully enacts the community's verdict (and insures that it is not carried out with Jack's raging vengeance). However, read from the closing sequence back, the narrative events are cynical toward the characters and the anticipated audience response. In this view, these moments are collapsed into a ruse that fills the time and the screen before the closer/kicker "punch line": Where apartheid is concerned, *plus ça change, plus c'est la meme*—and *it is the victims themselves who demand that it be that way.*[4]

Timothy is depicted as a truculent but fiercely proud black man who will not pretend to have been co-opted into the liberal white project implemented by Grace merely to please her. Across the narrative, he appears to become haltingly recruited into the project. However, in the closing sequence, Timothy is exposed as a hustler and a fraud. His "pride" is an instrument to secure access to women and money that is not his. The emphasis on the character being called "Proud Timothy" may readily be taken as an indictment of notions such as "Black Pride" since he closely follows the racially chauvinistic "script" enunciated at the beginning by the openly racist father. The father's world-weary racism is further confirmed by vigilante black-on-black killing occasioned by Timothy's theft of the community's patrimony. However, the white patriarch is not the only character to hold these hoary views. Wilhelm does too (although he phrases his chauvinism with more verbal skill than the father); and *Manderlay*'s narrative and stylistic grammar affirm their deeply held views.

However, Grace is constructed as needing to be socialized into knowing what racists like her father and Wilhelm already know. Grace speaks the language of contemporary liberalism, earnestly but stiffly and without the rigors of worldly experience behind her: "We made them what they are." She follows this up by putting the ruling family on notice that, "If you don't obey the law, we will compel you to do so." An idealist has, in other words, arrived at Manderlay. However, her flaws as an idealist are in play in her implicit threat of force while upholding laws that are laudable in themselves. Grace also uses the muscle that backs her words to effectively enslave the white family. In doing so, Grace peremptorily rejects an effort toward integration within a framework of racial and class equality. She merely reassigns the signifying valence of skin color. Her demand that the whites of the former ruling family serve dinner in black face underscores this—as she belatedly realizes but not before betraying her character's racial insensitivity (again, in contrast with the father's and Wilhelm's unerringly clear-eyed vision).

As a von Triersian idealist, Grace's well-meaning plans occasion one train wreck after another. In some cases, the failure is personal as when she confuses Jack with Jim. Worse still, Grace dismantles Mam's orchard—where the blacks had presented themselves to white authority hovering above—in a showy act of symbolic politics. The gesture leaves Manderlay vulnerable to the dust storm. Shorn of the shield furnished by the trees, the storm suffocates the crops and occasions severe deprivation for Manderlay's residents. It is an unsubtle hint that the "stable" hierarchy of racist tradition provided paternalist "benefits" and "protection" against the ineffably deep forces of an untamed nature.

The "one" through "seven" classification system into which each black subject of Manderlay is inserted is exclusively composed of pejorative categories ("chameleon," "loser," "clown") aside from the baldly incongruous category of "proud." Given the unmistakably derogatory qualities of "two" through "seven" (and the fact that an ostensible "one"—Elizabeth—can pass as a "seven" and vice versa for Timothy), the question is begged: "Proud" *of what, exactly*? However, the most insidious aspect of this detailed blueprint for humiliation and oppression is that it was authored by Wilhelm to keep his fellow blacks in submission. Moreover, Wilhelm's blunt endorsement of apartheid is apparently shared by the black community since he lets Grace in on the "secret" in front of the whole group with their apparent approval. In this view, race *should in fact* be coterminous with destiny and a person's potential should be tightly harnessed in what little variability that hardcore traditionalism allows for a given identity. Via Wilhelm, the "idealist" fanatic whose ideas seem to "work," *Manderlay* enthrones patently unjust traditionalist stasis over messy progress toward betterment.

In other moments, Grace's repeated and abstracted emphasis on the construct of "freedom" for the blacks makes her sound like a neo-conservative—particularly as the film was contemporary with early phases of the ongoing invasion/occupation of Iraq. The final VO refers to the perils of refusing the United States' "helping hand" while von Trier makes the link between text and global context manifest in an interview (Nicodemus 2005). Remarkably, for a filmmaker who goes to such lengths to deny naive sentimentality in the world of his films, von Trier indicates credulousness about certain moments within "real world" politics. In contrast with the vast majority of European citizens, von Trier slips beyond gullibility if he had seriously believed that the neo-conservatives' motives for the invasion and occupation of Iraq corresponded with the associated PR campaigns emphasis on "democracy" and "human rights"—rather than a bare-knuckled resource grab, cynically and criminally engineered under false pretenses. Moreover, von Trier's claims do not fit with *Manderlay* since, significantly, Grace's flaws demonstrably do not include assuming authority indefinitely or doing so for her own material aggrandizement. Moreover, if *Manderlay* is victim-blaming the African Americans, von Trier's defense of it as an allegory may recycle the same victim blaming cast of mind toward the people of Iraq. Despite the egregious Hussein regime, Iraq has not been a "basket case" in recent history. It was a prosperous nation up through 1990 prior to the advent of the 1991 Gulf War and economic sanctions (Goss 2002).

Numerous examples put the lie to von Trier's dismissal of formerly oppressed people's capacity to rise to the occasion of self-determination. As deprived a nation as Nicaragua, long a nationwide Somoza family plantation until liberation in 1979, instituted a disciplined, functioning, and enduring republic under highly unfavorable circumstances after its revolution (Rossett and Vandermeer 1983). The nation where I reside, Spain, presents a living organic monument to people's efficacy in changing the course of their governance from fascism to a vibrant liberal order. And, of course, there are other examples.

While noted for making marked shifts across films with respect to genre and style, in *Manderlay*, von Trier leans heavily on the concepts rehearsed in *Dogville*. As in *Dogville*, the film is shot on a soundstage while VOs by John Hurt furnish back-story peppered with sardonic commentary. *Manderlay*'s closing credit sequence is a powerful moment, although it extends the debt to *Dogville*. The closing credits musical selection—David Bowie's "Young Americans"—is reprised from *Dogville* and is once again accompanied by a montage of squalor and desperation within the world's "richest," "most powerful" nation (in this case, as these conditions intersect with the lives of black citizens). Civil rights demonstrations, Martin Luther King, Jr. (in his casket), neo-Nazi demonstrators ironically guarded by black police officers, black shoe shiners kneeling before white customers, U.S. poverty at third world standards, and lynchings—all feature in the extended montage of photos. The final image presents a black man cleaning a statue of Abraham Lincoln. The discourse of *Manderlay*, as channeled through Wilhelm, asserts that black subjects scripted out their status in cognizance of not being "prepared" for more (while "preparation" for improvement is deferred beyond the horizon). To witness and appraise *Manderlay* is to see a filmmaker whose edgy qualities have unfortunately succumbed to tired and cynical ones.

SECTION IV
MICHAEL WINTERBOTTOM

CHAPTER 9

"Lost Without Him"

Michael Winterbottom describes himself as having had a "'worrying number of retrospectives'" on his work by the time he was 42 years old (quoted in Bedell 2004: 1). Retrospectives have been launched in Spain, Italy, and Germany while Geraldine Bedell (2004) characterizes recognition in Winterbottom's native United Kingdom as more grudging. Reviews of, and box office for, Winterbottom's films have been variable; consider, for example, the critical bipolarity that greeted *Code 46* (Goss 2007). At the high end of the spectrum, British commentators weigh in with lofty appraisals of Winterbottom's work. The *Guardian*'s Peter Bradshaw et al., claim that British film would be "lost without him" (2003: 8) while the *Daily Telegraph*'s Sukhdev Sandhu hailed Winterbottom's *In This World* as "'the best British film of my lifetime'" (quoted in Bedell 2004: 3). *Jude* and *24 Hour Party People* stand out as the Winterbottom films that reached "a large audience . . . as well as critical success" (Allison 2005: 1). Winterbottom has yet to achieve the stature of Almodóvar or von Trier (both of whom are older and began their cinema careers during the 1980s). However, the striking qualities of Winterbottom's work indicate a filmmaker reaching his prime as an international presence crafting innovative, resonant, and often political films with a human rights accent.

Born in 1961 in Lancashire, Winterbottom read English at Oxford. He trained for a year in a film and television course in Bristol after which he landed an assignment for six months "'holding Lindsay Anderson's cup of tea'" (quoted in Bedell 2004: 5). Thereafter, with training as an editor, he worked in television at Thames and then with the British Broadcasting Corporation (Allison 2005). After breaking out of the editing suite, his first efforts in the director's chair were two documentaries on Ingmar Bergman followed by several made-for-television dramas.

Table 9.1. Winterbottom's Feature Films

A Mighty Heart (2007)
The Road to Guantanamo (Co-directed with Mat Whitecross)(2006)
A Cock and Bull Story (2005)
9 Songs (2004)
Code 46 (2003)
In This World (2002)
24 Hour Party People (2002)
The Claim (2000)
With or Without You (1999)
Wonderland (1999)
I Want You (1998)
Welcome to Sarajevo (1997)
Jude (1996)
Butterfly Kiss (1995)

During his early work in television, Deborah Allison claims that Winterbottom formed "the most important collaborative relationships that came to dominate his working ethos" across more than a decade (2005: 2). Allison cites Winterbottom's creative liaisons with scriptwriter Frank Cottrell Boyce and producer Andrew Eaton as foundational. Boyce penned the television drama *Forget About Me*, broadcast in 1990, and has since written six screenplays for Winterbottom's cinematic releases. In an effort to leave television and its attendant mores behind, Winterbottom and Eaton formed Revolution Films in 1994. The company has since been behind all but one of Winterbottom's films and has also backed several other directors' efforts. Winterbottom's other frequent collaborators include film editor Trevor Waite, who cut Winterbottom's first seven films, and Mark Tildesley, who has executed production design on six features. In front of the camera, several actors have made multiple appearances in Winterbottom's corpus—Shirley Henderson, Steve Coogan, Rob Brydon, and Christopher Eccleston.

Winterbottom is prolific: "In a country in which it is notoriously difficult to make films, Michael Winterbottom works at a prodigious rate" (Bedell 2004: 6), a fecundity that is in itself "an unparalleled achievement in the contemporary British cinema" (Allison 2005: 2). Since his cinematic debut, *Butterfly Kiss* in 1995, he has steered 13 more features to the screen through 2007's *A Mighty Heart*—an average of more than one film per year. The corpus of films is further noteworthy for hurtling across genres while presenting a farrago of "mainstream conventions and avant-garde excesses" (McGill 2004: 10), both across and within particular films. Where genre is concerned, the curriculum vitae includes a drama (*Jude*) and a Western (*The Claim*), each adapted from nineteenth-century source material, bio-pic/comedy (*24 Hour Party People*), romantic comedy (*With or Without You*), road film/black comedy (*Butterfly Kiss*), erotica (*9 Songs*), science fiction (*Code 46*), and documentary (*Road to Guantánamo*).   Like a number of other noteworthy filmmakers (e.g., Stanley Kubrick, Francis Coppola, Satyajit Ray), Winterbottom has frequently adapted from previously existing literature. *Jude, The Claim, A Cock and Bull Story, Welcome to Sarajevo*, and *A Mighty Heart* are adaptations; the first three were works of fiction and the latter two were journalistic efforts. He also flirted with, and backed out of, directing U.S. product *Good Will Hunting* (Gus Van Sant 1997) and *The Cider House Rules* (Lasse Hallström 1999) due to wariness about studio interference (McGill 2004).

After having co-founded Revolution Films, Winterbottom has maintained a measure of artistic control over his output. Nevertheless, securing funding to make films can be harrowing. Winterbottom was incredulous about obtaining monies to make *In This World*. "'We approached the BBC and The Film Consortium. There was no script, and we wanted to use non-actors. A lot of it was going to be in a foreign language'" (quoted in Bedell 2004: 2). Indeed, Winterbottom did not understand much of the dialogue that was largely reconstructed in post-production (Allison 2005). Despite the atypical profile of the film, the BBC and Film Consortium came forward with a very modest budget of 1 million pounds (1.45 million USDs as of January 1, 2002 [www.x-rates.com/cgi-bin/hlookup.cgi]). The film's fortunes and visibility were raised when it captured the Golden Bear at the Berlin International Film Festival, beating out the better-known and more generously budgeted *The Hours* (Stephen Daldry 2002). The prize helped trigger extended international distribution.

To both publicize and fund *9 Songs*, Team Winterbottom exhibited the film "in market" at the Cannes Film Festival. He says, "We were showing it because we needed to raise money to complete the film as we were funding it ourselves . . . (P)eople were queuing to try and get into it, they had to put on extra screenings . . ." (Hennigan 2005: 3). A taste for being daring has helped the cause as *9 Songs* has been called "the most sexually graphic movie to be passed by the UK censors" (Hennigan 2005: 1). From this experience, Winterbottom draws the conclusion that, "Weirdly, it shows that filmmakers have been censoring themselves much more than the BBFC (British Board of Film Classification) has been censoring them!" (Hennigan 2005: 3).

More recently, Winterbottom exhibited *Road to Guantánamo* at the Berlin International Film Festival in February 2006 as a means of arranging exhibition deals in as many countries as possible (Stone 2006). When the film made its general release in March 2006, Team Winterbottom opted for simultaneous distribution via British television, the Internet, and DVD in the hopes that the channels would all synergize each other (as they did to some extent in the United Kingdom via journalistic attention, e.g., Rose 2006). Their interests were not solely (or even primarily) commercial. The filmmaker and his collaborators took timeliness as a matter of great importance given ongoing abuse at Guantánamo—of prisoners and of legal precepts, as appraised, for example, by lawyers from prestigious U.S. law schools (Holmes 2006; Horton 2008a, 2008b, 2008c).

A Brief Survey of the Winterbottom Signature

A couple of Winterbottom's early films appear to traffic in conventional sensibilities (*Jude, With or Without You, The Claim*). In this vein, *Jude* looks at first blush like an accomplished exemplar of what Mike Wayne (2002) refers to as a British heritage film. Seeing it through the prism of Winterbottom's later films reveals *Jude*'s experimental and challenging touches. Stylistically, these touches include razor-sharp cutting between scenes that are not a frame longer than they have to be, changes in film stock, montages to convey character's subjective recollection (along with thematic motifs that would reemerge later: the horrors of childhood, "outsiders," and forbidden love in a rigid world). Six years later, with *In This World*, Winterbottom's methods are less devoted to *Jude*-style "beautiful" craftsmanship. He says that, for *In This World*, "'We didn't tell the characters to be happy or sad, because we couldn't do that, we didn't share their culture. We simply organized the journey, the mechanics'" and then filmed as they struggled toward asylum (quoted in Bedell 2004: 3). Shooting on location, and often spontaneously as well, is central to the method of filming that has emerged across Winterbottom's career. The director's playful tendencies extend the tradition of the French New Wave as when characters blast through the "fourth wall." In one such instance, a janitor cleans the bathroom in *24 Hour Party People* as an unremarkable background character. He suddenly abandons character and addresses the camera. He identifies himself as Howard Devoto and claims to not recall the just-finished scene, ostensibly recreated from his own life. During the scene, the actor (Martin Hancock) who plays Devoto as a man a quarter-century younger "shagged" Tony Wilson's wife Lindsay in a nearby bathroom stall.

Winterbottom pulls virtually all of the cinematic tricks from the toolkit in his corpus of films. He can be characterized as a showy, post-MTV filmmaker whose films liberally use formal techniques of camera, sound, and editing to create heightened effects. The toolkit includes different film stocks within and across scenes (including shifts from color to black-and-white and back), frequent hand-held shots, fast- and slow-motion, overexposure, split screens, sound bridges, archival footage, irises, subjective point-of-view (POV) shots, and frequent montages. Even title cards are given an imprimatur as in the undulating, rave-inspired ones for *24 Hour Party People*. Novelty becomes Winterbottom as *A Cock and Bull Story* uses a black screen to simulate the blank page in Laurence Sterne's 1759 novel, *The Life and Opinions of Tristram Shandy, Gentleman*.

A scene in the opening sequence of *24 Hour Party People* presents a stylistic *tour-de-force* that showcases many of Winterbottom's tendencies. In the scene, Tony Wilson (played by Steve Coogan) provides first-person narration that reconstructs the Sex Pistols 1976 show in Manchester, United Kingdom. Wilson addresses the camera in order to narrate from the perspective of the early twenty-first century present, even as he is clad in 1970s costume with his arm around his wife of the time (played by Shirley Henderson) while they witness the show as audience members. Thus, Wilson simultaneously enacts being the narrator and providing first-person non-diegetic recollections about the past *and* being within the film's diegesis in the past. Wilson then inventories other notables in the same audience, such as the members of Buzzcocks and Joy Division/New Order. Archival footage provides flashforwards (within the ongoing flashback) to these bands' later successes (modest in commercial terms for the Buzzcocks, massive and mainstream for New Order as demonstrated by footage of an arena show). The Sex Pistols are played by actors reconstructing the 1976 concert and, in other shots, are captured in archival footage of the original band in grainy film stock. Boundaries between the document and the reconstruction are thus toyed with. In a couple of shots, actors playing the audience members "pogo" (dance) in front of back-projected archival footage of the Sex Pistols; thus, the document and the reconstruction are literally placed into the same frame.

Pop music is also an important touchstone of Winterbottom's films. Indeed, three of his films take their titles from pop songs that also appear on the soundtrack: *I Want You* (Elvis Costello), *With or Without You* (U2), and *24 Hour Party People* (Happy Mondays). The importance of pop music in the films begins with the cinematic debut *Butterfly Kiss* as Eunice parries her victims in convenience stores by asking about a song she cannot name (that turns out to be New Order's "World in Motion"). All of *24 Hour Party People* revolves around the music industry, with a Manchester accent. In Winterbottom's world, non-diegetic music at times transmits commentary about what is on screen: Coldplay's "Warning Sign" accompanies a devastated Maria's recollections in the final scene of *Code 46* (with the repeated lyric, "I miss you"). Bobby McFerrin's "Don't Worry, Be Happy" sonically—and sardonically—garnishes the arrival of oblivious UN functionaries to the implosion of the Federal Republic of Yugoslavia in *Welcome to Sarajevo*. The closing credit sequence of *24 Hour Party People* cleverly uses musical cues that telegraph the temporal and narrative trajectory. The musical selection segues from Joy Division's early post-punk "Love Will Tear Us Apart" to the same Manchester band's later incarnation as New Order as it delivers an upbeat dance cut, "Here to Stay."

Some repeated formal elements are particularly significant in Winterbottom's films. For example, cutting is at times so rapid (e.g., establishing shots of a second or two) as to evoke the restless modern experience of "channel surfing." Despite having generally gone out of style, VOs are used in many of Winterbottom's films. First-person VO furnishes the audience with privileged access to a character's thoughts that may also foster identification with the character (Wood 2002). In a similar vein of identification, many Winterbottom films cue their concern with accessing characters' phenomenal experiences in heavy use of flashbacks (e.g., *I Want You*, *A Cock and Bull Story*, *A Mighty Heart*) that sometimes frame the whole narrative (*Butterfly Kiss*, *The Road to Guantánamo*, *9 Songs*). Hallucinations (*I Want You*, *24 Hour Party People*) and dream sequences (*Code 46*, *A Cock and Bull Story*) also endow the audience with privileged access to characters' interior worlds.[1]

Where narrative is concerned, Winterbottom's films can appear meandering and choppy. For example, *Welcome to Sarajevo*'s plot is amorphous and "ambient" (war-zone setting) until the protagonist Henderson seizes on the orphanage as a cause almost 30 minutes into the runtime. This is partly deliberate. Collaborator Frank Cottrell Boyce comments that in his scripts, "'Characters disappear then reappear unexpectedly, or make a huge splash and never turn up again. I love films that float like that. They exist more in the present tense somehow, because you can't see where they're going'" (quoted in Allison 2005: 6). Nonetheless, in the recent *A Cock and Bull Story*, complicated shifts in chronology are handled in bravura fashion. The film's jig-sawed time-shifts are incorporated into the comic motif of Steve Coogan as Tristram Shandy repeatedly noting that he is getting ahead of himself in the story—given that his character has yet to be born!

As with the French New Wave and its many echoes through film history, Winterbottom's films are often characterized by significant and provocative vignettes that prompt moods and inferences. The tendency contrasts with the "A → B → C" chains of causality that typify classical Hollywood narratives. This is partly because Winterbottom relies heavily on improvisation. Moreover, Winterbottom posits, "I think scenes where characters sit down and tell each other their history, or what's going on inside their head, are fake. I prefer to watch people, and hope that if you watch them closely enough, you might be able to imagine what's going on inside their heads" (Hennigan 2005: 2). Thus, in constructing and presenting the characters, gestures and offhand comments weigh heavily. In an uproarious example, reluctant dad-to-be Eddie in *Wonderland* betrays his doubts about becoming a father by brandishing a video of David Lynch's *Eraserhead* (1977)—that is, a horror-style film about a deformed monster/baby.

In the balance of this chapter, I will examine several thematic motifs that characterize Winterbottom's films. First, I will discuss his treatment of the family, an "Ideological State Apparatus" (Althusser 1994), and its various spin-offs. I take the construction of gender, romantic relationships, and children as being implicated within the presentation of the family as an ideological institution. Within Winterbottom's world, romance is not simply a dyadic and hormonal-driven matter but is immersed in tensions between social convention and taboo. Hence, forbidden love is a regular feature of the narratives. The pattern begins with the proto-lesbian serial killers of the debut film *Butterfly Kiss* and then extends to the scandalously unmarried, mixed parentage family of *Jude* and the Oedipal taboos of *Code 46*. In Winterbottom's films, implication within (primal) crimes also clinches bonds between characters through the "transfer of guilt." Chapter 10 follows with a cross-examination of Winterbottom's films and their intriguing posture toward realism and truth. Winterbottom's style and generic material (including bio-pic and documentary) at once foreground reflexivity and also probe the question of realism and, more importantly, the issue of truth. Several films in the corpus concern media and media workers and exhibit abiding concern with the constructions of reality more broadly in media-saturated societies. Chapter 11 turns to the presentation of the United States in Winterbottom's films. In stark contrast with von Trier's corpus, in Winterbottom's fictional films, the United States is presented in a manner that is often favorable to its guiding mythologies about itself *(*e.g., with regard to capitalism and class mobility in *The Claim*). Chapter 11, and this section on Winterbottom, concludes with a detailed examination of human rights as they are implicated, and championed, in several of Winterbottom's films.

Fraught Affiliations

In situating Winterbotttom's filmic discourse, I begin with the premise that the family is an ideological institution. Indeed, it is construed as one of Louis Althusser's Ideological State Apparatuses (ISAs) in his groundbreaking 1968 essay, (along with, e.g., the educational system, the church, culture industries) (Althusser 1994: 90). In Althusserian terms, this means that, within the family, the ruling ideologies of a given time and place tend to be put into practice on a massive scale. Althusserian ideology is profoundly "hands on" and deeply concerned with the practical, everyday rituals that seem "natural" and "centering" for subjects of them. For Althusser, recruitment into ideology is like answering to the call of one's name and, as such, hardly seems to require reflection (1994: 108). In this view, to be an ardent Catholic need not require fluency in explaining arcane dogmas on which belief ostensibly pivots (e.g., how a blessed bread host becomes literal body and blood via ritual). Rather, being Catholic is embodied in organizing one's time around the mass, being seen (and seeing who else is) in the church and its ritual, encountering the people whom one knows on this terrain with the attendant cues, expectations and practices. As a corollary, ideology in action is typically *not* rational since most social organization requires (sometimes massive) deferral of (individual and/or group) interests. In this view, ideology plays on emotions, desires, and idealizations more than playing on what *is*. Nevertheless, it cannot be stitched from whole cloth; material reality must be alluded to in some measure for ideology to make and maintain a claim on the subject.

The ideology that one expects to be reproduced in the family is the ideology of the ruling class for its commanding role in steering the social organization of production. In this view, gender status may be taken as part-and-parcel of class striation in which economic rewards are differentially allocated to men and women. Class division outside the home may be thusly reproduced and recast as gendered status within the home (for males, typically backed by "bread-winner" status). Also notice that Althusser is alive to hiccups, slip-ups, and fumbles, such that ruling class ideology is never mechanically (but is often grudgingly) reproduced. Even as the family reproduces ruling ideology, that same ideology simultaneously depends upon having prevailed, bottom-up, in the ISAs such as the family.

How does this intersect with Winterbottom's corpus? A significant share of Winterbottom's films orients to the family and some of the family's subsidiaries and spin-offs: namely, gender practices, the romantic couple, and the child. Of course, emphasis on the family animates many films; "rom-coms," for example, in which the formation or preservation of the germ of the family in the heterosexual couple is at stake. What is different about Winterbottom's treatment? I posit that Winterbottom's presentation of the family (often, but not always) tugs on and strains the threads that hold the family-oriented ideology together. In this manner, Winterbottom's films at times reveal the fragile contingency of the ruling ideology. In turn, ruling ideology depends on being renewed and reproduced in order to hold subjects of society within the centrifugal force of existing authority and its material concomitants and practices.

In looking at the question of the family as an ISA in Winterbottom's corpus, I decompose the issue further. Most generally, gender practices find their Ground Zero within the family. In Winterbottom's films, as in the world generally, men are by tradition "on top." A recent report from the United Kingdom demonstrates the extent to which, despite laudable gains of several "waves" of feminism, gender traditionalism forms a large part of the template through which subjects are compelled to live. To wit, the Equal Opportunities Commission of Scotland reports that, "sex equality is still generations away" as it "calls for urgent action to close the stubborn gaps that persist in pay, family life, public services, justice, safety, and power"—indicated, for instance, by full-time wages that are 14 percent lower for women than men (Equal Opportunities Commission 2007: 1). Given that men have come to recognize the fragility of traditional privileges, Winterbottom's films capture some of the anxiety about what men have to lose.

However, social conventions reach deeper than the pay stub and demand further elaboration. In the psychoanalytic account of development, the Oedipal drama endows the male child with a deeply ingrained sense of taboo; in particular, to suppress the sexual feelings harbored for mother (Freud 1991: 372–382). However, this is not simply a case of keeping a lid on something and acting stoical. The lesson goes to the soul of the subject in society. The post-Oedipal child internalizes a complex of relationships in which the more powerful parental authority is in a position to lay down the law and stake claim to the spouse, issuing veiled threats to the erotically fired child from a position of authority with all of its attendant pomp. In other words, the child internalizes a model not only of the family—but of the functional behavior of an entire social order. This order is reproduced not only through sanction and taboo but via elaborate schedules of reward. In abiding by the family hierarchy, the likelihood is proffered that the male child may one day behave as father (i.e., enjoy the pleasures of carrying on with someone like mother, wield authority in the domain of the family) as the cycle is reproduced. If nothing else, the Oedipal drama's wide circulation as a master Western myth speaks to the abiding concern with the internalization of social order, submission to authority and its taboos—and their proximity to the enticements of reward.

The cycle that reproduces authority and its internalization is, however, disrupted if one posits that fixation on the Oedipal drama is not the end of the story—in part, because it is not the beginning. Gaylyn Studlar (2000) confronts the male-enthroning Oedipal drama that posits woman as lacking. She emphasizes that the earlier (more "primal") fixation with mother is never wholly or even mostly papered over. In this view (entertained earlier with respect to Pedro Almodóvar's *Talk to Her*), the mother is primordial, all-encompassing, a world onto herself for the young child. The masochist's idealization of mother is chased through a hall of mirrors in infinite regress, so that he or she never reaches the desired object (i.e., successful masochism). In Winterbottom's menagerie, Jude (*Jude*), Martin (*I Want You*) and Matt (*9 Songs*) present instances of male masochists while Eunice (*Butterfly Wings*) enacts the female version.

Some other mechanisms that bring people together into a tension-laden order in Winterbottom's films include variations on "primal crime" scenarios; they evoke "transfers of guilt" of the type that characterize Alfred Hitchcock's plots. Jacqueline Rose (2004) discusses the primal crime via Freudian theorization. Within the legend from which it is drawn, the primal crime consists of the brothers ganging up on the revered/resented father and murdering him. In doing so, the father's monopoly on valuable resources (including women of the group) is broken to the brothers' benefit. However, one consequence is that the crime of murder occasions a charged and uneasy truce among the perpetrators: "Once the deed was done, only guilt, plus the dawning recognition of the danger each brother presented to the other, caused them to bind together and lay down their arms" (Rose 2004: xiv). The brothers keep an eye on their backs, in this complicated amalgam of affiliation and fear, that binds the group together—not so much through high ideals held in common, but in being "aghast at its own history, its own actual and potential deeds" (Rose 2004: xiv). So it is with Miriam and Eunice (*Butterfly Wings*) and William and María (*Code 46*); the pairs are bound together by crimes that Miriam and

William witness, actively cover up to become complicit after the fact—and later emulate in order to be still more like their loved ones. As in the Hitchcockian theme of the "transfer of guilt" (e.g., *Blackmail* [1929], *Strangers on a Train* [1951]), one character's knowledge of another character's secret transgressions implicates (binds) the first character with the second. Rather than facilitating liberation, knowledge occasions coupling forged through shared guilt and a need for cooperation in a perilous milieu.

With these touchstones in mind, below, I survey and discuss Winterbottom's construction of the family ISA, the gender theorization entailed within it, and the presentation of childhood.

With or Without You: Reproducing Ruling Ideology

Alongside the filmmaker's reputation as a controversialist animated by politics (Left-leaning), Winterbottom's corpus also contains works that contradict the audacious image. A couple of convention-bound entries in Winterbottom's corpus set up contrast with later, more challenging works. In this vein, *With or Without You* is at once a predictable film and one that mainly hits the notes on the family/gender traditionalist song sheet. This film was "primarily made for television but was granted a limited release in its home territory" (Allison 2005: 5), hence I have included it in the discussion. However, as Allison adds, "The film did little to develop Winterbottom's directorial repertoire" (2005: 4).[2]

With or Without You features few stylistic touches that suggest Winterbottom's thumbprint. Exceptional moments mainly occur toward the beginning of the film (namely, an expository and expressionistic montage that charts Vincent and Rosie's fertility problems). The film bluntly endorses the ostensibly sturdy, traditional triad of Man-Woman-Child in the final shot. It is a posed photo of the extended family assembled around the reconstituted marital dyad sutured together with newborn child. The scene rings false as for most of the film the couple has descended into boredom peppered with contempt for each other. The hollowed-out quality of the relationship is manifest in cutting comments—Rosie halts a bid for sex from Vincent with a castrating, "Don't start something you can't finish"—and the partners' respective "affairs."

Vincent's affair consists of spontaneous, vigorous sex with the voluptuous Cathy (who, despite her relative brevity onscreen, appears in full-shot nudity whereas Rosie never does). Rosie opts for a form of infidelity with Benoit that is prolonged with romantically tinged experiences (dancing, eating, concert going, finally absconding together to sleep in the woods). The outcomes of the affairs are also along gender stereotypical lines. Vincent vents his anger at Cathy as he exits her bedroom. A more interesting character than Rosie, Cathy is humbled via his hostile, peremptory departure from the situation that she set up. Along with being sexually assertive, Cathy is also financially independent with her own business—and the film's verdict goes against her. For her part, Rosie exits her entanglement mainly via a letter to Benoit telling him that their nascent affair is over since leaving Vincent would be tantamount to leaving part of herself—appearances during the previous hour of runtime notwithstanding.

In the film's endgame, Vincent rediscovers virility in part by acting out his former police officer role during sex with Cathy ("You have the right to remain silent . . . ")—an interlude that appears far more spontaneous and pleasurable than anything enacted with Rosie. He subsequently deals with Benoit in masculinist fashion, un-retiring his gun to shoot bullets into the sand around his cowering would-be rival. Rosie finally disposes of the romantic and thoughtful Benoit via her castratingly perfunctory response to his phone call during the baby's christening ceremony. The sturdiness of this couple is tested—but only so that baby may be parachuted in as deus ex machine to cement the family together. High-fidelity ideological reproduction demands this plotline and closes off any hint that a baby would exacerbate (rather than annul) the relationship's internal problems.

Hey, Jude

Jude is an early entry in the corpus that orients toward an array of enduring, interpenetrating concerns in Winterbottom's films: the family, forbidden love and the situation of the child. In symptomatic terms, the film is also timely as, by 2006, 44 percent of children in the United Kingdom were born out of wedlock (*Mail* Online 2007). While this loosening up of mores may be welcome as an exit from stifling (often misogynist) tradition, it comes with other costs in anomie. Multiple sets of parents generate thorny problems (with respect to, e.g., visitation rights, appropriate degrees of contact with former partners). While *Jude* does not engage with the paint-by-numbers reproduction of ruling family ideology as is found in the closing of *With or Without You*, its criticisms of the ideology are chimerical and implicit.

In the opening sequence of *Jude*, the title character dreams of university. The audience would expect a successful quest by classical Hollywood convention. However, the tone of *Jude* darkens as it proceeds. Love tests, mainly hatched by Sue, dominate the early phases of the narrative. She tempts Jude into a seemingly compromised night at his house that triggers his "guilty" implication in her (desired, melodramatic) expulsion from her strict school. Upon learning that Jude has an estranged wife, Sue immediately presses the wooden Phillotson for a marriage proposal. And, in a gesture that jabs cruelly at Jude's sexual jealousy while positioning Phillotson to be ever "looking over his shoulder," she asks Jude to give her up in the marriage ceremony—to the orphaned Jude's father figure!

After they dispose of the starchy Phillotson via their affair, Jude and Sue's shared life quickly turns grim. A taboo "Brady Bunch" family before its time, their three children hail from two pairings (Jude and Arabella, Jude and Sue). Moreover, on Jude's flinty insistence, he and Sue do not get married, thereby constructing a barrier between them that occasions degradation and disaster. Jude fits the masochist's profile, as he insures that he does not finally "reach" the obsessed-over Sue via marriage. The family is in turn subject to prejudice against unwed parents at all turns, losing work and being denied housing. Jude insists that they persevere, from town to town, for "as long as it takes for the world to change." The pressures on the family and scorn from outside are acutely felt by the younger Jude. He is presented as a morose and withdrawn child of sketchy origins who has also been subject to rejection by multiple mothers; Arabella jettisons him from the grandparents' home in Australia (off-screen) while Sue never warms to him. After Sue expels him from the parental bedroom, in his final act, Jude the younger murders his two half siblings and then hangs himself.

On one hand, the elder Jude seems admirably willing to challenge convention and its prejudices, as he dismisses marriage as a "piece of paper" (echoing Sue's earlier, glib dismissal of it, with which Jude clearly becomes fixated). However, Jude sets up a masochistic double bind where the piece of paper is "the law" that he abides by and that governs the enduring status of the relationship to Arabella —and, simultaneously, the flouting of such a paper in defiance of tradition vexes the liaison with Sue. Moreover, Jude's desires—a woman and children at his side—are entirely orthodox. In lieu of being married, Sue learns to lie about their *de jure* marital status so as not to be expelled to the street with the three children in tow.

In the closing sequence, Jude's largely stilted reaction to the death of all three of his children is in itself disturbing. By contrast, Sue is shattered and returns with a vengeance to the religion about which she had long harbored ambivalence. In the register of masochism, Jude keys on his relationship to Sue, which is one of separation, distance, and idealization of their perpetually troubled, barrier-laden past. Jude's final words—"We are man and wife, if ever two people were on this earth"—speak to core traditionalism on his part. Specifically, he channels the desire for marriage as "man and wife"—that is, man as given in state of nature, wife as possession and social construct—and not the egalitarianism of "man and woman." The closing scene also keynotes the masochistic project of an infinite regress of separation via Jude's repeated vow to Sue, "I won't stop trying" to stoke the relationship again. They share a passionate (if quick) kiss—and Sue makes a hasty, resolute exit from the chilly blue-grey graveyard, leaving Jude alone with his unrequited desires in the final shot.

Jude is set in the nineteenth century and has many of the markings of a British heritage film. As such, it presents the emphases on costumes and period music as well as being drawn from Britain's robust literary tradition. The more recent *Code 46* is set, by contrast, in a near future that has amped-up many of the dystopic features of the present (Goss 2007). Nevertheless, in abstracted terms, *Jude* and *Code 46* have a strong resemblance in their shared emphasis on social taboo and its intersection with economic class. In particular, the "Code 46" of the film's title refers to international law in the film's visioning of the future. Due to pervasive technological interventions into the reproduction of the species, people often do not know who their biological relatives are. The purpose of Code 46 is to proscribe subjects from mating, wittingly or otherwise, with partners possessing their parents' genetic material. In other words, the film presents a futuristic spin on the ancient Oedipal myth and its deeply ingrained taboo.

Like Jude and Sue, William and Maria go on a voyage in order to pursue their forbidden love affair that contravenes Code 46.

However, due to viruses that remotely police Code 46 violations, they are apprehended. Thereafter, William's memory of the affair is erased (a techno-mediated concomitant to the psychoanalytic concept of repression). He is parachuted back into his comfortable life as a white-collar worker "Inside" the globally hegemonic company. By contrast, Maria is expelled from her lower rung on the class-striation ladder on the Inside of the metropole's checkpoints to the absolute pauperization in the environmentally despoiled "Outside." In the final shot of the film, she looks to be on the path to death from want and exposure to dangerous sunlight. In *Code 46*, violating the taboo that anchors society is more readily forgiven in the case of the white collar/white man than for the working-class woman with a Latin surname. Both *Jude* and *Code 46* are attentive to taboo and the social conventions (e.g., surrounding social class) that condition subjects and distort and disrupt relationships. At the same time, the narrative vectors of both films also thumb their noses at convention; in particular, the happy endings of Hollywood convention that prescribe consummation of heterosexual pairing prior to the end credits.

"Guys and Dolls": Theorizing Gender

I Want You is another entry in the Winterbottom corpus that dwells on gender relations in terms that exhibit resonance as well as tension with tradition. In this case, Helen embodies two gendered tropes, exchanging one for the other as the narrative unfolds. Initially, she is emplotted as "woman in jeopardy." Later, she behaves as a femme fatale. The film initially appears to be a thriller in which an attractive 20-ish woman is stalked by Martin, a disturbed former boyfriend. Their earlier liaison terminated most unhappily according to the dialogue toward the start of the film, Martin killed Helen's father, who took umbrage on discovering the sexual relationship while she was still a minor. However, as the narrative plays out, Helen more closely resembles the "spider woman" of a film noir.

In a sequence about one-third through the film's runtime, Helen brushes off flirtations from a taxi driver en route to a club where her recently deposed boyfriend Bob toils as a DJ. Helen encounters an acquaintance, Sam, at the club while Bob is compelled to witness the unmistakable dance floor flirtation from the decks. After the club closes, Helen rebuffs Sam's criminally aggressive demands for spontaneous sex, and is rescued by Martin who materializes from nowhere and slams Sam with a bottle. Frightened, Helen rebuffs Martin. Honda, a traumatized mute 13-year-old whom Helen had earlier asked (flirtatiously) to zip up her dress, has been surreptitiously watching the whole sequence of events. Shaken, Helen restores equilibrium by confiding in Honda in the privacy of his beach-boat "retreat." So, five minutes of runtime, five males, five stock figures: bathetic old guy (taxi driver), the jilted lover (Bob), the predatory and slimy pretender (Sam), the brutish but, in his own damaged way, "loving" thug (Martin), the sensitive voyeur (Honda). All gravitate toward Helen and collide within a short sequence of scenes in which Helen is the center of the universe.

Helen's trajectory from seeming victim to "Venus Fly Trap" is completed in the final reel. She kills Martin in front of the mute Honda after Martin reveals (plausibly) that Helen killed her father and that he took the rap for it in a literal transfer of guilt. A second transfer of guilt is in motion when Honda helps Helen dispose of Martin's dead body as Martin had previously done with Helen's father; the transfer of guilt onto Martin that absolved Helen is now partly discharged onto Honda. He becomes a co-conspirator after the fact, bound to Helen and her crime by the shared guilty secret.

Wonderland is another entry in Winterbottom's corpus that takes up gender, largely within the family, via a series of contrasting subjectivities that tend toward de-essentializing the categories of "man" and "woman." This is accomplished in part by upsetting some gender tropes and by generally de-idealizing the ensemble of characters via their (mostly) everyday-type flaws. *Wonderland* is also Winterbottom's only film that is structured as a Robert Altman-like ensemble of intersecting stories that in turn invites analysis of characters via comparisons. Although a family is the center of the film, its members are never all in the same place at the same time—a symptom of a fractured millennial tribe. While the film is called *Wonderland*, the London that it envisions may also be taken as an alienated capitalist wasteland. For example, potential romantic entanglements "market" themselves to Nadia during the audio montage of dating service messages from men eager to turn her toward their "brand."

The three sisters present striking contrasts with each other in mapping out contours of female subjectivity. Nadia is a bohemian who works in a café and is desperate for romance. The film opens with her meeting a mediocre dating service "lifer" in a crowded bar. Molly is "uptight," married, and in an advanced state of pregnancy. Her valorization of convention frightens her skittish husband Eddie who clings to illusions of rebellion. Debbie is an unashamedly vulgar "ladette" who has trysts with two men during the course of the weekend. In the middle of the beauty salon workday, she boasts at having enjoyed being pregnant for its swelling of her breasts ("tits" in her parlance).

The mother of the family is a bitter and hyper-aggressive woman who eventually kills the neighbor's dog with poison. She is living a life parallel in time and space (but not *with*) a correspondingly passive husband. He, nonetheless, takes a few tentative steps toward asserting himself during the course of the weekend. The rest of the cast is largely composed of AWOL or otherwise troubled males: Darren is the estranged son/brother who has left the family and makes several guilt-tinged efforts at phone contact. While Debbie is a ladette who maintains household cash flow and consummates various trysts, Dan, the father of their child, is a near useless male. After begging Debbie for cash upon picking up their son Jack, Dan assays several hook-ups with women (including Nadia) to no avail. The laddish father leaves Jack home on Saturday night to watch a video that the youngster has already seen while he launches unsuccessful campaigns to womanize (but only realizes smashing success in imbibing heavily). Unsupervised into the next day by his self-absorbed lad/ladette parents, Jack wanders to the amusement park to see fireworks where he is viciously beaten by a gang.

In another plotline, Eddie exits to shop for food in order to avoid a confrontation with an incensed Molly over quitting a sales job that he detests. He awkwardly puts on his moped helmet before he leaves the apartment in a gesture of defense against his wife that also externalizes his desire for escape. Eddie subsequently roams London on a moped for the ensuing 24 or so hours, evading his unwanted fate as "family man" while Molly goes into labor. Eddie's sub-*Easy Rider* "Born to Mild" adventure concludes with an accident that leaves him hospitalized. Other men in the film exhibit contrasting defects. While lonely Franklin is defensive and sexually repressed, Tim is narcissistic and sleazy. Nadia is used by the latter and the film ends on a hopeful note of mutual interest with the former.

The large ensemble and multiple storylines work against traditional gender tropes that the film plays with and recombines. Moreover, the family that subsumes gender endures—more or less—in *Wonderland*; although no one seems certain as to why the family continues to lurch onward (anomie? inertia?) and its present form is certainly threadbare. The family is de-idealized within the capitalist cityscape of *Wonderland*'s London—a place that is at once clotted with people and lonely, full of stimulation, and hollow. These antimonies in *Wonderland* suggest the deep-seated need for affiliation that, if not fulfilled by families *per se*, requires some substantial channel.

Critique of gender animates the comedy *A Cock and Bull Story*. The film revolves around the making of a film-within-a-film, *Tristram Shandy*, based on the famous novel. Winterbottom's version of the source material, *A Cock and Bull Story*, dwells on and lampoons male status anxiety. Contrast is telling between Steve's attempting to play eighteenth-century characters Tristram and Walter Shandy in the *Tristram Shandy* film-within-a-film and Steve on the twenty-first century set. In the eighteenth-century sequences, the men are in command of the situation to absurd degrees. The informally convened "men's club" on the estate consults a hilariously prolix compendium of "phrases for all occasions," oblivious while Elizabeth Shandy suffers agonizing birth pains at the same time in the same house (emphasized via cross-cuts). By contrast, in the twenty-first century sequences that depict the making of the *Tristram Shandy* film-within-a-film, the men are still privileged, albeit with more sense of vulnerability in a world in which change is afoot, however slowly, and men are "on top" but conscious of slipping. Thus, while a *Cock and Bull Story* does not present a "New Man," it takes jabs at a still privileged man, hanging on by his fingernails, who knows that his status is precarious.

More specifically, Steve is implicated with two contrasting women named Jennie/Jenny. The first Jennie is a Brit of African origin who is a dedicated and articulate production assistant. The second Jenny is the girlfriend with whom he recently had a child. Jennie is attractive and astute within the remit of her work outside the home. Flirtations with Steve result in two moments of kissing (one on screen, the other referred to as having occurred the "other night"). The second Jenny is consistently with the baby and identifies with her role as mother/Steve's girlfriend. As Jennie/Jenny is split, Steve is similarly a split character dwelling within a subjectivity divided between "dad" and "cad." He is further split as "Tristram Shandy/Steve Coogan" that in turn implicates the split into "The *real* Steve Coogan/The *reel* Steve Coogan" that plays on the actor and his image (Hayward 2006: 375–384). His efforts to trump up his manhood where dad and cad may intersect—"Time for sexual intercourse" he awkwardly jokes to his coworkers upon leaving with Jenny for their hotel room—are further betrayed by private insecurity, such as asking Jenny whether he has a "star"'s nose or that of a "character actor."

A Cock and Bull Story's most tense relationship plays out between Steve and Rob Brydon in their androgenic clashes over status. The film begins and ends in bookend fashion with (seemingly improvised) exchanges between them that focus on their looks, standing—and twenty-first-century male anxieties about the same. A running joke concerns Steve's desire for shoes that will make him appear "taller" in order to "dominate" (his word) scenes, both visually and narratively, with respect to Rob's Uncle Toby. When told by interviewer Tony Wilson (playing himself and also the subject of *24 Hour Party People*) that Brydon impersonates and criticizes him, a jolted Steve rejoins that it is actually "flattery" and lets slip that he believes Rob "acts like he's taking a piss but he's actually obsessed by me." When the subplot with Gillian Anderson as Widow Wadman is added to the script to assuage the anxious producers, Rob corners Steve to get him worked up over the enhancement of his part as Uncle Toby. Rob makes a final dig at Steve's careening masculinity by claiming that Jenny suggests his libido has decreased since the advent of the baby.

After encountering Rob, Steve exhibits no interest in Jenny in their hotel room even as she pleads, "I have traveled 200 miles by train with a baby to have sex with you." Instead, Steve frantically surveys the damage to his leading role status by skimming through the original *Tristram Shandy* novel (which he has not read although he affects having done so) to see how prominent the Widow Wadman subplot is. Thereafter, he has a nightmare in which Rob gives a bravura performance as Uncle Toby, skillfully parrying Wadman's queries about his war-injured penis—and thereby maintains the appearance of intact manhood. Meanwhile,

Steve shrinks to fetal size off-camera during the shoot—a metaphor of ebbing status and autonomy—literally cabined within a woman's dominance, in contrast with Toby who successfully negotiates obstacles with Wadman. Upon waking, Steve subsequently (provisionally) patches up his masculinity through a guilt-laden kiss with Jennie before returning to bed with Jenny.

The Kids: Not Alright

Of a piece with an often critical perspective on the family, and the vicissitudes of romantic pairings, childhood is not sentimentalized in Winterbottom's world. Indeed, to present preadolescents in troubling circumstances is to conjure a world in which horror is often visited upon relative innocents, where family or state may not be sufficient shelter (they may, indeed, be the origin of the horror). *Jude* inaugurates the pattern. Jude the elder is an orphan brought up by a catastrophizing aunt and is first seen being thrashed by an adult in the fields. In the final reel, Jude the younger murders his step-siblings before hanging himself. The child thusly explodes a "guilt bomb" in the middle of his parents' increasingly troubled relationship that shatters their life together. In *Wonderland*, Jack is left to his own devices by his separated, youngish parents who are too (self-)centered on a hedonistic life style to notice his whereabouts during the course of a day. Jack is beaten viciously by bullies at the amusement park. The police subsequently categorize him as a runaway—although the description is more fitting for the parents. In *Welcome to Sarajevo*, the orphanage of vulnerable youngsters in a war zone crystallizes as the center of Henderson's conscience as he reports on the implosion of the Federal Republic of Yugoslavia. In another variation, *I Want You*'s Honda is an orphan who discovered his mother's dead body in the bathtub (suggesting suicide) and whose trauma is such that he has not spoken since. He is befriended by the treacherous Helen, also an orphan, who apparently killed her father before doing the same to the boyfriend who assumed the guilt for her initial crime.

As discussed above, family life often presents deep fractures in Winterbottom's presentation of it that refuses many "soft-focus" aspects of tradition. However, Winterbottom ratchets up the darker view of the family in general by depicting childhood as an unsentimentalized period of vast vulnerability and precocious implication in the troubled world of adults.

CHAPTER 10

Real Art

This is a dramatization inspired by certain actual events. Some of the names have been changed and some of the events, characters, dialogue, and chronology have been fictionalized for dramatic purposes.
—Closing title card in the credit sequence of *Welcome to Sarajevo*

The relationship between art and artifice that implicates what is called "realism" presents an enduring issue in cinema. While the word "realism" tends to be overused in everyday discourse to the point of fatigue, it has simultaneously become an increasingly amorphous signifier. Moreover, an everyday concept of realism is not equal to all of the gradations that may accompany the concept. Thomas de Zongotita (2005) offers a useful exercise on this score as he sifts through dozens of distinct concepts of realism that arise in a mass-mediated environment (e.g., "real real," "staged real," "edited staged real," "staged hyper real," etc.). The word itself— *realistic*—denotes not a direct encounter with the real thing itself but a presentation that may impact to pass muster as being *as if* it is real. Where film and realism are concerned, any given film may be evaluated as *relatively* formalist (i.e., showy technique, such as rapid MTV-style montage) versus realist ("fly on the wall" transcription of pro-filmic events, as via minimal cutting)(Easthope 1993).[1]

In his brief survey of the history of realism in film, Robert Stam (2000b) spotlights several claims that ground further discussion. In Stam's appraisal, what counts as realism is inseparable from conventions and expectations, often tied up with formal technique, that differ across time and place. Black-and-white film stock, uninterrupted long takes, Dolby sound, hand-held camera work: All have been heralded as preferred emblems of realism at one time or another. However, the realism game is given away in construing it as necessarily anchored in the idioms of formal technique. On this view, "seeing realism simply as a constellation of stylistic devices, a set of conventions that at a given moment in the history of art, manages through a fine-tuning of illusionistic technique, to crystallize a strong *feeling* of authenticity" (original emphasis; Stam 2000b: 224).

The achievement of realism via formalist "fictional codes" also includes generic conventions. These conventions may, in turn, be taken as exemplars of realism; they do, indeed, correspond with *something* familiar, namely other films and their culture-bound tropes, if not the world beyond one's salon. As an example, Stam marshals the generic narrative convention in which the uptight father takes umbrage at his daughter's show-biz aspirations. But, as the script demands in the final reel, the father applauds the daughter as her quest is realized in spectacle on stage; a plot line that may correspond with tropes more than lived realities.

Conversely, the rise of reflexive filmmaking in the 1960s via a tide of New Waves pulled strongly in a counter-direction. Garnished with dollops of Brechtian influence, reflexive films cashier many of the pretenses that underwrite illusionistic codes in favor of film that is self-conscious of its representational strategies. Stam observes that this tendency persisted into the 1980s–1990s albeit with its reflexivity noticeably altered into the idiom of "a less politicized 'intertextaulity'" (2000b: 225).[2] However, Stam reframes received opinion about the "realism versus reflexivity" issue by positing that it is not a dichotomy. Instead, he proposes a "coefficient" between realism and reflexivity that would weigh a film as more or less realistic in a variety of registers (2000b: 227). Stam is cognizant of the (often cynical) irony that is inscribed in many contemporary reflexive moves, notably in advertising that tactically foregrounds its own manipulations. Nonetheless, Stam also posits that media's implication into lived experience and subjectivity make reflexivity one of the constituent parts of what is real. Stam judiciously resolves the issue as follows: "The challenge now...is to avoid a naively 'realistic' view of artistic representation, without acceding to a 'hermeneutic nihilism' whereby all texts are seen as nothing more than an infinite play of signification without reference to the social world" (2000b: 228).

Beyond presenting striking artistic signature, discussed earlier, Winterbottom's style has taken positions on the relation between reality and artifice to a greater extent than most contemporary filmmakers. Winterbottom's interest in testing the demarcations and intersections of realism and reflexivity is one of the cardinal aspects of his work (Allison 2005). The claim is supported by the prominence that Winterbottom endows to journalists—who, in turn, are ostensible tribunes of the real and its associated truth. Specifically, *Welcome to Sarajevo*, *24 Hour Party People*, and *A Mighty Heart* all feature journalists in addition to the explicit documentary turn of *The Road to Guantánamo*.

In one instance of experimentation with realism, Winterbottom employed a cinematographer (Sean Bobbitt) whose background was exclusively in documentary to shoot the fictional *Wonderland*. Winterbottom assayed to realize a documentary "look" for a fictional film on contemporary London to generate an edge of realism. In filming on location in London's bars and cafes, "We tried to just be three people in the corner and not control the set" (Kaufman 2000: 3). Winterbottom recalls,

> (At) the beginning of the film, in the bar, we went to do some tests without lights, without boards, without microphones. We shot there and they didn't pay any attention to us. As soon as we put a small light up, everyone was very aware. So what we did was try to find exactly the right places for the story to happen, shoot at the right time for the story. Like in the bar we had to wait until everyone was drunk and it was closing time and shoot very quickly in and amongst what was happening and try to capture those moments. (Kaufman 2000: 3)

Winterbottom uses technique to channel realism, at times enabled by contemporary film technology (such as less obtrusive, highly portable digital cameras). At the same time, Winterbottom also traffics in the reflexive tradition that Stam discusses by, for instance, dismantling the "fourth wall" or employing showy techniques (such as extended montages) that manifest the film as being a film. However, Winterbottom's abiding concern with truth is a unifying element in these tendencies; this commitment, in turn, prompts politicized confrontations with some loci of authority, such as the traditional family and abusers of human rights.

Capturing Truth

There is realism, an artistic strategy; then there is the overarching question of truth. This investigation is grounded in the assumption that truth is not a function of idiosyncratic perceptions that reduce to a subject position (as in the aphorism, "Where you stand depends upon where you sit"). Rather, truth *is*. It is an external and knowable condition against which texts may be compared with regard to their truth value that may be appraised by empirical methods. Truth is not assumed to be a binary (yes/no) concept, as appealing as that idea may be, but it can be grasped to specify "high," "low," or "no truth value" in evaluating a text (where a text may be, e.g., a statement, news report, or film). This is a conventional view with respect to the Enlightenment heritage, one that has in recent decades been challenged by well-meaning but flabby postmodernism that eschews grand narratives and lines of causality in favor of an emphasis on subject position as alpha and omega of knowledge.

The stakes are high with regard to truth. Consider that contemporary Rightists have found it highly serviceable to hijack the retreat from Enlightenment concepts of an external truth that is subject to empirical inquiry. Strategic (and unscrupulous) ambiguity, one may call it. Under the dizzied sign of the postmodern, statements about external reality—e.g., "Climate change is an observable condition already in motion, due to human activity" (see Union of Concerned Scientists 2004) or "Gore Won the 2000 US Election" (see Wolfe 2000)—collapse into ineffable mysteries and indecipherable hieroglyphics. In turn, the tactically deployed dense fog of postmodern agnosia that clouds vision on the ground provides cover to strategically install definite specifications of "reality" (procedures, laws, invasions) to Rightist specifications.

Nevertheless, reading a newspaper, a government document, a menu, or a repair manual all make very different demands and require very different strategies of divining truth than reading a work of fiction such as a dream, a novel, or a film. A newspaper can (indeed, should) be read and evaluated with respect to what it does and does not say about the external truth, as a substantial body of scholarship has demonstrated (Bennett 2001; Herman and Chomsky 1988). Reading a film is, however, different in the first instance since it is generally one form of fiction or another. Moreover, style in fictional expression is of much more moment than the style of a newspaper, or a phonebook, or a scientific write-up (each of which should, by convention of their respective genres, largely eschew stylistic flourishes for straightforward clarity).

The artist is not a historian. To take one example: Shakespeare's historical plays are poetry, not documentary evidence. Winterbottom's films have implicitly endorsed this view as well. For example, when Steve exclaims in *A Cock and Bull Story* that he cannot get his head around (or his hands in) the low pockets of his eighteenth-century costume, he is informed that the costume is in fact historically accurate. Steve counters that, "It can be historically accurate and still be contrived"; a defensible (if, in Steve's case, a self-serving) observation. By contrast, the character of the historical advisor in the same film channels a narrowly crabbed concept of historical accuracy. He assays to distribute names to the actors so they can call out "plausible" appellations to each other as they die on cue during the battle scene (as if "smartly" producing answers to trivia questions with their dying breaths). The literal-minded historian reveals a tin ear to the poetics of reconstructing the past for the present.

At the same time, it is glib and anti-intellectual to assume that there are no stakes involved in teasing reality and fiction apart when circumstances may demand that they be carefully collated. Moreover, representations of the past may implicate ethical challenges that a thoughtful observer should not airily wave away or gloss over (Christians et al. 2004). In this vein, a recent and highly decorated film, *The Lives of Others/Das Leben der Anderen* (Florian Henckel von Donnersmarck 2006), addresses Honecker-era East Germany. In the film, a Stasi agent's conscience awakens and he spares one of the state's victims. Anna Funder, author of the historical study *Stasiland*, posits that the plotline of *The Lives of Others* could not have occurred within the Stasi's tight and impenetrable latticework. Funder describes the film as at once fictitious and richly deserving of "its public and critical acclaim. It is a superb film, a thing of beauty" (2007: 14). Nevertheless, however severe it may be in conjuring a stunningly drab and oppressed land, *The Lives of Others*' underlying premise about loopholes in the Stasi's conduct of surveillance does not correspond with the documentary record. It is a disturbing, powerful account of totalitarianism—even if it does not "go far enough" with respect to literal historical truth.

Other distinguished films have similarly begged questions about the tension between historical fact and the poetic license that they have adopted (e.g., *Bonnie and Clyde* [Arthur Penn

1967]) or events that, while "typical" episodes, are nevertheless fictionalized in their specifics (e.g., *The Magdelene Sisters* [Peter Mullan 2002]). In these and numerous other instances, one may ask whether the films illuminate "higher truths," above and beyond a collection of facts, that poetically express and transcend specifics of the source material. It may be most judicious to assess each film on its own merits, provisionally granting artistic license while being wary of filmmakers who abuse it to, for example, score cheap ideological points. In any event, as a filmmaker who regularly adopts a political stance, Winterbottom's fidelity to established facts is at stake in some entries in the corpus.

Creative Tensions

Winterbottom's films regularly step out of an illusionistic presentation of the pro-filmic events via stylistic flourishes that celebrate the film *as film*. One method of doing this is to dismantle the transparent "fourth wall" through which the audience agrees to peer unobtrusively in on the world of the characters in exchange for the some measure of an illusion of realism. In the opening scene of *24 Hour Party People*, a notable moment in this register occurs when Steve Coogan, playing media maven Tony Wilson, walks toward and addresses the camera. He claims that, while he does "not want to spoil the film," his hang-gliding misadventures of the opening scene resonate with the story of Icarus—and with subsequent events in the narrative at hand. Hence, the actor steps away from illusionism by acknowledging that he is in the first scene of a film. Nonetheless, addresses to the camera aside, Coogan as actor plays the part of Wilson to otherwise conventional specifications, "being" him for the film's purposes. Moreover, the address-to-the-camera gesture is made in this instance in the service of the time-honored fictional convention of foreshadowing; namely, Wilson's ambitious and romanticized plans will overreach.

The later film, *A Cock and Bull Story*, trades heavily on disposing of the "fourth wall." Early in the runtime, Steve Coogan steps out in costume to announce that he is, "Tristram Shandy, the main character of this story, the leading role." He subsequently spends most of the film shorn of his eighteenth-century costume (indeed, he is often arguing about how that costume should look) and being status-obsessed, insecure actor Steve rather than the character whom he ostensibly plays. Hence, Steve Coogan plays Steve, and only sporadically positions as Steve playing Tristram Shandy. Moreover, when in costume in the film-within-a-film, Coogan the actor does not actually "do" much more than introduce other characters and make commentaries on them. In this vein, Steve's Tristram Shandy is dismissive toward the child actor playing him as a pre-adolescent who gets his penis caught in a window frame. "Best of a bad bunch" of child actors, he posits from the other side of the same room and earns immediate rebuke from the child actor who steps out of "character" to address his critic. Shortly thereafter, Coogan announces he will play Tristram Shandy's father Walter as well, as he fits a new wig onto his head.

Drama-mentary

A Cock and Bull Story is a clever film in pulling at the seams of realism and artifice as it brings a difficult novel to the screen. In a more squarely political vein, Winterbottom's other efforts probe the membrane between filmed fiction and documentary. These interventions are perhaps most ambitious, as well as politically charged, with *In This World*. The method of making the film is inseparable from its challenges to strongly drawn distinctions between fiction and documentary film. *In This World* was initially researched via Winterbottom's and screenwriter Tony Grisoni's discussions with refugees in London. Thereafter, the two collaborators took a hiatus in taxis and on the backs of trucks from Pakistan to Turkey in order to get first-hand understanding of the particulars of a refugee's journey ("Behind the Scenes with Michael Winterbottom and Tony Grisoni" 2003). Casting was conducted at the Peshawar, Pakistan, refugee camp, playing on the tradition of neo-realism in eschewing trained actors for the instincts of someone "living it." Sixteen-year-old Jamal was cast in the lead. The family that he is depicted leaving behind is in fact his family at the camp that he left to undertake the filmed odyssey. As the journey played out, a tiny crew staged and followed the action. During most of the shoot, the crew consisted only of Winterbottom, cinematographer Marcel Zyskind, and sound recordist Stuart Wilson along with the actors. Filming was done in secret in parts of Afghanistan and in Turkey's Kurdish zone in order to evade "security-conscious" local authorities (although the filmmakers regarded

France as the most hostile place in which they filmed! ["Behind the Scenes with Michael Winterbottom and Tony Grisoni" 2003]).

Winterbottom did not script dialogue but explained the dramatic situations to Jamal (who speaks some English, like the character he plays) who then explained what he understood to Enayat (who does not speak English). Hence, the characters' relation on the "set" are in parallel to what one sees in the film, as Jamal at times uses English to communicate internationally when Enayat cannot. Moreover, the crew and cast were similarly in the parallel situation of requiring "fixers" to ease their problems in moving Jamal and Enayat across semi-porous borders without documents. The filmmakers paid bribes to make up for what they could not furnish with respect to necessary documents—again, as the characters frequently do on camera. In one scene, an Iranian officer boards the bus to check documents and expel wayward Afghans attempting undocumented transit. The officer was bribed into playing along and not expelling Jamal and Enayat—except as staged for the camera—with the promise of a role in the film as himself ("Behind the Scenes with Michael Winterbottom and Tony Grisoni" 2003). Jamal's trajectory into the United Kingdom finishes with the refugee's petition for asylum. He is rejected although given a stay until the day before he turns 18, according to one of the closing title cards.

Alongside audible echoes between the lives of the players and the events depicted on screen, there are significant deviations for narrative impact. To wit, Enayat perishes during the journey—as many asylum seekers do although, in this case, the realistic narrative turn is not backed by off-camera "reality." *In This World* also exhibits characteristics of a professional film production with respect to its division of artistic labor. Where sound is concerned, the credits include a "foley supervisor/editor," "foley artist," "foley assistant," and "foley recordist"; that is, a team dedicated to enhancing under-recorded sounds from the principal photography in order to create a better artistic fit of the aural landscape to the imagery after the fact. The credits also include a "score mixer" and a "supervising sound editor," among other sound specialists who labored on the film. The artifice of non-diegetic music, in turn, buttresses emotional impact of the narrative as in a "conventional" production (notably, after Jamal reaches Europe, while Enayat has suffocated on the same clandestine voyage by freighter). Thus, the realism of *In This World* often cuts close to the bone. It should nonetheless be regarded as the—highly unconventional, challenging, politicized—fictional film that it is, one that arguably channels more textures of truth than are often found in journalistic efforts in newsprint or over the airwaves.

Meet the Press

Many Winterbottom films address mediation and reality via a focus on media workers, particularly journalists. In this vein, *Welcome to Sarajevo*, presents a largely affirmative view of news media. Early in the film, the news stringer Flynn makes a hazard-laden walk though sniper fire in order to assist in moving a victim's body, while Henderson later makes an enduring commitment by adopting one of the orphaned victims of the events on which he reports. The film acknowledges that a large share of news media does not behave to these lofty standards, as when a Royal Family fiasco eclipses the Balkans War as the lead story in British news. Nonetheless, *Welcome to Sarajevo* shows reporters in a war zone taking vast risks to transmit the truth to a wide audience—and assaying to mobilize social betterment.

A Mighty Heart constructs a similar binary within journalism, while mainly accenting the noble journalist. Although he is on screen for little of the 100-minute runtime, reporter Daniel Pearl is treated as a high-minded truth seeker who places himself in dangerous situations in order to investigate. In the same film, Asra claims to have become a reporter out of idealistic motives when her dinner guests chide her. She seems to abide by her stated creed while, as a Muslim and an Indian, absorbing suspicion and harassment from both U.S. officials (Platt of the FBI) and from the Pakistanis. Nonetheless, the same film presents a series of less scrupulous pack journalists. Anonymous scribes mass outside Marianne's lodgings with Asra as well as outside the home of Pearl's bereaved parents. A television interviewer asks Marianne a question that manipulatively goads the grieving widow while John Bussey of the *Wall Street Journal* defends the paper's collaborations with the CIA in a seeming concession to convenience over principle.

In *A Cock and Bull Story*, one subplot concerns Gary, a predatory journalist who stalks Steve. Steve's discomfort is driven by the knowledge that Gary has information on his tryst with a stripper.

Via this form of blackmail, Steve reluctantly agrees to an interview that turns out to be a puff piece on "fatherhood" in support of the upcoming *Tristram Shandy* (i.e., the film-within-a-film). Hence, in this subplot, journalism is presented as opportunist and tawdry—and as *quid-quo-pro* promotion by another name, a plot turn that resembles facts on the ground with respect to a tame, private sector-dominated and deferential "Fourth Estate."

24 Hour Party People's Wilson is also a journalist. In contrast with Henderson—the dignified, cause-driven man on the beat in *Welcome to Sarajevo* —Wilson finds many of his assignments degrading. He covers stories such as hang-gliding, a dwarf washing an elephant, and sheep herding. As the host of *Wheel of Fortune*, Wilson also assays to shoe-horn in "high-brow" philosophizing on the nature of chance—to the producer's chagrin who insists that the monologue be cut. In this manner, *24 Hour Party People* critiques mass media when it behaves to largely commercial specifications; a critique that is not particularly new and that is also leavened with humor. Nonetheless, Wilson's media critique is given weight when he combats the mainstream music oligopoly and forms his own company. Moreover, he fashions Factory Records as a cooperative with the artists, a commitment that he writes out in blood. When financial problems arise, he therefore has no assets to sell off.

In a monologue to the camera, Wilson also engages the audience from the posture of a media worker/maven making editorial comment about media and its newer, "enabling" technological substrates. He claims that, with the rise of DJs and raves in Manchester in the 1980s, fans communed with the medium and not with the band; and "even the white man starts dancing," he observes, suggestive of wider cultural "democratization" and boundary-leveling as efflux to the DJ spinning. Wilson's commentary is also heavily shaded with local pride as it is preceded by a journalistic discourse on Manchester's lead role in the advent of industrial production. The implication is that the recent rise of a "participatory" form of popular culture out of Manchester—namely, raves—is part of the same trajectory of world-shaking innovation (in this case, from industrial to "leisure" production). Along with aggrandizement of Manchester, the monologue also implies that sounds and experiences have supplanted more durable industrial goods as the "base" of the economy. In this manner, the film steps away from critique to celebrate the "National Entertainment State" as part of the pageantry of a presumptive "March of Progress."

Emotional Realism, with Style

9 Songs illustrates Winterbottom's investment in gender and relationships. The film also stresses stylized capture of the phenomenal experience of a relationship that is recalled after the fact via a palimpsest of re-representation in the filmic medium. As a later entry in the corpus, *9 Songs* is consistent with the daring approach that characterizes Winterbottom's more recent work. In this case, the film transmits the experience of recollection and loss through seemingly little plot as connotation and innuendo are played heavily. In the emphases on memory, hints of Matt's backward-looking masochism are in play. Along with its consistencies with other aspects of Winterbottom's auteur tendencies, *9 Songs* is illustrative of strategies of realism in the service of channeling the "emotional truth" of the relationship.

The film occurs within Matt's unfolding, episodic recollections of the relationship with Lisa. It is tightly organized in its 64-minute runtime via the deceptively simple scheme of eight (mainly rock and roll) concerts during the course of their relationship.[3] The ninth concert is a coda that occurs after Lisa has left Britain and returned to the United States. The concerts furnish "chapters" that organize the material while Matt and Lisa's relationship traverses from the roiling excitement of new sex partners; to tenderness; to boredom and contempt; and, finally, to a polite break-up. The chapter-like punctuation cues the audience to evaluate and assess each phase of the relationship via the revealing vignettes of sex, banter, and their excursions as a couple outside the apartment. In this manner, the audience may compare each vignette with preceding ones in reconstructing the trajectory of the relationship.

Aside from a couple of brief scenes of Matt's work as an Antarctic investigator, the narrative coils around the couple. This stands in contrast with more sprawling, at times cluttered, narratives in Winterbottom's earlier films. Through Winterbottom's reliance on VO, Matt furnishes subjective commentaries; the technique interpolates the audience to identify with him by accessing the narrative through the prism of his recollection. In the first VO, Matt states, "When I remember Lisa, I don't think of her clothes or her work, where she was from, or even what she said. I think about her smell, her taste, her skin touching mine" over close-up shots of moan-laden intercourse between them. This provides an early indication that the film is both a memorial "reconstruction" as mediated through the narrator and his (sense-heavy) recollections.

Lisa is from the United States (as is immediately evident from her accent). Aside from her energetic vulgarity, the film does not much dwell on her origins. Nevertheless, Lisa clearly bears the imprimatur of being from the New World; the dance moves that she demonstrates to Matt in one scene are mainly Latin American, explained in her later aside that she had prior boyfriends from Brazil, Colombia and Argentina. Matt is perhaps more strongly constructed as a British "type" as few words pass through his "stiff upper lip." After Lisa departs for the airport, leaving Britain behind, Matt goes home and boots up his computer in a ritual of restraint. Moreover, Matt's work in the majestic starkness of the Antarctic presents hints of someone with a deep (or, largely "frozen") internal life.

Along with being national "types" to an extent, Matt and Lisa may be construed as older man (early 30-something) and a *jejune*, impatient younger woman (age 21); this is perhaps the lynchpin of each identity within the dyad. In a VO about halfway through the film, Matt recalls Lisa as she is captured in montage behaving as an uninhibited disco queen staged against nightclub lighting. In his accompanying VO, he appraises her as having been 21 years old, beautiful, and egotistical. Matt's criticisms of her collide with fetishizing presentation of her easy expressions of animal attractiveness that are, in turn, inflected with a masochistic recollection of what is no longer attainable.

Hints of coming apart begin subtly. Lisa rejects Matt's bid to do something together on one of her national holidays (Thanksgiving) because she has plans with people whom Matt "would hate." In this manner, she brackets part of her life off, with shadings of contempt for his social acumen. Shortly after, Lisa is entranced by a female lap dancer while Matt sits next to her. He wordlessly exits, leaving her in the seedy venue. In a beautifully staged POV shot, Matt later discovers Lisa masturbating vigorously. Backlighting out the bedroom window generates a blinding glow around her genitals as she writhes on the bed in long shot. The POV shot underscores his idealizing—and painful—recollection of being left out. Matt attends the next *9 Songs* concert alone, in "reply" to her vigorous solo sex. When the couple resumes their sex life, the S&M has a far more aggressive edge to it. Lisa steps on him in high-heeled boots that inflict visceral threat and pain, even while she "distances" herself via the costume and semi-ritualized sex.

Despite dispensing with the costumes in their final love scene, sadism is evident: Lisa elects Matt's birthday as the occasion to announce she is leaving Britain. Matt characterizes their final week in London as an "orgy"—of sightseeing and buying souvenirs. The parting is "friendly" but distant, ensconced in the safety of commoditization and touristic ritual. In her final shot, Lisa is alone in the back of the taxi looking inscrutably out the window. Distance between the former lovers is now immanently, literally Atlantic. Matt's reserve—and masochism—gets externalized in the last of the nine songs, as the Black Rebel Motorcycle Club sings, "Now she's gone and love burns inside me." The credit sequence is shot, post-concert, in blurred telephoto with echo-y and muffled sound effects as a lingering patron stomps on beer cans. It evokes a blearily "buzzed" evening out, seeking the next love affair to spontaneously generate out of *being there*. The audience to *9 Songs* witnesses the ineffable chemical reaction implicated in coming together as a couple and the ensuing coming apart, while the closing credits proffer the possibility of the cycle playing out again.

The film exhibits tensions between style and the verisimilitude of the recollections that it channels. On one hand, Winterbottom did not use a script for the film, thereby going "beyond" what Dogme95 calls for in its celebrated back-to-basics approach (von Trier and Vinterberg 1995). Moreover, leads Kieran O'Brien and Margo Stilley are not experienced erotic actors. Where the tension between realism and formalism is concerned, the filmmakers used three cameras to unobtrusively record the concert experiences as they unfolded. Similarly, a small crew was on hand in the apartment for the love scenes. Alongside the formal idiom of realism, the episodic structure is not the randomness of the real but a carefully calibrated construction that is clinched via the editing process. This structure enables the viewer to dwell on connotation and mystery concerning the character's internal states that surround, for example, Lisa's growing impatience, hunger for "variety," or perhaps a desire to fastidiously close down her commitment prior to returning to the United States. Indeed, Lisa's nation of origin furnishes a key emphasis within the chapter to follow.

CHAPTER 11
Rights and Wrongs

This section finishes with an appraisal of Winterbottom's distinct interest in politics on an international plane. It is an unsurprising interest for a British artist; in this vein, consider the United Kingdom's historic role in fashioning (or, more pointedly, mal-forming) the contemporary world via its imperium and exports that include the spectacalized mass republic and industrialization tailored to capitalist specifications. The first half of the chapter addresses Winterbottom's measured views of the United Kingdom's former colony, the United States, that has taken up the United Kingdom's former place as global hegemon after WWII. One of the United States' keynote inventions after WWII has been the formation of international institutions (United Nations, World Bank) and codification of international laws that include human rights conventions. Marking the intersection of human rights-oriented concerns with the film texts completes the analysis of Winterbottom's corpus.

A Transatlantic View

The earlier chapter on von Trier presents a detailed account of the filmmaker's posture toward the United States. This is because the von Trier corpus features several films set in the United States—*Dancer in the Dark*, *Dogville*, *Manderlay*—that make unmistakable bids to critique the world's presumptive hegemon. Winterbottom's corpus also devotes attention to the United States, most notably in *The Claim* and *The Road to Guantánamo* (both of which will be discussed in detail later). Several other films in the Winterbottom corpus present a quickly glossed and surprisingly "conventional" view of the United States. In *A Cock and Bull Story*, the extent of U.S. command over the filmscape gets play. In one scene, a cellular phone call from Steve Coogan's agent dangles a part in a film by noted U.S. independent Alexander Payne. The call is greeted with Rob Brydon's jealous taunts from the backseat: "You fucking asshole," he repeats in what turns out to be an impersona-tion of Al Pacino, but also channels his aggrieved sense of being imminently left behind in the British industry. In the final scene of the film, Brydon reveals that his models for acting are Pacino, Barbra Streisand, and Anthony Hopkins; that is, two Usonians whose careers have benefited from the U.S. distribution apparatus and a British-born actor who (in contrast with, e.g., Robert Car-lyle) has effectively become a Hollywood star.

When the rushes of *Tristram Shandy*, the period film-within-a-film in *A Cock and Bull Story*, are exhibited, the producers are un-der-awed. The remedy seized upon to salvage the film is to enlist a "star" for the marquee. Studio "B-Lister" Gillian Anderson is the designated "star" with U.S. imprimatur whom they pursue. In re-sponse to the offer of a part in *Tristram Shandy*, Anderson and her agent (clad in a workout style "get-up") enthuse in a caricature of cloying U.S. friendliness ("Hiiiiii!", "I looooove the book!"). In one of *A Cock and Bull Story*'s final scenes, a brief bulletin on the car ra-dio reports Bushite Washington's faith-based insistence that its occupation of Iraq is being effectively implemented in the face of resistance. It furnishes a hint that, while Hollywood sustains its prominence on screens, facts on the ground suggest a nation in paroxysms of decline due to its disastrous political leadership and shambolic acumen in the international arena beyond the multiplex cinema.

In *Welcome to Sarajevo*, Flynn is a Usonian character played as a natural extrovert and opportunist (unburdened with ponderous intellect). He is first seen walking through sniper fire in order to assist in evacuating a body, an action that he later ascribes to an instinct for publicity (although one suspects the motives are not so crass). Later, he reports that he is making a "fortune" selling in-ternational phone service while the former Federal Republic of Yugoslavia implodes around him—*Mother Courage and Her Chil-dren*–style wartime capitalism, in other words. However, in con-trast to the otherwise dedicated reporter Henderson, Flynn becomes better acclimated as he learns conversational Bosnian.

Beyond these briefer visionings, *The Claim* presents Winter-bottom's most sustained vision of the United States in a fictional work and it mainly traffics in accepted mythologies. The film con-cerns a nineteenth-century California frontier town, Kingdom Come, established around the discovery of gold. It is the fiefdom of

local strongman Daniel Dillon. Although Dillon rules without en-
cumberances of democracy, he is characterized as almost "liberal"
by "Wild West" standards by, for example, not killing an accused
thief but merely dealing out 25 lashes. When the railroad company
surveys the area in order to determine an optimal route through it,
Dillon exerts pressure for the railroad to stop at Kingdom Come in
order to ensure the town's continued expansion. Nonetheless, the
chief engineer, Dalglish advocates a route away from Kingdom
Come and into the nearby valley on scientific grounds. All parties
understand that this development will negate any need for the
continued existence of Kingdom Come along with Dillon's privatized dominion over it. A couple of shoot-outs follow in which Dillon
kills two of the railroad's men before he accepts defeat, a defeat
hastened by the dissolution of the family that Dillon had traded
two decades earlier for the town's deed and that has left him again
via death (wife Elena) and willful abandonment (daughter Hope).

In *The Claim*, Winterbottom largely affirms U.S. mythology
about itself. First, most of the characters are immigrants from
elsewhere starting with Dillon. He was once a penniless Irish
transplant who still speaks with a thick brogue. Thus, in the film,
modest origins are surmountable in the New World with its embrace of the "poor huddled masses." Second, the march of technology is presented as driving broad liberalization of social life. In this
vein, a woman, Dillon's former lover Lucia, is the leading citizen of
the new town in the valley that is Kingdom Come transplanted
and upgraded. The corporation is presented as the racing heart of
progressive change. The grandee of the railroad, a business
man/visionary, presides over the official ceremony in which he aggrandizes the gathered masses' place in U.S. history and unveils
the name of the new town: Lisboa (Lisbon), in deference to Lucia's
Portuguese roots. The public naming ritual for the town and the
wedding ceremony are enacted with earnest John Ford-style celebration of the Usonian frontier community.

Third, despite the uncritical appraisal of the impact of (ostensibly liberalizing, corporate-sponsored) new technology, *The Claim*
also slips in the counter direction. During the closing sequence, the
film valorizes the traditional order of the "maximum leader" as it
came to be embodied in Dillon. In the register of the personal, Lucia pays homage to her deceased former lover as his body passes.
Then it is Dalglish's turn for sentimentality. The proximal cause of

Dillon's downfall, Dalglish solemnly intones on the broader significance: That "pioneers, people like Dillon, they came out here when
there was nothing and built these towns and ruled them like
kings." *The Claim* thus hits all the notes in affirming touchstones
of U.S. ideology and makes few concessions to critique. Specifically,
the film celebrates liberalizing change, technology and the corporation (or, capitalism generally). At the same time, *The Claim* is garnished   with   (contradictory)   sentimentality   for   illiberal
traditionalisms as embodied by the monarch-like Dillon. Given
these moves, it's all good in the United States, according to *The
Claim*.

Notice that Winterbottom's visioning of the nineteenth-century
United States in *The Claim* contrasts strikingly with his earlier
presentation of nineteenth-century England in *Jude*, another
Thomas Hardy adaptation. In particular, Dillon arrives in California penniless and with dependents. While the deal he makes to
take ownership of Kingdom Come is a stunning (subsequently
guilt-laden) betrayal of his family, Dillon ends up realizing huge
wealth, local power, and a measure of affection. Jude, by contrast,
is constantly thwarted in his efforts toward class promotion. Following Phillotson's fatherly advice that university is the means to
open doors of opportunity, Jude makes a failed quest for college.
He is denied admission in an unashamedly classist rejection letter
that informs him that manual labor more closely fits his station in
life. At once proud and bitter, Jude observes that he has assayed
class promotion in one lifetime that was traditionally accomplished
over the course of generations (if at all). In Winterbottom's treatment, the U.S. protagonist in the same time frame is not so constrained in class terms.

In a more critical register toward the United States, Winterbottom constructs the character of Randall Bennett in *A Mighty
Heart*. Although not as menacing as the Usonians in *The Road to
Guantánamo*, Bennett hails from the shadowy world of what he
calls "diplomatic security." While the character looks like a be-
yond-his-shelf-life 1980s "new wave" hipster (receding hairline,
sunglasses, earring), Bennett is a creepy figure. He interprets each
piece of news on the kidnapped (subsequently murdered) Daniel
Pearl as "not a negative thing," sunny, U.S.-style optimism that is
proven wrong at each turn. More unsettling is his desire to see torture meted out. In one scene, he breaks the somber mood to en-

thuse at the anxious Marianne that the Pakistanis will not use restraint in interrogating suspects and that he desires a "front row seat" to witness beatings with sticks. Subsequently, the captain takes him on a series of raids during which Bennett, while peripheral, stands out as the only Euro-descended and "civilian" presence. Bennett thrills as he accompanies a raid in a slum ("I love this town!"), cocooned as he is from its grinding poverty and caught up in the hot-pursuit spectacle of state power. The closing title card states that he subsequently moved on to Iraq.

More Than a Cameo: Human Rights

In the projects that his team has adopted and in the subsequent treatment of the material, human rights animate many of Winterbottom's films. The films that make clearest contact with human rights issues are *Welcome to Sarajevo*, *In This World*, *Code 46*, and *The Road to Guantánamo*. Moreover, *Murder in Samarkand* is currently "in production" and will most likely ratchet up the human rights campaign on the screen. The film is drawn from the memoir of former British diplomat Craig Murray, who has made stringent critique of the human rights negligence of British foreign policy in the Blair era as it intersects with the abusive governance of the Central Asian nation of Uzbekistan (Human Rights Watch 2001).

What, more precisely, does "human rights" mean and how is it pertinent? Indeed, human rights are not a monolithic set of concepts with their associated practices. Are rights construed as what a person is endowed with as a human being (the "positive rights" emphasis)? Or, are they better understood as what cannot be done to the person ("negative rights")(Fields 2003)? Positive rights include the right to adequate housing, health care, caloric intake and education. A negative right assures not being unduly interfered with, such as proscriptions against a subject being tortured or unfairly suppressed, for example, with regard to speech/cultural practice. On the more expansive (positive) view of rights, starvation or a lack of adequate schooling is not a mere bureaucratic foible or shrug-inducing "market failure"; rather, it rises to the level of human rights abuses toward deprived populations. Although human rights may take off and extend from a wide range of commitments (Fields 2003: 44–67), the unifying elements are concern with human dignity and the liberation of human potential from injustices that compromise it. For the moment, however, the for-mulation of human rights far outruns their implementation on the ground. To read the United Nations' (1948) "Universal Declaration of Human Rights" is to survey a blueprint for a world that does not exist; but, if it did, it would be unrecognizable in global terms with respect to the lived situation of the vast majority of the world's population.

Winterbottom's films make stout contributions to human rights discourses. The films orient to rights as they impact on real/realistic people faced with diminished possibilities based on the arbitrary matters of who and where they are: Residents of a war zone (*Welcome to Sarajevo*), refugees (*In This World*), impover-ished "Outsiders" exiled from prosperity in a ferociously classist social order (*Code 46*) and detainees held in Guantánamo for years without being charged with a crime (*The Road to Guantánamo*).

In this World, *Welcome to Sarajevo*, and *Code 46* emphasize subjects' movement across boundaries that have been constructed by State/private authority. Indeed, movement in Winterbottom's corpus often assumes the form of an "illicit journey" (Allison 2005: 9). *In This World*'s actors/characters sojourn through Pakistan, Af-ghanistan, Iran, Kurdistan, Turkey, across the Mediterranean to Italy, France, and finally to London—doing so without documents. The illicit journey theme is also strongly inscribed in *Code 46* as *papeles* are necessary to move among the world's metropoles and evade the flyover areas that are "Outside" in which deprivation and shantytown desperation are the rule. *Welcome to Sarajevo* also presents this emphasis on documents as enablers of international movement in the effort to transport children out of besieged Sara-jevo and to Italy. By contrast with *In This World* and *Welcome to Sarajevo* in which barriers are traversed in a geographically marked, political quest for greater opportunity, movement in *The Road to Guantánamo* is mainly downriver—deeper into the horror of statism, inflected on detainees who do not know "if or when they will be released or brought to any form of judicial process" but have nonetheless been presumed guilty via indeterminate incar-ceration (Amnesty International 2007: 1).

Heart of Darkness

The Road to Guantánamo presents a clear instance of Winterbot-tom's abiding interest in human rights. In this case, support for human rights is necessarily couched within implicit criticism of the Bushian "Long War" as brutal—and inept with respect to its ostensible goal of securing a safe environment. Whether committed by non-state actors or by states, terrorism is a heinous crime by the lights of human rights and by any concept of common sense. For this reason, the Bushite failure to effectively counter it in strategic terms is disturbing as discussed at length by aghast officials of the U.S. security apparatus who witnessed craven neo-conservative managerial clowning at close quarters (Clark 2004; Scheuer 2004).

As the film neared its premiere, Winterbottom was cautious about not appearing to paint 300 million Usonians with the same broad brush: "America has lots of good things as well. There are lots of people who are anti-Guantánamo in the United States" (Stone 2006: 2). Winterbottom registers eagerness in the same interview to have the film distributed in the United States for optimal impact since citizens can pressure their own government; a logical desire. However, *Road to Guantánamo* opened on June 23, 2006, in the United States in a limited distribution on 15 screens, nationwide, reaching a high of 25 screens in its third week of July 7 (The Numbers 2007a). During the same week, no-holds-barred social consciousness raisers such as *Pirates of the Caribbean: Dead Man's Chest* (Gore Verbinski) and the Adam Sandler masterpiece, *Click* (Frank Coraci), were piped into 4,133 and 3,458 cinemas, respectively, by corporate *diktat* (The Numbers 2007b).[1]

In *The Road to Guantánamo*, Winterbottom and co-director Mat Whitecross pursue a strategy reminiscent of U.S. documentarian Errol Morris (e.g., *The Thin Blue Line* 1988) by enabling the protagonists to tell their stories and giving the audience space to evaluate testimony and tease out implications. Although it is a staple of the Winterbottom corpus of fictional films, the documentary convention of VO is used only sparingly and at the end. Despite what seems to be an effort to avoid heavy-handed outlines of the story's contours by largely eschewing third-person VO, the film's politics are unmistakable in advocating for human rights by presenting a situation where they have been taken out of play. The film centers on four young British men of Southeast Asian origin—Asif, Shafiq, Ruhel, and Monir—as they get sucked into the riptides of unfolding history. For being in the wrong place at the wrong time, they endured two-and-one-half years of nightmare captivity beyond scrutiny and the reach of human rights conventions, an account that squares with what has been independently discovered about Guantánamo (Amnesty International 2007). One of the four (Monir) did not survive, having been lost in 2001 in the chaos of the Northern Alliance's campaign in Afghanistan and never found. He is assumed dead. The surviving trio is known as "The Tipton Three" with reference to their home area in Great Britain.

The implied message of the film can be pulled together straightforwardly in human rights terms: If Bush's alleged confrontation with terror was being waged justly and efficaciously—and not with head-spinning viciousness and caprice—the Tipton Three would not have endured what they did. For this and a raft of other reasons, it is a difficult and disturbing film to watch. The three young men give their testimony with stunning understatement and command of their emotions. In the final sequence, Shafiq claims that the experience of the incarceration made him a better person (presumably for surviving intact), Ruhel reports that he has become more religious, and Asif states that he is looking forward and not back; it is the closest that any of them comes to embittered commentary.[2] Nonetheless, the closing sequence of the film is unclear on how, in particular, the cell doors were pried open. A brief epilogue presents footage of Asif's wedding in Pakistan in July 2005, which had been the group of friends' original reason for traveling to Southeast Asia in autumn 2001.

The United States first appears in the film via a brief prologue in which Bush indicates that the war against terror is being waged against "bad people." As a British-made film presented first to a British audience via television, the archival footage includes Tony Blair's supportive stance as part of the prologue. Bush verbalizes; Blair is spoken of and pantomimes steely resolve on cue in Winterbottom and Whitecross' witty abstraction of the puppeteer quality of the transatlantic relationship. Any person of decency is in favor of apprehending "bad people" bent on mass murder; a point that requires no further elaboration because it is screamingly obvious. Rather, the question begged by the prologue is how the stated Bush (and Blair) project is answered by events depicted in the documentary. Moreover, the fact that the Blair government, with its arsenal of state authority and power, was by far the most supportive and high-profile lieutenant to Bush's project may account for the extent to which the Winterbottom-Whitecross film avoids polemic; the United Kingdom is implicated in the events not only as victim (the Tipton Three) but also as the Bush team's deputy.

The first half of the film mainly presents the thuggery of the Northern Alliance, the U.S.-supported faction against the Taliban (although the United States unleashes destruction from the sky in Afghanistan with seemingly indiscriminate aerial bombardment). The second half of the film portrays the methods at Guantánamo at closer quarters. Asif gives a quick overture when he states that, growing up in the United Kingdom, he had long looked favorably on his nation's former colony in the United States. With notable restraint, he posits that his experience of Bush's gulag destabilized his assumptions. Bush is summoned from the news archive around the midpoint of the film's runtime to state that the enemy is composed of "killers who don't share our values." A cut to Rumsfeld furnishes a slight verbal twitch toward the truth; he states that Geneva conventions have been followed, adding the qualifier, "for the most part." Thereafter, the Tipton Three provide accounts of the riot squad-equipped "Extreme Reaction Force," in reconstruction, as mobilized against a prisoner who is unarmed and who had lost his mind. The suspect is beaten with a baton, kicked, and bloodied in what is explicitly intended as an example to the other captives. Toward the end of the film, Winterbottom and Whitecross present a harrowing depiction of the torture techniques that were described to them: In particular, stress postures in which the suspect is chained to the floor in an excruciating squat ("short shackling"), subjected to ear-splitting music and strobe lights, and denied access to the tiolet for extended periods.

The U.S. Department of Justice's Inspector General corroborates that these techniques have been used on detainees at Guantánamo (Department of Justice, Office of the Inspector General, Oversight and Review Division 2008), that is, against persons described as "illegal combatants" ("a status unrecognized in international law") who have "not been charged or convicted" but whose guilt has nonetheless been assumed (Amnesty International 2007: 6, 5).[3] The Inspector General's report entertains the term "war crimes" in conjunction with the United States' conduct in the Bush era at Guantánamo (2008: xxii). Retired U.S. Army Major General Antonio Taguba corroborates this in a recent statement on Guantánamo and other theatres: "After years of disclosures by

government investigations, media accounts, and reports from human rights organizations, there is no longer any doubt as to
whether the current (Bush) administration has committed war
crimes" (2008: 1).

The film is grounded in the young men's accounts of the tidal
circumstances that swept them into Guantánamo. However, in being so dedicated to their riveting and deeply disturbing first-hand
accounts, the film misses openings to underscore the convergence
of multiple lines of evidence on Guantánamo. This is an opportunity missed to nail down the case with VOs or title cards that
would likely not have interfered with the structure and flow de-
vised for the film. Among the many salient facts that the film does
not mention in sticking closely with the testimony of the Tipton
Three is that U.S.-allied forces in Afghanistan made captures "in
at least some cases in exchange for bounty payments" (Human
Rights Watch 2004: 1). Journalist Naomi Klein observes that payments ranged from 3,000 to 25,000 USDs and that Afghans were
informed of the bounty via flyers that read in part, "'Get wealth
and power beyond your dreams'" (quoted in Klein 2007: 11). This
led to at times indiscriminate seizure of people subsequently fun-
neled into Guantánamo under a "blanket determination" without
having "accurately determined…who was a combatant and who
was not, who posed a grave security risk and who was just a
farmer in the wrong place at the wrong time" (Human Rights
Watch 2004: 2). In this vein, Klein reports that the Pentagon calculated that 86 percent of Guantánamo prisoners were fingered
after the bounties had been publicized (Klein 2007: 11). The captives were then denied "individualized determinations of status in
competent tribunals as required by the Third Geneva Convention
and its (United States') own regulations" to separate out combatants from people "in the wrong place in the wrong time" (Human
Rights Watch 2004: 2). Prior to Bush-Cheney-Rumsfeld, the conventions had been followed by U.S. forces.

A Mighty Heart, also grounded in actual events, is more
equivocal—even backsliding—on torture. In a brief scene, the captain orchestrates the torture of Suleiman, hung by his wrists in a
seedy interrogation room. However, in a volte face from the un-
stinting criticism in The Road to Guantanamo, A Mighty Heart
may be read to suggest that "torture works" as the captain obtains
actionable intelligence. The sequence contrasts with the contention

that torture spins its victims heads around so far that they will say anything—as noted by former CIA agent Valerie Plame in an interview, an observation that she attributes to U.S. Military consensus on the matter (Horton 2007). The FBI strongly corroborates the dubious view on coercive interrogation methods (Department of Justice, Office of the Inspector General, Oversight and Review Division 2008: xiii). As with *The Lives of Others*, the "flaw" of *The Road to Guantánamo* may be it does not go far enough in depicting the black boot of statism.

On the Road

Another entry in Winterbottom's corpus deals with a form of warfare that is less obvious; namely, an internationalized class war waged through want and its impact on people's aspirations. *In This World* claimed the Golden Bear as well as the Peace Film Prize at the Berlin International Film Festival in 2003 (Internet Movie Data Base 2003). The premise of *In This World* is that Jamal, a refugee, embarks on a hazard-laden journey to the United Kingdom with his cousin Enayat in order to apply for asylum. In itself, this presents a rarely observed emphasis on one of the world's most marginal groups: Refugees, the ultimate outsiders.

The human rights banner is raised almost immediately as the film opens with a montage around the camp in Peshawar. VO gives a rapid orientation. To wit: The first refugees arrived in Peshawar from Afghanistan following the 1979 Soviet invasion. Many children have since been born in the camp and have known no other environment. The next large wave of refugees arrived following the U.S.-led bombing that commenced in October 2001. One million refugees are located in the camp ("Behind the Scenes with Michael Winterbottom and Tony Grisoni" 2003), making it a de facto large city—but one with no future, a temporary place that through neglect has become a largely unnoticed dead end.

Code 46, a science fiction effort, was released a year after *In This World* and it evidences a number of human rights themes rehearsed in the earlier film. Specifically, *Code 46* depicts a ferociously classist social order in the trappings of the "near future." In the film, movement is carefully regulated between the "Inside," where prosperity reigns, and the largely pauperized and despoiled areas "Outside." One cannot pass into the Inside without *papeles* that are also coded with genetic information as the state/corporate gaze of surveillance extends deep into the subject (including "character" issues!). As Winterbottom observes,

> Because Andrew (Eaton) and I were off making *In this World*, about two refugees, we got this idea of people having no papers and trying to travel from one place to another and problems that creates. And a lot of that world—refugee camps, people in deserts, people outside the system, without papers, excluded—these elements are part of the social fabric of *Code 46* as well. (Mitchell 2004: 2)

The emphasis on migration and class segregation survives the pronounced generic shift from the quasi-documentary of *In This World* to the science-fictional *Code 46*. Moreover, the two films in tandem forcefully indicate that the infrastructure of international classism is being implemented via control over movement. The issue plays out in real lives each day; for example, in the waters around Spain's Canary Islands where impoverished economic refugees arrive in unsteady vessels seeking entry into Europe. Thousands arrive each month, taking an enormous chance that is calculated as preferable to pauperization and slow death for patiently "playing by the rules" and staying home. To take one case, at least 50 Africans died in one unreliable vessel attempting the journey in mid-July 2007 (Tremlett 2007a). Winterbottom's ostensibly futuristic treatment presents a highly resonant vision of market-induced want and desperation with class segregation spatially marked and enforced.

As striking as these films are, not all of Winterbottom's corpus is as deft or as auspicious on the human rights front. While the earlier effort *Welcome to Sarajevo* is laudable in addressing a contemporaneous issue of considerable moment in the political and human rights arena—mainly, Yugoslavia's implosion—it also presents some flaws. The film presupposes a fair amount of knowledge about the lines of conflict in the former federal republic. It can thus be taken, to an extent, as denouncing "the violence" as if violence is animated by its own life force within a Southeastern European milieu (and even as individual characters are presented as decent people). By contrast, *In This World* effectively frames the causes and stakes of the refugees' situation with a brief but compelling VO at the outset on the ongoing, largely unnoticed crisis.

Welcome to Sarajevo also has its moments of "Atrocity Exhibition" (Joy Division 1980) during which horror appears as an ambient feature of a grimly "exotic" locale. Risto pulls a book off his shelf—and is promptly assassinated by an unseen assailant without further explanation (aside from an unelaborated earlier reference to his having "lost his innocence," presumably by having killed someone). The viewer may similarly be queasy upon seeing Henderson's subdued congratulations to another reporter on locating the "scoop" of the war in internment camps (that, moreover, look disconcertingly like WWII-era camps). In this case, many people's misery behind barbed wire becomes one person's career advancement as acknowledged by the characters within the confines of the editing suite.

Moreover, *Welcome to Sarajevo* echoes "white man's burden" ideology that is transposed to Southeastern Europe. In particular, Henderson's act of adopting Emira is a stand-up move on behalf of a child orphaned in a war zone. When her mother turns out to be alive and makes a claim on her daughter, Henderson returns to Sarajevo to secure the mother's signatures on the adoption documents. Despite acknowledging she has been a "bad mother," she is initially recalcitrant about signing over her child. Henderson then places a phone call in which Emira addresses her nonplussed mother in English before code-switching to tell her in Bosnian, "I am happy here, this is my home now, goodbye." The mother signs immediately.

There is no serious doubt that a child is better off leaving a war zone and not being encumbered by a mother who had been a nonpresence in her life. Nevertheless, *Welcome to Sarajevo* also aggrandizes Britain—history's arch imperialist where imperial bells still chime. Emira's devotion to the English language functions as tribute to Britain as guardian of human rights and as protectorate to the world's vulnerable. *In This World*, by contrast, depicts the young men's sentimental attachments to family in Peshawar alongside the understandable desire for a better life—and it does so without echoes of a "white man's burden" largely because Jamal and Enayat display notable resourcefulness and courage during their quest for material betterment.

There are disappointing aspects of *Welcome to Sarajevo*, mainly those that are shaded with (to some extent, "always already" unavoidable) nationalism and otherizing. However, Winterbottom's dedication to fashioning cinema that is ripe with hard-nosed, contemporary human rights themes stands out as exceptional in the sweep of big screen history. Moreover, along with orienting to fundamental social concerns—the family, class, outsiders, taboo—the corpus has not retreated into a stuffed shirt, wince inducing, pedantic series of films since the corpus playfully incorporates lighter moods and intelligent comedy (*24 Hour Party People, A Cock and Bull Story*). In transmitting such varied content with an original stylistic signature, Winterbottom has staked out a distinctive niche among filmmakers.

CHAPTER 12
Afterword

In this volume, I have attempted to unpack and analyze bodies of films that have been crafted by three current European directors. Along with characterizing their stylistic signatures, I have pursued an abiding concern with tracing out the politics (both cultural and formal) that are embedded within the films. The effort has been grounded in a detailed characterization of the international film industry that circumscribes each director and employed the auteur theory as a sturdy and flexible method to organize analysis into each director's corpus.

As always, there are further considerations—the background music that may not be noticed at first blush—that inform the choice of subjects and the subsequent treatment of them. Where the former is concerned, the choice of European directors is partly a small riposte and symbolic blow against the presumptive Empire of Hollywood and all that comes in its train. Fareed Zakaria comments, "Americans take justified pride in their own country—we call it patriotism—and yet are genuinely startled when other people are proud and possessive of theirs" (quoted in Burke 2008: 3). More pointedly, Usonians often act as if they carry a caricatured social-geography of the world within their internalized schemata. In this caricature, the rest of the world sits in abject despair and dullness, punctuated by occasional bursts of stilted interaction with the other people near at hand who similarly dwell within a stasis occasioned by their archaic and simplistic cultural environs. In this view, only when Usonians arrive with lantern shows to regale these abject peoples via archetypically resonant tales of Southern California teens struggling with Prom Night does the non-Usonian come to life, exit his or her torpor, and liberate his her or her formerly latent inner Usonian. This book is one gesture, however limited, against such caricature in putting the emphasis in the first instance on what is interesting in current European cinema. Moreover, as the end of history is not yet at hand, nor is it due to arrive in the foreseeable future, Hollywood's dissolution in internationalized finance/ownership terms may yet occasion shifts where product is concerned—or it may not. In any event, industrial trends accompanied by emerging substrates of production and distribution may occasion as yet unknowable challenges to the previously prevailing political economy of the film industry.

On the Zentropa Web page, von Trier recounts in a video that, "As a young man, I saw film companies as completely closed. I was madly interested in film but was always met by a closed door" (Zentropa Productions 2003). While the chief function of the Zentropa Web page is promotion for the production company that von Trier co-founded (and that is now run as a quasi-cooperative with its employees), one can mine further implications that surround his commentary. First, it is evident that a rising generation of younger people has grown up in an exceptionally sophisticated visual culture that presents intensifying global reach. Anecdotally, across the past decade, I have often been astonished by the quality of the outcomes that my students at University of Illinois-Urbana and Saint Louis University-Madrid realize when given the option of using a camera and "editing suite" to fashion academic work. The students' facility indexes the visual and narrative forms in which they have been immersed all their lives. It is one respect in which one can say things may be "getting better all the time!"—and, to the extent that it is so, the situation has been given a boost in practical terms by the availability of relatively inexpensive digital cameras. Film stock was once extremely expensive to purchase and develop. Hence, Robert Rodriguez (born 1968, hence middle-aged but younger than the three auteurs discussed here) circumvented the limitations of film stock and learned the trade of filmmaking with his father's video camera, low-cost videotape, crash editing between VCRs, with his many siblings to furnish a cast (Rodriguez 1996). Digital cameras are still more user friendly, particularly with regard to ultra-mobility and computer-based editing enabled by the transfer of digital information. In turn, fora such as www.youtube.com furnish a ready distribution channel in addendum to the narrowcast distribution channels (film fests) that Rodriguez utilized in first gaining exposure in the early 1990s. Even if at the margins, independent and international production has beachheads on which to maneuver.

As a species, we cannot help but tell stories to ourselves and to each other. Tales and their lamina of embellishments organically arise in rehearsing an account of one's day to share with others as one walks home, in dreaming by night or daydreaming at the workbench—or in scripting an international cinematic sensation. In pulling together this volume's concern with politics, there is an urgent need for us to mobilize each other with stories—ones that are resonant with truth—about crises that we have inherited and that are ongoing. Global society's egregious and grotesque maldistribution of wealth will continue to hothouse general social instability and avoidable conflict while, in parallel, the phalanx of climate change-driven disruptions to planetary existence in the slightly longer term is a bracing matter. Creativity and courage are what the moment demands. All need be mobilized in the effort to reverse this real-life narrative trajectory, from a von Triersian donnybrook toward Almodóvar-style reconciliation.

NOTES

Chapter 1: Introduction

1. Winterbottom and Almodóvar are preparing to ease into the director's chair with new projects soon to be inaugurated with the snap of the clapboard. However, von Trier announced his retirement from the director's role in May 2007 at age 52 (Burke 2007), as this volume was preparing for takeoff. Von Trier will continue to have a role in filmmaking, as a producer and scriptwriter, via the Zentropa studio that he co-founded. For the moment, until a more extended future shakes out, he may still be regarded as a contemporary filmmaker since his last film, *The Boss of It All/Direktøren for det hele* (2006) realized international cinematic distribution in 2007.

2. "Usonian" (i.e., U.S.-onian) is the term that I will use in lieu of the more familiar "American" in order to more accurately differentiate nations of the Americas (North, South and Central) from each other. Although English speakers have not widely taken up the term Usonian, there is an equivalent in Spanish that circulates (*estadouniduense*, from the noun Estados Unidos).

3. However, original sources on and documents by the PNAC on "full spectrum dominance" are now scarce since, as of June 2008, its Web page bizarrely reads: "This Account Has Been Suspended. Please contact the billing/support department as soon as possible." Despite apparently falling on tough times, former members of PNAC are known to include Dick Cheney, Dan Quayle, Donald Rumsfeld, Lewis Libby, and Jeb Bush among other high-profile figures.

4. In this vein, Lane Crothers (2007)'s project as a tribune of "globalization" implicitly folds the whole concept into "Americanization" (with more folding along the way; e.g., "the west" is used interchangeably with "the U.S." with unswerving insistence, while "markets" are taken as cognate to "democracy"). Crothers' case studies dwell on extra-Usonian cultures' response to U.S. media product, with their resistances to it largely reduced to sentimental attachments and parochial nuisances (in, e.g., France [2007: 124–129]). In this treatment, media "globalization" is retooled into shorthand for "one-way channel that runs, exclusively, from the U.S. outward."

Section I: Industries and Auteurs

Chapter 2: The International Film Industry

1. Co-productions figure prominently on the list. For instance, *The Lord of the Rings* trilogy (Peter Jackson) is a United States–New Zealand–Germany co-production. Also notice that The Numbers' rankings are denominated in non-inflation corrected USDs. Hence, more recent films are advantaged by the mere fact of inflated ticket prices.

2. Given the drift of the different prevailing cultures and modes of production, watching films in a European cinema can be a jarring experience with respect to the trailers that precede the feature, many of which are for U.S. films

while others are for European entries. Thus, the contrast between U.S. and European films is often more stark for being abstracted into the two-minute montages of the films presented, back-to-back, in trailer versions. During trailers for European films, one often witnesses: A boisterous large meal, people talking. A walk in the countryside, an argument, candlelight. Kisses. And the U.S. trailers? Blaring sound effects and agitated voiceover! Explosions, annihilation, severed limbs everywhere! Look: Swarthy terrorists speaking broken English! The steely president is on the phone surrounded by grim-faced advisors! Battalions of helicopters move in formation! And finally the lone hero emerges out of some CGI fireballs! He sports carefully cultivated stubble and is dusted with some designer bloodstains, accessorized "babe" on his arm. The world has, thankfully, been saved!

3. For example, *Live Free or Die Hard* (Len Wiseman 2007), featuring Bruce Willis' increasingly arthritic "action hero" shtick, was released in Spain under the less "in-your-face" title, *La Jungla 4.0* (*The Jungle 4.0*).

4. To take one grimly funny contrast in European efforts to attract film production: The Liverpool (UK) Film Commission offers Liverpool as a "'lookalike for ... Nazi Germany'" (quoted in Miller et al. 2001: 75).

5. As Eleftheriotis observes, there is high historical irony in Europe's exercise of "defensive nationalism" against the onslaught of U.S. screen product. In particular, the vast swaths of the globe colonized by Europe undertook similar defensive quests in support of their unique identities.

Chapter 3: The Auteur Theory

1. In this vein, a recent trend in book publishing is toward an analogue to director's cuts for films with respect to novels. In particular, novels that had previously been published after titles and significant passages had been amended by editors have been realigned with the author's original vision of the work. Raymond Carver's *What We Talk About* has already been given this treatment in a way that cancels Gordon Lish's editorial pruning that had refined much of what is regarded as Carver's laconic voice. James Joyce, William Faulkner, and Sylvia Plath are also due for similar "director's cuts" that, in any event, problematicize the romanticized image of the monadic scribe (Campbell 2007).

2. Careful attention to method is important in avoiding theoretical and empirical pratfalls or reification of an authorial presence. A homely example concerning reification will suffice. On DVD, I recently watched the Alejandro González Iñárritu-directed *Amores Perros* (2000) for the first time. I was agog at the opening scene, a car chase through Mexico City that was shot as a silent film. As the scene unfolded, I began to rehearse auteurist talking points on González' similar bravura use of sound and silence in *Babel* (2006) and in his segment of *11.09.01* (2002)—when I realized, during the second scene of two characters talking at breakfast, that the first scene was *not* in fact shot silent. Rather, the cables on my DVD player were not connected properly, occasioning image without sound until I became aware of the problem; and thus exploding this particular auteurist thesis for the moment.

3. Sarris takes a drastic detour when he places the auteur theory into the ser-vice of unashamed Usonian nationalism (that coincides with the fevers of the Kennedy era). He admits having long experienced a deep sense of inferiority as a Usonian, subject to Hollywood commercialism, with respect to Europe and its ostensibly rarified culture. By 1962, however, he raves that "film for film, director for director, the American cinema has been consistently supe-rior to that of the rest of the world from 1915 through 1962." On this view, auteurism may be instrumentalized "as a critical device for recording the his-tory of American cinema, the only cinema in the world worth exploring in depth beneath the frosting of a few great directors at the top" (1985: 535).

Section II: Pedro Almodóvar

Chapter 4: "'It was Almost Impossible to Dream That...'"

1. Notice, however, that editing a text on Spanish popular culture is not coter-minous with an apparent high regard for it. In a startling moment of conde-scension in her "Introduction," Kinder characterizes Antonio Banderas' career arc into Hollywood as a promotion from "prior minor league stardom in a peripheral national cinema" (1997: 7). More generally, writing on Almodóvar and Spain is often larded with orientalisms (Said 1979) even from ostensible admirers. Kinder presents such in her 1987 interview with Almodóvar in which she assays a theoretical takedown on what she construes as a fascist aesthetic in his early films (along with several asides that, on pa-per, read as barbed)(Kinder 1987). Although it is not central to his argument in the Kinder-edited volume, an otherwise admiring Paul Julian Smith more briefly (if advertently) orientalizes by positing pre-cognitive primitivizations. He claims that Almodóvarian cinema "neglects logical sense for aesthetic sensation, (and) produces inexplicably powerful emotions in the spectator" (1997: 194). In the same volume, Peter Besas (1997) steers away from classic orientalism and toward seemingly bored condescension while he character-izes the Spanish film industry as an admixture of the Mafia-style clannish with Potemkin Village charades of industriousness staged mainly to pocket subsidy checks. Orientalist discourse on Spain is of a piece with a good deal of U.S.–UK journalistic coverage of the nation (Goss 2004a).

2. Controversy surrounds the year of Almodóvar's birth. In his book-length study, Ernesto Acevedo-Muñoz reports it as 1951 (2007: 1).

3. The virtuoso editing in Almodóvar's later films belies the small budgets and necessarily rough technique of the earlier ones. In *Pepi, Luci, Bom . . .* a se-quence of shots in which Pepi answers the door and sits down with the po-liceman was shot across three occasions (June 1979, December 1979, June 1980) and then spliced together in the final cut of the film (D'Lugo 2006: 21)!

4. In another register of identity, Paul Julian Smith (2000: 184) praises the thoughtful portrait of David as disabled. *Live Flesh* sensitively depicts his dif-ficulty in getting into a car in a series of jump-cuts. During a sex scene in the bathtub when David orally pleasures Elena, the film also demonstrates how able a person in a wheelchair may be.

Chapter 5: A Dedication

1. An exception: A brief scene with a sympathetic Civil Guard officer in *Law of Desire* outside the unit's building. However, the officer transmits useful narrative information to the protagonist Pablo, thus he may also be a construed as a "plot device." The inspector in *Matador* also presents as competent, although he depends on the psychic Ángel to lead him to the final crime scene.
2. The pattern echoes a Hitchcockian thematic motif. In particular, Hitchcock protagonists such as Hannay (*39 Steps*, 1934), John Robie (*To Catch a Thief*, 1955), and Roger O. Thornhill (*North by Northwest*, 1959) exhibit more resourcefulness and skill than the professional cops whom they outmaneuver in the quest for truth.
3. Almodóvar on his nation's "peculiarly Spanish" form of Catholicism: "Spanish people take religion as part of their daily life; that doesn't mean that they don't take it seriously, my mother took her saints very seriously. But not mass" (quoted in Mackenzie 2004: 158). Almodóvar's divided posture toward religion is similarly channeled by Tina in *Law of Desire*. She assembles a shrine for earnest bouts of prayer. The shrine is composed of the Virgin Mary, Barbie dolls, and Marilyn Monroe iconography. Mother Superior in *Dark Habits* has constructed a similar shrine in her convent office. It is in the type of gesture that Luis Buñuel described as characteristically Spanish in being devout—albeit, on idiosyncratic terms (de la Colina and Pérez Turrent 1992: 155–156).
4. Jordan and Morgan-Tamosunas' line of argument gains further force from sickening news from Austria this week in May 2008. Josef Fritzl imprisoned his daughter as a sex slave in an underground dungeon for almost 24 years. There is no serious question to be asked regarding the misogynistic ideology that drives such a crime. While, strictly speaking, it is not fair to compare Almodóvar's fiction with a hideous crime revealed two decades after *Tie Me Up . . .*'s release, the nature of sexually oriented kidnapping in its real-life manifestations gives considerable pause.

Section III: Lars von Trier

Chapter 7: *"Agent Provoc-Auteur"*

1. The phenomenon does not just reside in Northern Europe. In Spain, one of the less multilingual zones of Western Europe, indigenous English-language films have also gained a toe-hold: *Darkness* (Jaume Balagueró 2002) and, more auspiciously Spain's Goya award winner as "Best Film" of 2006, *The Secret Life of Words/La vida secreta de las palabaras* (Isabel Coixet 2005)—a film with von Trier's *Breaking the Waves* written into its DNA.
2. Another link between the noted surrealist Buñuel's film and von Trier's corpus is that Viridiana enters into trance-like states several times (beginning with an episode of sleepwalking in the opening ten minutes of *Viridiana*).
3. Notice that the character's name also bears an association with trances (Mesmer, mesmerize).
4. One sees here how von Trier's artistic schemes fall short of Buñuel's *Viridiana*, discussed earlier, in the construction of the failed idealist. Buñuel's ide-

alist is intelligent and absolutely sincere—in contrast with Tom—and she still fails. Thus, Buñuel conveys the thesis about idealism as itself harboring the germs of its destruction with greater confidence and elegance—and less hint of "cheap shots" against his own characters to ease the unfavorable outcome.

Chapter 8: Old World/New World

1. The Icelandic character is unsympathetic and explosive. And he may be taken as a "jokey" reference to von Trier's unhappy experience of previously directing the world's best-known Icelander, Björk, in *Dancer in the Dark* (Deneuve 2005).
2. The three films of von Trier's "Golden Heart" trilogy are *Breaking the Waves*, *The Idiots*, and *Dancer in the Dark*. The "U-S-A" trilogy's first two legs are *Dogville* and *Manderlay* with *Wasington* (in preproduction) slated to be the third leg, although complicated by von Trier's current retirement. However, *Dancer in the Dark* bridges not only temporally to the "U-S-A" trilogy that it immediately precedes, but the film is also conceptually proximal to the critique enacted within the "U-S-A" trilogy.
3. As withering as the portrait of Dogville is, its citizens' one redeeming characteristic is that they summarily reject the one exemplar of the ruling class among them—Tom—for his pretences of rallying them (e.g., toward "moral re-armament"). U.S. populations are in reality often less savvy on this score and more credulous toward ridiculous, pampered scions of unfathomable privilege who offer themselves up as "leaders" of the heartland. To take one index of the phenomenon: In a speech in Madrid, Spain, in April 2005, former Democratic presidential candidate Michael S. Dukakis observed that in the 2004 federal election, George W. Bush carried the 18 poorest states in the United States. In other words: a detached aristocrat, groomed from the cradle within the nation's most elite sanctums of prep schools and country clubs, with a policy portfolio to match, was delivered into office by relatively deprived people.
4. Other films in the corpus similarly present a surprise—and new, important characters—in the final scene. In *Epidemic*, the psychic only appears in the final scene, and it is here that the audience sees that the plague vector has extended off the pages of the Lars-Niels script and into Copenhagen. Grace's father appears only in the final sequence of *Dogville* (although his voice is heard through the car window earlier). Similarly, in *The Idiots*, the audience learns the horrific psychohistory concerning Karen's family in the last scene when Anders (the abusive husband) is glimpsed for the first time. The technique of a "kicker" in the final scene does not meet these more auspicious standards in *Manderlay* as noted.

Section IV: Michael Winterbottom

Chapter 9: "Lost Without Him"

1. There are other motifs in Winterbottom's films that are more curiosities than "keys" to them. Nonetheless, to indulge these, his corpus includes numerous shots depicting blurs of passing traffic (one such shot indeed opens the debut film, *Butterfly Kiss*); graphic scenes of childbirth (*Jude*, *Wonderland*, *A*

Mighty Heart); nightclub scenes with strobe lights (*I Want You, Code 46, 9 Songs, A Mighty Heart*) or strobe-light effects (e.g., as Miriam drowns/strangles Eunice in *Butterfly Kiss*); and several important characters who are hairdressers (*I Want You, With or Without You, Wonderland*).

2. Conversely, *Go Now* (1995) was made for British television and was not cinema distributed in the U.K. home territory (Allison 2005). Given its cabining on the small screen, I do not discuss it here.

Chapter 10: Real Art

1. A film may be saturated with showy technique and, paradoxically, present characters' phenomenal experience more closely. Steven Soderbergh's prismatic editing techniques in the opening sequence of *The Limey* (1999) present this quality (Goss 2004b). Sound bridges, flash-forwards, and flashbacks present Wilson and Eduardo as they tensely feel each other out over the course of an evening. Nonetheless, *The Limey*'s complicated nonlinear cutting—its juxtapositions between words and images, leaps forward and back in time—may more closely represent the non-linear qualities of consciousness and communication. The characters warily circle around each other, gradually showing their cards and elaborating earlier, more tentatively proffered observations as the discourse plays out. In contrast with the hand-held camera that is taken as contemporary grammar of realism for its ragged edges, this sequence is an exquisitely constructed montage that, via heavy stylization, captures sophisticated social/cognitive processes (. . . "realistically").

2. Indeed, the mania for identifying intertextual references reaches a feverish pitch for the generation that grew up in the 1980s–1990s and/or was trained in graduate school during this epoch. In this vein, Caroline Bainbridge's (2007) book-length study of Lars von Trier devotes a whole chapter to exhaustively cataloging influences on the filmmaker (from, e.g., Bertolt Brecht to David Bowie)—without explaining the *why* behind this impulse and its implicit assumption that "more intertextural!" collapses into "better!"

3. The 64-minute runtime refers to the Region 1 (North American) DVD on which I took my veridical set of notes for this book. However, the first version of the film that I witnessed, in revival, at Madrid's Cine Dore Filmoteca in August 2006 was the 67-minute version. The 64-minute North American DVD version trimmed some of the more erotic images. In any event, as with many films, more than one version circulates across time and place.

Chapter 11: Rights and Wrongs

1. Of *The Road to Guantánamo*'s worldwide theatrical gross of 1.078 million USDs, 30 percent (0.327 million) was U.S. box office (The Numbers 2007a). When I mentioned *The Road to Guantánamo* to colleagues in Spain—where the film was endowed with very visible distribution—they assumed that it had been banned in the United States. A ban, while illiberal in principle, may have prompted a measure of publicity. The limited release, however, rendered it "un-banned"—and close to invisible due to infinitesimal distribution.

2. A salient aside: For all of my adult life, I have heard U.S. conservatives extol private initiative with full-throated demands to "get the government off the

people's back," a key theme (and talking point) of Ronald Reagan's paradigm-shifting 1980 campaign. The U.S. Right's subsequent indifference to, or enthusiasm for, Guantánamo puts the lie to one of the alleged pillars of its movement with regard to a restrained state—although this unashamed "flip-flop" on the tailoring of state authority is consistent with social psychologist Bob Altemeyer (2006)'s characterizations of Right-wing authoritarians' talent for compartmentalized thinking and bald double standards.

3.   Almost half of the 450 FBI agents who performed tours in Guantánamo either observed or heard about coercive interrogations, and the U.S. Department of Justice's Inspector General's report reiterates that the FBI (its agents at Guantánamo, its leadership in DC) was troubled by the interrogation techniques directed at detainees. In turn, the FBI identifies the coercive techniques with the Department of Defense, where some of the most virulent neo-conservatives were setting the tempo (starting with Rumsfeld).

REFERENCES

Acevedo-Muñoz, Ernesto (2007). *Pedro Almodóvar*. London: British Film Institute.

Af Geijerstam, Eva (2003). "A Conversation with Lars von Trier, Henning Bendtsen, and Ernst-Hugo Järegård." In *Lars von Trier Interviews*, edited by Jan Lumholdt, pp. 64–70. Jackson: University of Mississippi Press. Originally published 1990.

Allison, Deborah (2005). "Michael Winterbottom." *Senses of Cinema*, May. Retrieved June 25, 2007 from: www.sensesofcinema.com/contents/directors/05/winterbottom.html.

Altemeyer, Bob (2006). *The Authoritarians*. Retrieved June 9, 2008 from: members.shaw.ca/jeanaltemeyer/drbob/Introduction_links.pdf.

Althusser, Louis (1994). "Selected Texts." In *Ideology*, edited by Terry Eagleton, pp. 87–111. New York: Longman. Originally published in English 1971.

Amnesty International (2007). "United States of America: Cruel and Inhuman: Conditions of Isolation for Detainees at Guantánamo Bay." Retrieved July 14, 2007 from: http://www.amnesty.org/library/print/ENGAMR510512007.

Bainbridge, Caroline (2007). *The Cinema of Lars von Trier: Authenticity and Artifice*. London: Wallflower Press.

Barnouw, Erik (1993). *Documentary: A History of the Non-Fiction Film*. New York: Oxford University Press.

Barthes, Roland (2001). "The Death of the Author." In *Theories of Authorship*, edited by John Caughie, pp. 208–213. London: Routledge. Originally published 1968 (French), 1977 (English).

Bedell, Geraldine (2004). "A Winterbottom's Tale." *Observer* (London), February 1. Retrieved July 14, 2007 from: film.guardian.co.uk/interview7interviewpages/0,,1136149,00.html.

"Behind the Scenes with Michael Winterbottom and Tony Grisoni" (2003). DVD Extra, *In This World*. UK: Optimum Releasing.

Beltzer, Thomas (2005). *Dogville*: An Addendum. Retrieved June 25, 2007 from: www.sensesofcinema.com/contents/directors/02/vontrier.html.

Bennett, W. Lance (2001). *News: The Politics of Illusion*. New York: Longman.

Besas, Peter (1997). "The Financial Structure of Spanish Cinema." In *Refiguring Spain*, edited by Marsha Kinder, pp. 241–259. Durham, NC: Duke University Press.

Bingham, Harry (2007). "You Say Potato, I Say Ghoughbteighpteau." *Guardian* (London), September 29, Review:3.

Bordwell, David (1989). *Making Meaning*. Cambridge, MA: Harvard University Press.

Bordwell, David and Kristin Thompson (2001). *Film Art*. New York: McGraw-Hill.

Bradshaw, Peter, Xan Brooks, Molly Haskell, Derek Malcolm, Andrew Pulver, B. Ruby Rich, and Steve Rose (2003). "The World's 40 Best Directors." *Guardian* (London), November 23. Retrieved January 16, 2004 from: www.guardian.co.uk/arts/fridayreview/story/0,12102,1084266,00.html.

Branigan, Tania (2005). "Let China Learn English, Says Brown." *Guardian* (London), September 22.

Brook, J. A. (1989). "Freud and Splitting." Presented to the Ottawa Psychoanalytic Society, September 1989. Retrieved May 23, 2008 from: http://http-server.carleton.ca/~abrook/SPLTTING.htm.

Brown, Royal S. (1985). "Hermann, Hitchcock and the Music of the Irrational." I, *Film Theory and Criticism*, edited by Gerald Mast and Marshall Cohen, pp. 618–649. New York: Oxford University Press. Originally published 1982.

Burke, Jason (2007). Dark Days for Film-making World as Depression Lays von Trier Low. *The Observer* (UK), May 13, p. 27.

——— (2008). "When Uncle Sam Goes to War." *Observer* (London), 22 June. Retrieved July 14, 2008 from: http://books.guardian.co.uk/reviews/politicsphilosophyandsociety/0,,2286940,00.html.

Buscombe, Edward (2001). "Ideas of Authorship." In *Theories of Authorship*, edited by John Caughie, pp. 22–34. London: Routledge. Originally published 1973.

Campbell, James (2007). "What a Carve-Up."*Guardian* (London), December 1, Review:21.

Canadian Broadcast Company (2006). "Fake Bum Important to *Volver*? Butt of Course, Says Almodóvar." September 9, CBC Arts. Retrieved April 14, 2008 from: http://www.cbc.ca/news/story/2006/09/09/tiff-volver-butt.html.

Cawelti, John G. (1985). "*Chinatown* and Generic Transformation in Recent American Films. In *Film Theory and Criticism*, edited by Gerald Mast and Marshall Cohen, pp. 503–520. New York: Oxford University Press. Originally published 1978.

Christians, Clifford G., Kim B. Rotzoll, Mark B. Fackler, and Kathy Brittain McKee (2004). *Media Ethics: Cases and Moral Reasoning*. Boston: Pearson.

Clark, Richard A. (2004). *Against All Enemies*. London: Simon and Schuster.

A Collective Text by the Editors of *Cahiers du cinema* (1985). "John Ford's *Young Mr. Lincoln*." In *Film Theory and Criticism*, edited by Gerald Mast and Marshall Cohen, pp. 695–740. New York: Oxford University Press. Originally published 1970 (French), 1972 (English).

Cook, David A. (1990). *A History of Narrative Film*. New York: Norton.

Corliss, Richard (1985). "The Hollywood Screenwriter." In *Film Theory and Criticism*, edited by Gerald Mast and Marshall Cohen, pp. 593–601. New York: Oxford University Press. Originally published 1970.

Crothers, Lane (2007). *Globalization and American Popular Culture*. Lanham, MD: Rowman and Littlefield.

Crowther, Bosley (1967a). "Screen: 'Bonnie and Clyde' Arrive." *New York Times*, August 14, p. 36.

——— (1967b). "Run, Bonnie and Clyde." *New York Times*, September 3, p. 2:1.

de la Colina, José and Tomás Pérez Turrent (1992). *Objects of Desire: Conversations with Luis Buñuel*. New York: Marsilio.

Deneuve, Catherine (2005). "Clash of the Titans." *Guardian* (London), September 21, pp. G2:10–11.

Department of Justice, Office of the Inspector General, Oversight and Review Division (2008). *A Review of the FBI's Involvement in and Observations of Detainee Interrogations in Guantánamo Bay, Afghanistan, and Iraq*. "Executive Summary," pp. i–xxxii. May. Retrieved June 8, 2008 from: www.usdoj.gov/oig/special/s0805/final.pdf.

D'Lugo, Marvin (2006). *Pedro Almodóvar*. Urbana: University of Illinois.

"Dogme Films" (n.d.). Retrieved July 4, 2007 from: www.dogme95.dk.

Eagleton, Terry (1991). *Ideology: An Introduction*. New York: Verso.

——— (1994). *Ideology*. New York: Longman.

Easthope, Antony (1993). "Introduction." In *Contemporary Film Theory*, edited by Antony Easthope, pp. 1–23. London: Longman.

The Economist (2007). "Spain: Economic Structure." November 13. Retrieved May 8, 2008 from: http://www.economist.com/COUNTRIES/Spain/PrinterFriendly.cfm?Story_ID=10086901.

Eleftheriotis, Dimitris (2001). *Popular Cinemas of Europe*. London: Continuum.

Ellul, Jacques (1965). *Propaganda: The Formation of Men's Attitudes*. Translated from the French by Konrad Kellen and Jean Lerner. New York: Knopf.

Elms, Robert (1992). *Spain: A Portrait after the General*. London: Heinemann.

Elsaesser, Thomas (2005). *European Cinema: Face to Face with Hollywood*. Amsterdam: Amsterdam University Press.

Equal Opportunities Commission (2007). "Final EOC Report Warns Sex Equality in Scotland Still Generations Away." July 24. Retrieved July 26, 2007 from: www.eoc.org.uk/Default.aspx?page=20559&theme=print.

Europa Cinemas (n.d.). "About Europa." Retrieved March 11, 2008 from: http://www.europa-cinemas.org/en/infos_europa/index.php.

Fields, A. Belden (2003). *Rethinking Human Rights for the New Millennium.* New York: Palgrave Macmillan.

Finney, Angus (1996). *The State of European Cinema.* London: Cassell.

Flew, Terry (2007). *Understanding Global Media.* New York: Palgrave Macmillan.

Foucault, Michel (1974). "Noam Chomsky and Michel Foucault: Human Nature: Justice versus Power." In *Reflexive Water*, edited by Fons Elders, pp. 135–197. London: Souvenir Press.

—— (1995). *Discipline and Punish: The Birth of the Prison.* Translated from French by Alan Sheridan. New York: Vintage Books.

—— (2001). "What Is an Author? (Extract)." In *Theories of Authorship*, edited by John Caughie, pp. 282–291. London: Routledge. Originally published 1969 (French), 1977 (English).

French, Phillip (2007). "Bye Bye, Good American Spy." *Observer* (UK), 19 August, p. 14.

Freud, Sigmund (1991). *Introductory Lectures on Psychoanalysis, Volume I.* London: Penguin.

Fuchs, Dale (2005). "Spain Acts to Stop Domestic Violence." *Guardian* (London), June 30, 2005.

Funder, Anna (2007). "Tyranny of Terror." *Guardian* (London). May 5, p. 14.

Galt, Rosalind (2006). *The New European Cinema: Redrawing the Map.* New York: Columbia University Press.

Goss, Brian Michael (2002a). "'Deeply Concerned About the Welfare of the Iraqi People': The Sanctions Regime Against Iraq in *The New York Times* (1996–98)." *Journalism Studies*, 3:1, pp. 83–99.

—— (2002b). "'Things Like This Don't Just Happen': Ideology and Paul Thomas Anderson's *Hard Eight, Boogie Nights*, and *Magnolia.*" *Journal of Communication Inquiry*, 26:2, pp. 169–90.

—— (2003). "Critical Essays and Reviews: *Understanding Disney* by Janet Wasko and *Global Hollywood* by Toby Miller, Nitin Govil, John McMurria and Richard Maxwell." *Journal of Communication Inquiry*, 27:2, pp. 215–23.

—— (2004a). "Foreign Correspondent: Spain in the Gaze of *The New York Times* and *The Guardian.*" *Journalism Studies*, 5:2, pp. 203–19.

—— (2004b). "Steven Soderbergh's *The Limey*: Implications for the Auteur Theory and Industry Structure." *Popular Communication*, 2:4, pp. 231–55.

—— (2007). "Taking Cover from Progress: Michael Winterbottom's *Code 46.*" *Journal of Communication Inquiry*, 31:1, pp. 62–78.

—— (2008). "*Te Doy Mis Ojos* (2003) and *Hable con Ella* (2002): Gender in Context in Two Recent Spanish Films." *Studies in European Cinema*, 5:1, pp. 31–44.

Gough-Yates, Anne (2003). *Understanding Women's Magazines*. New York: Routledge.

Hafez, Kai (2007). *The Myth of Media Globalization*. Cambridge: Polity.

Hall, Stuart, Charles Critcher, Tony Jefferson, and John Clarke (1978). *Policing the Crisis: Mugging, The State, and Law and Order*. New York: Holmes & Meier.

Hammond, Wally (2003). "Edge of Darkness." In *Lars von Trier Interviews*, edited by Jan Lumholdt, pp. 103–105. Jackson: University of Mississippi Press. Originally published 1995.

Harsin, Jayson (2006). "Von Trier's Brechtian Gamble: On *Manderlay*." February. Retrieved June 23, 2008 from: http://www.brightlightsfilm.com/51/manderlay.htm.

Hayward, Susan (2006). *Cinema Studies: The Key Concepts*. Oxon, UK: Routledge.

Hebdige, Dick (1988). *Subculture: The Meaning of Style*. London: Routledge.

Hennigan, Adrian (2005). "Michael Winterbottom *9 Songs*." Retrieved July 14, 2007 from: www.bbc.co.uk/films/2005/03/03/michael_winterbottom_9_songs_interview.shtml.

Herman, Edward S. and Noam Chomsky (1988). *Manufacturing Consent: The Political Economy of Human Rights*. New York: Pantheon.

Hjort, Mette and Ib Bondebjerg (2001). *The Danish Directors: Dialogues on a Contemporary National Cinema*. Bristol, UK: Intellect.

Hobsbawm, Eric (1996). *The Age of Extreme: A History of the World, 1914–1991*. New York: Vintage.

Hoffman, Lars (2003). "He'd Rather Watch a Cop Show Than Himself." In *Lars von Trier Interviews*, edited by Jan Lumholdt, pp. 3–4. Jackson: University of Mississippi Press. Originally published 1969.

Holmes, Stephen (2006). "John Yoo's Tortured Logic." *Nation*, April 13. Retrieved April 20, 2006 from: http://www.thenation.com/doc/20060501/holmes.

Hooper, John (1995). *The New Spaniards*. London: Penguin.

Horton, Scott (2007). "Six Questions for Valerie Plame." *Harpers*, October 25. Retrieved May 26, 2008 from: http://harpers.org/archive/2007/10/hbc-90001505.

——— (2008a). "Challenging Torture." February 4. Retrieved February 5, 2008 from: http://harpers.org/archive/2008/02/hbc-90002305.

——— (2008b). "Gitmo and the G.O.P. Election effort." March 29. Retrieved May 29, 2008 from: http://harpers.org/archive/2008/03/hbc-90002751.

——— (2008c). "The Great Guantánamo Puppet Theater." February 21. Retrieved May 29, 2008 from: http://harpers.org/archive/2008/02/hbc-90002460.

Hughes, Dominic and Phillips, Benedict (2000). *Oxford Guide to Successful Public Speaking*. London: Virgin.

Human Rights Watch (2001). "Human Rights Watch World Report 2001: Uzbekistan." Retrieved May 16, 2005 from: http://www.hrw.org/wr2k1/europe/uzbekistan.html.

——— (2004). "United States: Guantánamo Two Years On." January 9. Retrieved July 14, 2007 from: http://www.hrw.org/english/docs/2004/01/09/usdom6917_txt.htm.

Instrell, Rick (1992). "*Blade Runner*: The Economic Shaping of a Film." In *Cinema and Fiction: New Modes of Adapting, 1950–1990*, edited by John Orr and Colin Nicholson, pp. 160–170. Edinburgh: Edinburgh University Press.

Internet Movie DataBase (2003). "Awards for *In This World*." Retrieved May 26, 2008 from: http://www.imdb.com/title/tt0310154/awards.

——— (2008a). "Awards for Lars von Trier." Retrieved June 22, 2008 from: http://www.imdb.com/name/nm0001885/awards.

——— (2008b). "Pedro Almodóvar." Retrieved April 4, 2008 from: www.imdb.com/name/nm0000264/.

Jäckel, Anne (2003). *European Film Industries*. London: British Film Institute.

Joiner, Whitney (2008). "Not Quite Americans." *Salon*.com, June 11. Retrieved June 11, 2008 from: www.salon.com/books/int/2008/06/11/orner/print.html.

Jordan, Barry (2000). "How Spanish Is It? Spanish Cinema and National Identity." In *Contemporary Spanish Cultural Studies*, edited by Barry Jordan, Barry and Rikki Morgan-Tamosunas, pp. 68–78. London: Arnold.

Jordan, Barry and Rikki Morgan-Tamosunas (1998). *Contemporary Spanish Cinema*. Manchester, UK: Manchester University Press.

Joy Division (1980). *Closer*. Manchester, UK: Factory Records.

Kael, Pauline (1985). "Circles and Squares." In *Film Theory and Criticism*, edited by Gerald Mast and Marshall Cohen, pp. 541–552. New York: Oxford University Press.

Kaufman, Anthony (2000). "Michael Winterbottom's *Wonderland*." July 28. Retrieved July 14, 2007 from: www.indiewire/people/int_Winter_Michael_000728.html.

Keeley, Graham (2008). "Spanish Cabinet Has Its First Female Majority." *Guardian* (London), April 15, p. 15.

Kinder, Marsha (1987). "Pleasure and the New Spanish Mentality: A Conversation with Pedro Almodóvar." *Film Quarterly*, 41:1 (Fall), pp. 33–44.

——— (1997). "Refiguring Socialist Spain: An Introduction." In *Refiguring Spain*, edited by Marsha Kinder, pp. 1–32. Durham, NC: Duke University Press.

Klein, Naomi (2007). "The Age of Disaster Capitalism." *Guardian* (UK), pp. G2:6–12, September 10.

Koplev, Kjeld (2003). "9 A.M., Thursday, September 7, 2000: Lars von Trier." In *Lars von Trier Interviews*, edited by Jan Lumholdt, pp. 170–204. Jackson: University of Mississippi Press. Originally broadcast 2000.

Lernoux, Penny (2003). *Cry of the People*. Garden City, NY: Doubleday.

Lévi-Strauss, Claude (2001). "The Structural Study of Myth." In *Theories of Authorship*, edited by John Caughie, pp. 131–135. London: Routledge. Originally published 1958 (French), 1969 (English).

Lumholdt, Jan (2003). "Introduction." In *Lars von Trier Interviews*, edited by Jan Lumholdt, pp. ix–xx. Jackson: University of Mississippi Press.

Mackenzie, Suzie (2004). "All About My Father." In *Pedro Almodóvar Interviews* edited by P. Willoquet-Maricondi, pp. 154–161. Jackson: University of Mississippi Press.

Mail Online (2007). "Babies Born out of Wedlock Rise by a Fifth." June 28, 2007. Retrieved May 29, 2008 from: http://www.dailymail.co.uk/news/article-465029/Babies-born-wedlock-rise-fifth.html.

Matthews, Peter (2004). "Lost in La Mancha." *Sight and Sound*, September, Retrieved November 9, 2006 from: www.bfi.org.uk/sightandsound/review/3381/.

McChesney, Robert W. (1999). *Rich Media, Poor Democracy*. Urbana: University of Illinois Press.

McGill, Hannah (2004). One Man's Diverse Wonderland. *Herald* (Glasgow), September 11, p.10.

Miller, Toby, Nitin Govil, John McMurria, and Richard Maxwell (2001). *Global Hollywood*. London: British Film Institute.

Mitchell, Wendy (2004). Michael Winterbottom on *Code 46*. *indieWire*, August 6. Retrieved June 3, 2005, from: www.indiewire.com/people/people_040806 winter.html.

Moss, Stephen (2007). "Late Developer." *Guardian* (London), November 7, pp. G2:7–7.

Nicodemus, Katja (2005). "'I Am an American Woman.'" *Sight and Sound*, November 17. Retrieved June 15, 2008 from: www.print.sightandsound.com/features/465.html.

Nowell-Smith, Geoffrey (2001). Visconti (Extract). In *Theories of Authorship*, edited by John Caughie, pp. 136–137. London: Routledge. Originally published 1967.

The Numbers (2001). "Crouching Tiger, Hidden Dragon." Retrieved March 22, 2008 from: http://www.the-numbers.com/movies/2000/DRAGN.php.

―――― (2007a). "The Road to Guantánamo." Retrieved July 26, 2007 from: www.the-numbers.com/movies/2006/GUANT.php.

―――― (2007b). "The Top Movies, Weekend of July 7, 2006." Retrieved July 26, 2007 from: www.the-numbers.com/charts/weekly/2006/20060707.php.

——— (2008). "All Time Highest Grossing Movies Worldwide." Retrieved March 14, 2008 from: http://www.the-numbers.com/movies/records/worldwide.php.

Parenti, Christian (1999). "The Prison Industrial Complex: Crisis and Control." CorpWatch, September 1. Retrieved June 27, 2008 from: www.corpwatch.org/article.php?id=852.

Pateman, Carole (1988). *The Sexual Contract*. Stanford, CA: Stanford University Press.

Pew Global Attitudes Project (2006). *America's Image Slips, but Allies Share U.S. Concerns over Iran, Hamas*. June 13. Retrieved June 25, 2008 from: http://pewglobal.org/reports/display.php?ReportID=252.

Place, Janey (1978). "Women in Film Noir." In, *Women in Film Noir*, edited by E. Ann Kaplan, pp. 35–67. London: British Film Institute.

Polanski, Roman (1984). *Roman*. New York: Morrow.

¡Que Me Dices! (2006). "Si, el Tamaño Importa." November 11, No. 504, pp. 60–63.

Refn, Anders (2004). "Special Features: Interviews: Anders Refn, Assistant Director." *Doc.ville* DVD. Hvidovre, Denmark: Zentropa Entertainment8.

Rodriguez, Robert (1996). *Rebel without a Crew*. New York: Penguin.

Roman, Sheri (2003). "Lars von Trier: The Man Who Would Be Dogme." In, *Lars von Trier Interviews*, edited by Jan Lumholdt, pp. 133–143. Jackson: University of Mississippi Press. Originally published 1999.

Rose, David (2006). "Using Terror to Fight Terror." *Observer* (London), February 26, Review:4–5.

Rose, Jacqueline (2004). "Introduction by Jacqueline Rose." In *Sigmund Freud: Mass Psychology and Other Writings*, pp. vii–xli. London: Penguin.

Rossett, Peter and John Vandermeer (1983). *The Nicaragua Reader: Documents of a Revolution Under Fire*. New York: Grove Press.

Rothman, William (1982). *Hitchcock: The Murderous Gaze*. Cambridge, MA: Harvard University Press.

Ryan, Michael and Douglas Kellner (1988). *Camera Politica*. Bloomington: Indiana University Press.

Said, Edward W. (1979). *Orientalism*. New York: Vintage Books.

——— (1994). *Culture and Imperialism*. New York: Vintage Books.

——— (1997). *Covering Islam: How the Media and the Experts Determine How We See the Rest of the World*. New York: Vintage Books.

Sarris, Andrew (1985). "Notes on the Auteur Theory in 1962." In *Film Theory and Criticism*, edited by Gerald Mast and Marshall Cohen, pp. 528–540. New York: Oxford University Press. Originally published 1962/1963.

Scheuer, Michael (2004). *Imperial Hubris*. Dulles, VA: Brassey's.

Schrader, Paul (1986), "Notes on Film Noir." In *Film Genre Reader*, edited by Barry Keith Grant, pp. 189–182. Austin: University of Texas Press.

Shin, Jeeyoung (2005). "'Cine-Mania' or Cinephilia: Film Festivals and the Identity Question." In, *New Korean Cinema*, edited by Chi-Yun Shin and Julian Stringer, pp. 51–62. Edinburgh: Edinburgh University Press.

Silverman, Kaja (2000). "Male Subjectivity and the Celestial Suture: *It's a Wonderful Life.*" In *Feminism and Film*, edited by E. Ann Kaplan, pp. 100–118. Oxford: Oxford University Press. Originally published 1981.

Simpson, Christopher (1988). *Blowback*. New York: Collier Books.

Smith, Gavin (2003). "Dance in the Dark." In *Lars von Trier Interviews*, edited by Jan Lumholdt, pp. 144–152. Jackson: University of Mississippi Press. Originally published 2000.

Smith, Paul Julian (1997). "Pornography, Masculinity, Homosexuality: Almodóvar's *Matador* and *La Ley del Deseo.*" In *Refiguring Spain*, edited by Marsha Kinder, pp. 178–195. Durham, NC: Duke University Press.

——— (2000). *Desire Unlimited: The Cinema of Pedro Almodóvar*. London: Verso.

Söderbergh-Widding, Astrid (1998). "Denmark." In *Nordic National Cinemas*, edited by Tytti Soila, Astrid Söderbergh-Widding, and Gunnar Iverson, pp. 7–30. New York: Routledge.

Staiger, Janet (2003). "Authorship Approaches." In *Authorship and Film*, edited by David A. Gerstner and Janet Staiger, pp. 27–57. New York: Routledge.

Stam, Robert (2000a). "The Author." In, *Film and Theory*, edited by Robert Stam and Toby Miller, pp. 1–6. Oxford: Blackwell.

——— (2000b). "The Question of Realism." In *Film and Theory*, edited by Robert Stam and Toby Miller, pp. 223–228. Oxford: Blackwell.

Stone, Susan (2006). "The Road to Guantánamo." February 17. Retrieved July 14, 2007 from: www.spiegal.de/international/0,1518,druck-401386,00.html.

Studlar, Gaylyn (2000). "Masochism and the Perverse Pleasures of the Cinema." In *Feminism and Film*, edited by E. Ann Kaplan, pp. 203–225. Oxford: Oxford University Press. Originally published 1981.

Suskind, Ronald (2004). "Without a Doubt." *New York Times*, October 17.

Taguba, Antonio (2008). "Preface to *Broken Laws, Broken Lives: Medical Evidence of Torture by the US.*" Physicians for Human Rights. Retrieved July 2, 2008 from: brokenlives.info/?page_id=23.

Tapper, Michael (2003). "A Romance in Decomposition." In *Lars von Trier Interviews*, edited by Jan Lumholdt, pp. 71–80. Jackson: University of Mississippi Press. Originally published 1991.

Thompson, Kristin and David Bordwell (2003). *Film History*. Boston: McGraw-Hill.

Tremlett, Giles (2007a). "180 Migrants Survive Voyage in Giant Canoe." *Guardian* (London), July 31, p.14.

———— (2007b). "After Franco, the Forgetting." *Guardian* (London), November 3, p. 24.

———— (2007c). *Ghosts of Spain: Travels through a Country's Hidden Past.* London: Faber and Faber.

Trimble, David (1998). "Looking for Peace within the Realms of the Possible." Nobel Lecture, Oslo, Norway, December 10. In *The Oxford Union Guide to Successful Public Speaking,* edited by Dominic Hughes and Benedict Phillips (2001), pp. 194–199. London: Virgin.

Truffaut, François (1967). *Hitchcock.* New York: Simon and Schuster.

———— (1976). "A Certain Tendency of the French Cinema." In *Movies and Methods,* edited by Bill Nichols, pp. 224–237. Berkeley: University of California. Originally published 1954 (French).

Turner, Graeme, Frances Bonner, and P. David Marshall (2000). *Fame Games: The Production of Celebrity in Australia.* Cambridge: Cambridge University Press.

Union of Concerned Scientists (2004). *Scientific Integrity in Policymaking.* Cambridge, MA: Union of Concerned Scientists.

United Nations (1948). *Universal Declaration of Human Rights.* Retrieved June 12, 2008 from: www.un.org/Overview/rights.html

Von Trier, Lars and Thomas Vinterberg (1995). The Vow of Chastity. Retrieved July 4, 2007 from: www.dogme95.dk.

Wasko, Janet (2002). *Understanding Disney.* Cambridge: Polity.

Wayne, Mike (2002). *The Politics of Contemporary European Cinema: Histories, Borders, Diasporas.* Bristol, UK: Intellect.

Williams, Mark (2000). *The Story of Spain.* Fuengirola, Spain: Santana, S.L.

Willoquet-Maricondi, P. (2004). Introduction. In *Pedro Almodóvar Interviews,* edited by P. Willoquet-Maricondi, pp. vii–xv. Jackson: University of Mississippi Press.

Wolcott, James (1999). "Death and the Master." *Vanity Fair,* April, pp.136–153.

Wolfe, Alan (2000). "Hobbled from the Start." *Salon.*com, December 15.   Retrieved June 12, 2008 from: www.salon.com/politics/feature/2000/12/15/trust/index.html

Wollen, Peter (1985). "The Auteur Theory." In *Film Theory and Criticism,* edited by Gerald Mast and Marshall Cohen, pp. 553–562. New York: Oxford University Press. Originally published 1972.

Wood, Robin (1971). *The Apu Trilogy.* New York: Praeger.

———— (1998). *Sexual Politics & Narrative Film.* New York: Columbia University Press.

———— (2002). *Hitchcock's Films Revisited.* New York: Columbia University Press.

Zentropa Productions (2003). *A Small Film About a Big Company/En lille film om et stort selskab*. Retrieved July 16, 2008 from: www.zentropa.dk.

Žižek, Slavoj (1995). *Mapping Ideology*. New York: Verso.

de Zongotita, Thomas (2005). *Mediated*. London: Bloomsbury.

INDEX

Intersections in Communications and Culture

Global Approaches and Transdisciplinary Perspectives

General Editors: Cameron McCarthy & Angharad N. Valdivia

An Institute of Communications Research, University of Illinois Commemorative Series

This series aims to publish a range of new critical scholarship that seeks to engage and transcend the disciplinary isolationism and genre confinement that now characterizes so much of contemporary research in communication studies and related fields. The editors are particularly interested in manuscripts that address the broad intersections, movement, and hybrid trajectories that currently define the encounters between human groups in modern institutions and societies and the way these dynamic intersections are coded and represented in contemporary popular cultural forms and in the organization of knowledge. Works that emphasize methodological nuance, texture and dialogue across traditions and disciplines (communications, feminist studies, area and ethnic studies, arts, humanities, sciences, education, philosophy, etc.) and that engage the dynamics of variation, diversity and discontinuity in the local and international settings are strongly encouraged.

LIST OF TOPICS

- Multidisciplinary Media Studies
- Cultural Studies
- Gender, Race, & Class
- Postcolonialism
- Globalization
- Diaspora Studies
- Border Studies
- Popular Culture
- Art & Representation
- Body Politics
- Governing Practices

- Histories of the Present
- Health (Policy) Studies
- Space and Identity
- (Im)migration
- Global Ethnographies
- Public Intellectuals
- World Music
- Virtual Identity Studies
- Queer Theory
- Critical Multiculturalism

Manuscripts should be sent to:

Cameron McCarthy OR Angharad N. Valdivia
Institute of Communications Research
University of Illinois at Urbana-Champaign
222B Armory Bldg., 555 E. Armory Avenue
Champaign, IL 61820

To order other books in this series, please contact our Customer Service Department:
(800) 770-LANG (within the U.S.)
(212) 647-7706 (outside the U.S.)
(212) 647-7707 FAX

Or browse online by series:
www.peterlang.com